Those Who Died Young

Marianne Sinclair was born in France and has lived, worked and studied in France, England and America. She has written two novels, *Paradox Lost* and *Watcher in the Park,* which were published in England and the United States, France, Germany, Holland and Scandinavia. She has also published a travel book, newspaper articles and eight translations, as well as book reviews, poems and literary essays. She was also editor of the Third World Series, which included Che Guevara's *Bolivian Diary.* She has travelled extensively for work and for pleasure to countries as far-flung as Peru, Korea, the Sudan, Egypt, Russia, Cuba and Mexico. She is at present living in France, where she is translating a book on Jack London.

THOSE WHO DIED YOUNG

CULT HEROES OF THE TWENTIETH CENTURY

MARIANNE SINCLAIR

Plexus, London

For Timon
may he live for ever

Sinclair, Marianne
    Those who died young.
    1. Performing arts – Social aspects
    2. Entertainers
    I. Title
    301.5'7   PNI590.S6
    ISBN 0-85965-029-4
    ISBN 0-85965-023-5 Pbk

Cover painting by Charlie Baird;
graphics and design by
Chris Lower and Bob Ughetti
Book designed by Chris Lower

Printed in Great Britain by
Acford, Chichester, Sussex

CONTENTS

RUDOLPH VALENTINO 1895-1926	**ZBIGNIEW CYBULSKI** 1927-1967
JEAN HARLOW 1911-1937	**BUDDY HOLLY** 1936-1959
MARILYN MONROE 1926-1962	**ELVIS PRESLEY** 1935-1977
CAROL LOMBARD 1909-1942	**EDDIE COCHRAN** 1938-1960
GÉRARD PHILIPE 1922-1959	**JIM REEVES** 1924-1964
JOHN GARFIELD 1913-1952	**GENE VINCENT** 1935-1971
MONTGOMERY CLIFT 1920-1965	**SAM COOKE** 1937-1964
JAMES DEAN 1931-1955	**OTIS REDDING** 1941-1967

BRIAN JONES 1942-1969	**MARC BOLAN** 1948-1977
JIMI HENDRIX 1942-1970	**KEITH MOON** 1946-1978
JANIS JOPLIN 1943-1970	**BRUCE LEE** 1940-1973
JIM MORRISON 1943-1971	**CHE GUEVARA** 1928-1967
DUANE ALLMAN 1946-1971	**JOHN KENNEDY** 1917-1963
'MAMA' CASS ELLIOTT 1943-1974	**ROBERT KENNEDY** 1925-1968
PAUL KOSSOFF 1950-1976	**EVA PERON** 1919-1952
GRAM PARSONS 1946-1973	**MARTIN LUTHER KING** 1929-1968

'Because I could not stop for Death
Death kindly stopped for me.
The carriage held but us
And Immortality.'

EMILY DICKINSON

'If we dreamt the same thing every night, it would have as much impact on us as the objects we see every day. And if a workman could be certain of dreaming for twelve hours every night that he was a king, I believe he would be almost as happy as a king who would dream every night for twelve hours that he was a workman.'

BLAISE PASCAL

'It's funny the way most people love the dead. Once you are dead you are made for life. You have to die before they think you are worth anything.'

JIMI HENDRIX

HOW IT WAS

Quite a few of the people discussed in this book were contemporaries of mine. A surprising number of today's legends were at the peak of their careers in the mid-fifties when I was entering the ranks of the teenagers and drinking in the popular culture of the West. Montgomery Clift, Marilyn Monroe, James Dean, Buddy Holly, Edith Piaf, Elvis Presley and Judy Garland were among the top stars of the 1955-1958 years; they are all dead today and none of them lived to old age. A second generation of legendary figures was growing up during that period: Brian Jones, Jim Morrison, Jimi Hendrix and Janis Joplin, along with all the other big stars of the liberated Sixties, experienced the unliberated fifties, as I did, during the most formative and rebellious years of their lives. In the small American town where I spent all my adolescence, I endured the pressure to conform that was a feature of the Eisenhower years. Janis Joplin was experiencing it a few thousand miles away in another small town identical to the one I lived in. Elvis Presley was at the height of his success then; the girls at my school raved about him and the boys copied his hair style, his pink shirts and suede shoes until they seemed to be wearing a uniform. Presley's songs were played on all the jukeboxes of America and it was not unusual to hear his latest hit played six times in a row in the drugstore during the half-hour it took to eat a banana split. Marilyn Monroe was by far the most popular female star of the day; she was a household name and I remember that the first man who ever tried to kiss me called me his little Marilyn – not because I looked like her (I was only thirteen at the time) – but because that was the highest compliment anyone could pay to a girl in those days.

Like all the other high school students in my town, I went to the cinema every Friday evening. It was there that I first saw Montgomery Clift in *From Here to Eternity* and James Dean in *East of Eden*. They were my heroes and I loved them, along with Marlon Brando, when they were just popular teen idols; it never occurred to me then that they would become cult-figures in a more general sense, that their films would be shown at cine-clubs to unborn generations, any more than I would have expected serious people of my parents' generations to respect them or even to go and see one of their films. They belonged to the teenagers who sat in the dark, chewing gum and smooching. They were like living symbols of our rebellion, our scepticism, our yearnings, though we certainly could not have expressed the feeling in terms of 'projection' or identification. When

James Dean died I cried, as I suppose most girls of my age did. I read the story of his death in the papers, saw the photographs of his wrecked car, yet still I could not believe it. It was the first death which had a strong emotional impact on me, and which eventually brought home the fact that death was not reserved for the old.

Most of the people discussed in this book, like these stars of the fifties, were youth heroes or stars of popular entertainment, and were enjoyed as such before their appeal reached the intellectuals, before anyone tried to construct cultural theories round them. There was no way of knowing in advance that they would die young, so that the element of awe and respect usually felt for the dead was lacking in the original appreciation of their merits. When they died, their images changed – death gave me a different perspective of their achievements, lending them a restrospective aura of pathos they did not possess to the same extent as when they were alive. Of course, we sensed Marilyn's vulnerability, James Dean's sensitivity, Montgomery Clift's inner conflicts, but it was only a part of their persona. They also seemed supremely enviable – they were good-looking, successful, rich and led far more interesting lives than any of us. Then, when they died, our impression of them was considerably modified. The shock and sorrow of their passing coloured people's reactions with compassion and pity. Seeing James Dean in *Rebel Without a Cause* when it was released soon after his death had a completely different impact than seeing him in *East of Eden* when he seemed to have his whole career ahead of him. Casting about for reasons and explanations as to why tragedy should strike people so young and so gifted, those characteristics were focused on which seemed to spell doom in them and the inevitability of an early end. The vulnerability became self-destruction, the feature by which they would be best remembered. The media helped of course, with all the articles, editorials, biographies and intimate revelations about the dead stars which came out immediately after their deaths. These pieces often brought out tragic aspects of the star's private life and chronicled inner torments which were not known to the public while he or she was alive.

Death gave a new awareness of these stars, a new vision of how they had really been or now seemed to have been. The hindsight of death gives new meaning to old responses, irremediably altering our emotional reaction to these heroes as well as our appraisal of them. It is this curious phenomenon which I have explored in this book.

MARIANNE SINCLAIR

1. WHAT'S IN A NAME?

What's in a name? When speaking of individuals like Rudolph Valentino, Marilyn Monroe, James Dean or Jimi Hendrix, Elvis Presley, Montgomery Clift, Janis Joplin or Bruce Lee, it is difficult to avoid using terms like 'hero', 'myth' and 'legend', even in the most casual reference to them. Even those who never admired them are aware that they were heroes to millions during their lifetimes, and have become the object of lasting cults since their deaths. How did it happen? Why did they become mythical and legendary after they died? They performed no miracles, they were not kings and queens set apart from birth to rule over others, they were not geniuses whose inventions revolutionized the lives of their fellow mortals or great military leaders whose campaigns and conquests altered the course of history. So why?

To begin with most were heroes and heroines to countless fans before an early death lent a mystical touch to their persona. The American poet, Wallace Stevens, defined the hero succinctly as 'a man beyond us yet ourselves'. A hero or a heroine is the personification of an ideal and thus it can be said that a man without heroes is a man without ideals. The hero possesses to a high degree the human qualities and accomplishments we value most. He is held up as an example of perfection; he is fervently admired and imitated. Those who hero-worship him seek to mould their characters and appearance on his, striving through emulation to become more heroic themselves. If the hero is of the opposite sex, which is often the case, love mingles with admiration. People can project their wildest fantasies onto their heroes because they appear so superior, and thus able to achieve with ease things which seem impossible to ordinary people. But on another level, modern heroes can be identified with, because they are real people who have problems and faults, who suffer and die like everyone else.

The nature of heroes has changed according to the times and circumstances in which they lived. In times of war and upheavals, the hero was warlike, his heroic deeds martial. Where religion was the all-pervasive influence, the hero embodied spiritual perfection and was often a saint or a martyr. When countries fought for national independence and struggled to shake off a foreign yoke, the hero was a patriot, a guerilla leader whose heroic feats were performed in the service of his country or his cause. In times of peace and prosperity,

the hero was often a contributor to his country's progress: an inventor, a statesman, a scientist or an explorer. But in the twentieth century, particularly in its second half, religion no longer plays an important part in most people's lives, political and military might are discredited and we are too technologically advanced to stand in much awe of science. Of course, heroes still emerge from those ranks: certain religious figures like Pope John XXIII, political leaders like John Kennedy or revolutionaries like Ho Chi Minh and Che Guevara. Astronauts are heroes to many – the Russians even have a Yuri Gagarin Day. But even the excitement generated by man's first steps on the moon has been tarnished by the enormous cost and subsequent cut backs of the space programme. There are sporting celebrities like George Best or Muhammad Ali who are *bona fide* heroes to their fans. There are national and even local heroes whom no-one outside their country or district know much about, just as there are international heroes like Albert Schweitzer who attract universal admiration for their dedication to the welfare of mankind. Yet the uncontested hero of this century, the one whose character and aptitudes strike the imagination of the greatest

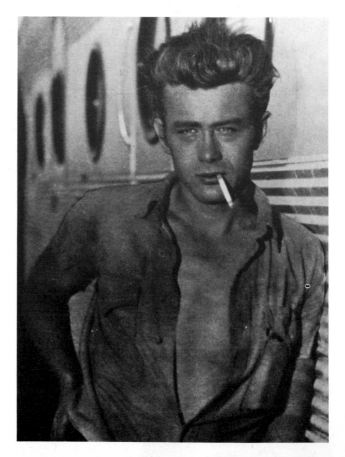

number of people, is the media hero. This is a natural enough development in an age where, for the first time in history, films, photographs, television and records make the name, face and voice of entertainers as well-known as those of one's closest friends. Free time and leisure activities play a far greater part in most people's lives than at any time previously, so it is also logical that heroes should be drawn from the ranks of those who entertain.

In other centuries, the hero's face was often unfamiliar; his features might never have been known or perhaps have only been glimpsed by the people who revered him. They had sometimes heard or read a vague, probably fanciful description of how he looked. At best, their curiosity could be satisfied by a painting of his likeness or by a blurred photograph, after photography had been invented. When books and magazines were not widely circulated and the great majority of adults were illiterate, people knew very little about their heroes in private life or ordinary situations. A hero was known only by reputation and it was entirely his deeds or achievements which made him famous, whereas today we have a detailed, overall picture of our heroes' characters, their lives past and present, their appearance, formal or informal, their personal views on every subject, even their secrets. This documentation, so minute and complete, makes us far more aware of the hero as an individual. The importance of his actual deeds

recedes and the impression of a larger-than-life personality becomes the motivating power in today's hero worship. The hero no longer has to *do* so much as to *be*. Even the talent which made him famous matters less than the person he is; fans go to a pop concert not so much to hear their idol sing as to see him in the flesh, to get a sense of what it is about him which makes him seem so unique and exciting. A faceless hero would be unthinkable now. It is the face itself which captures the interest first and makes people want to know more about the achievements. Che Guevara's life and actions were probably as genuinely heroic as those of any legendary hero of the past, but in the twentieth century it had to be his face which made his heroism famous; people who saw photographs of the handsome guerilla leader wanted to find out more about his life and death. Had there been no photographs of Che, his legend would never have spread the way it did. Today's hero cannot be nondescript to look at. Ugly or handsome, he must be strikingly photogenic and immediately identifiable visually.

In previous eras, people loved their heroes for their virtues, overlooking such faults as they had and which seemed unimportant compared to their merits. But today heroes are admired almost as much for their failings as for their qualities. Having a larger than life image, their faults also take on an exaggerated quality which often appeals to the imagination: Carole Lombard swore like a trooper, Judy Garland drank herself into a stupor, James Dean drove like a maniac, endangering not only his own life but that of others on the road, Brian Jones slept with two or three girls at a time and then kicked them out unceremoniously. We might be distressed and shocked by such conduct on the part of a sister, a sweetheart or a friend, but we accept it and even find it appealing in our cult figures. The ancient Greeks too were delighted by the goings-on of their gods, their drunken, adulterous and dishonest behaviour. After all, these were gods whose power lent glamour and prestige to activities which would have been considered degrading and immoral in a mortal. Everyone chafes at the restrictions imposed upon pleasure by society and by one's own conscience; there is a deep satisfaction in identifying with someone better-placed who gets away with it. Yet there is also resentment; retribution must come sooner or later. The price modern heroes should pay for being so lucky, so rich and self-indulgent must either be unhappiness or death, often both. This explains why the most adoring fans are so eager to read about the private misfortunes of their idols and why, when a popular star dies, there seems to be something satisfyingly inevitable about his death, whatever grief the news inspires. Further, a hero really must die young to preserve his credibility and to seem mythical. He must die at the peak of his fortunes, his looks and his fame, long before the fans have started

tiring of him. Decline of any kind is a sad process and in a hero seems almost a failing. His early death will confirm and reinforce his heroic status and increase his stature: his admirers will feel that here was one who lived life to the hilt and then died before time could take its revenge. At Carole Lombard's funeral, the officiating minister thundered in his eulogy: 'Only those who are not afraid of death are fit to live!' Carole Lombard did not choose to die when she did, but early death lent her an aura, gave her life a sort of significance it could not have had while she was alive. Dying young is what makes today's living hero tomorrow's legend.

It is only in terms of the dead that we can usually speak of myths and legends. Cults generally spring up after the death of an individual rather than during his lifetime. No star or entertainer, however popular and famous, can really be considered a 'myth' if he lives to a ripe old age and dies at ninety. Basically, these terms are reserved for stars who die young and tragically.

The words 'myth' and 'legend' are used in common parlance, but what in fact do they *mean*? The dictionary defines a myth as 'a person or thing existing only in imagination or whose actuality is not verifiable. A transcendental or semi-mystical belief which is given uncritical acceptance by the members of a group'. The definition of a legend is 'a popular myth, usually of

current or recent origin; one having special status as a result of possessing or being held to possess extraordinary qualities that are usually partly real and partly invented'. What is interesting about both these definitions is their ambivalent meaning: a legendary figure owes his status to the possession of extraordinary qualities *or* he is only held to possess them. His qualities may have been real *or* they may have been invented by his admirers. A myth exists only in the imagination or, at best, it is not verifiable. In the same way, 'hero worship' is defined as either 'the recognition and just evaluation of illustrious individuals' *or* as 'foolish and excessive adulation'. Thus legends, myths and heroes are people who either were truly extraordinary or who were only held to be so by uncritical adorers. Obviously, the creation of legends and of myths about dead heroes is an extremely subjective process. What supreme arbitrator can decide whether adulation is justified or ill-founded? The point has probably been contested for every hero who ever lived, but perhaps never as hotly as today when, as was stated earlier, it is the hero's overall personality which counts more than his actions. Achievements can be evaluated objectively in a way that character cannot. Even deadly enemies would have been forced to acknowledge that El Cid fought bravely in battle or that Napoleon was a remarkable general. But when it comes to assessing an individual's per-

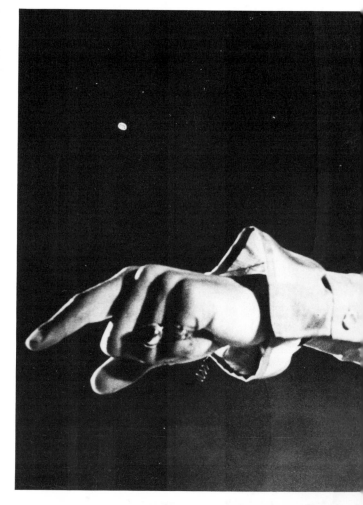

sonality, opinions can be radically opposed. To some, Brian Jones or Jimi Hendrix were repellent drug freaks, to others they were heroes.

The dictionary also provides interesting clues concerning the origin of words like cult or legend. Legend comes from the Greek word 'to collect', the word 'cult' comes from the Latin 'to cultivate' and the term 'fan' is an abbreviation of fanatic which, in its original sense, meant 'frantic, inspired by a deity'. Myth is akin to the Lithuanian word 'mausti' which means 'to desire ardently'. To collect, cultivate and desire ardently are very active states, not at all passive ones. We often forget this because fans, however, devoted, are anonymous and their obscurity makes them seem an insignificant factor in the creation of a cult around a dead or a living hero. Yet it is the fans who create a legend, who perpetrate a myth, who keep alive the memory of a beloved figure or allow it to fade away. The hero incarnates the myth, but fans are the original creators of that myth and its custodians once he is dead. For what really gives birth to myths is not any individual star so much as the collective hunger for myths, the universal need to believe in something or someone which results in the singling out of a chosen few who seem to personify the tastes and ideals of their age.

Myths have been described as 'expressions or objectifications of collective wishes'. Our twentieth century myths wholly reflect the aspirations of Western culture with its emphasis on youth, good looks and material success. Today's popular myth is unlikely to be, as he might have been at other times, a wise old hermit who scorns wordly possessions and meditates on spiritual perfection alone on a mountainside. But today's myths also show up the more negative aspects of our culture, its anxiety, dissatisfaction, lack of purpose and loss of faith. Our heroes are young, good-looking and rich, but they are often neurotic, self-destructive and rebellious.

In a pessimistic age, many young people do not identify with positive, well-adjusted heroes. They prefer anti-heroes who reflect their pessimistic outlook, their distrust of established values. Some of the great twentieth century literary figures who died young, often in tragic circumstances, might fit this pattern. From the twenties on there have been writers and poets whose lives and work have reflected the modern malaise, people like F. Scott Fitzgerald and Sylvia Plath in America, Brendan Behan in Ireland, Dylan Thomas in Britain, Albert Camus in France. In their work we find all the pre-occupations with despair, futility and frustration that modern youth appears to identify with, but it is in the nature of literature, in which a private relationship between writer and reader is built up, that although all are recognized as artistically great, none (except perhaps Fitzgerald) have achieved the mass adulation of the film or popular music heroes. This also applies to the jazz singers and musicians who also succumbed to the introspection of their art, men like Charlie 'Bird' Parker, John Coltrane and Roland Kirk, and women like Billie Holiday and Bessie Smith. Often they were victims of the same pressures as rock stars like Hendrix and Joplin, but their music being so much less accessible meant that while sadly missed, death did not always add to their legendary stature.

But they were undoubtedly anti-heroes, following an individualistic rebellion to which today's youth often relates. Disliking the world as it is and yet unable to find alternative solutions, others have taken refuge in a hedonistic lifestyle; sex, drugs, dancing, music, speed. No wonder that so many of their heroes seem to personify these things. 'To heck with work', John Garfield said in one of his early films, and it made him famous because the words echoed the disillusion people felt during the Great Depression of the thirties, with the bleakness of everyday life and the pointlessness of effort when it so often went unrewarded. 'To heck with everything!' a later generation of cult figures said,

taking the bitterness a stage further. 'I'm here to have a party, man, as best I can while I'm on earth. I think it's your duty to', Janis Joplin once declared; this odd concept of duty, the dedication to the principle of 'having a party' even if it wrecks your health and ultimately kills you, made Janis seem to many every bit as heroic as Florence Nightingale.

Jimi Hendrix summed up this nihilistic rejection of all convictions which has become a form of conviction, in an interview in 1967. Of religion he said: 'There are so many different beliefs that something must be phoney. I used to go to Sunday School, but the only thing I believe in now is music.' Of politics, he said: 'All I know is what I read in the papers. I don't care, so long as they don't drop the bomb before I get a chance to make money.' What has gone wrong? The decline of religion? The threat of nuclear holocaust? Pollution of the environment? The decay of morality? Perhaps

left) died at 35; virtuoso Roland Kirk (below) at 41; Billie Holiday (right) was 44 when her tragic life ended in 1959; Bessie Smith (bottom right) and John Coltrane (below right) both died aged 40.

Hendrix expressed it best when he said, 'The mechanical life – where cities and hotel rooms all merge into one – has killed . . . enjoyment for me. So I've just got to get out. Maybe to Venus or somewhere. Some place *you* won't be able to find me.' Hendrix confirmed his disgust with the 'mechanical life' by dying at the age of twenty-seven. In this respect he was as true to this conviction that life was not worth living as heroes who in the past proved their dedication to a cause or an ideal by dying for it. Marilyn Monroe, James Dean, Montgomery Clift, Brian Jones, Janis Joplin and even Elvis Presley showed the same contempt for the principle of self-preservation and this made a lot of people identify with them even more strongly after they died than while they were alive. It is impossible to categorize such a wide variety of people who became cult figures after their deaths and who died in such different circumstances. But the general message seems to be that young people in the latter part of the twentieth century have wanted to know from their heroes that life does not have much purpose, that adult society is a mess which cannot be got straight and that, therefore, the sooner you stop the world and get off the better. This explains why, more than ever before, they mythologize those who die before middle-age. Bill Graham, the pop entrepreneur, confirmed this when he said: 'I would talk to a lot of the kids; and what it amounted to was they wanted to live very fast, die very young, and have a good-looking corpse.'

All the dead entertainers discussed in this book fulfilled these requirements, however much they differed from one another. Perhaps later generations, less disenchanted and with a surer sense of purpose, will ask themselves what today's myths and legends had to show for their status apart from their egocentricity and their complexes. Still, myths and legends do for their times. They change constantly and few survive the passage of centuries. What never alters, however, is the human impulse to collect, to cultivate and to desire ardently; that, more than any single individual's achievements, is what gives birth to the cult of heroes and the mythology of those who die young.

17

2. THE LOVE GODS

Rudolph Valentino died in 1926, the summer Marilyn Monroe was born. He had come from Italy and she was born in Hollywood where the film industry had started. He was as dark as she was fair. Valentino was 'radiantly self-assured' and supremely European and those two traits were important ingredients in his success; whereas Marilyn was a typically American girl and, as the cameraman on one of her films described it, half her appeal lay in 'the inferiority complex which, coupled with such beauty, gave her a look of mystery'.

When we look back on Rudolph Valentino and Marilyn Monroe, whose lifespans only coincided for two months in the summer of 1926, who had nothing in common except their Hollywood screen fame, we find them linked indissolubly like two halves, the him and her of the same phenomenon. Their impact on the public had everything in common: they were the superstars of superstars because they embodied, in its most primal, unalloyed sense, the principle of LOVE, and love is what stardom is all about. Love is what makes fans scream, what makes audiences rush to the cinema, what turned 'otherwise intelligent men into frenzied baboons' when Marilyn appeared, what made law-abiding, mature women shriek, faint and clobber policemen over the head with their matronly handbags when they caught a glimpse of 'Rudy'. There have been many other love-gods and goddesses in the history of the movies and yet, when we sift through the evidence and try to determine who came the closest to the love ideal on the screen, the names of Valentino and Marilyn inevitably come first. If there were a prize, an ultimate Oscar which would be awarded to *the* most popular and adulated actor and actress of all time, the most manically adored in his or her lifetime, the most mourned and

romanticized after death, it could scarcely fail to go to Valentino and to Marilyn. They are the king and queen of twentieth century movie romance, the incarnation of its ideal of erotic love. There are obviously quite a number of runners-up. Thousands, perhaps millions of fans might disagree with this verdict, insisting that Tyrone Power was more handsome than Valentino, that Greta Garbo had far more class than Marilyn, that Marlon Brando is the better actor, that Marlene Dietrich was more beautiful, that Gregory Peck had more dash or Joan Crawford more personality. Many film stars can make valid claims to achievements that were outside the scope of Valentino or Monroe, but love is what we are talking about here. What both had to an uncommon, probably unique, degree was a kind of flesh appeal, a compelling presence which made audiences, in their imaginations, bridge the gap between cinema seat and screen, the fantasy becoming as real as reality, the emotion aroused almost as vivid as if Rudy or Marilyn had actually been sitting in the seat next to them, holding their hands.

The erotic impact of these two stars was quite straight: it was not cerebral, spiritual or even perverse. It was a direct, unmitigated invitation to have sex: 'Come with me to the Casbah', 'Let's make love'. You could not mistake the gleam in Rudy's eye; his eager, leer, his love-crazed expression, his flaring nostrils all meant one thing: *lust*. Marilyn's jiggle and wiggle as she walked, her half-closed lids, her parted lips contained one message only: 'Take me to bed; you won't regret it'. And yet, if their appeal had only resided in sex it wouldn't have been enough. Few people want to cope with the starkness of raw sex; they want it packaged in fantasies of potential passion; sex with a sizzle is great, but the possibility of True Love, of finding a mate worthy of one's loftiest aspirations, must gild the pill. The tart and the gigolo promise to give us all the sexual thrills that only tarts and gigolos can, but must

also make us feel that they are good people. Rudy will seduce you, how exciting, but do not worry, he is also a man of principle and will marry you in the end. Sure, Marilyn's a blonde bombshell who is not wearing any underwear under the gold sequins, but you can tell at a glance that she's a fine sort really, who does not want to break up anyone's marriage and who will prove to be a true sweetheart to the lucky fellow who gets her.

Good looks and sexiness are not enough to drive fans crazy, to turn a star into a living legend or a myth after death. John Gilbert was handsome and he died young, Jayne Mansfield was sexy and she died young. But we are still firmly under the influence of the great idealization of romantic love which has been an integral part of Western culture since the Middle Ages; we expect the object of our lust to also be worthy of us, or else the fantasy falls flat. In this respect, Valentino and Monroe outshine all their rivals; supremely sexy, expert at arousing desire, there is nothing too primitive or crude about their sex appeal, though it is obvious and devastating.

Must love gods died young to realize the ideal synthesis of *eros* and *thanatos* – love and death, as two complementary aspects of the same life process: regeneration and degeneration, procreation and destruction? Or, more prosaically, must true love gods die young in order to preserve their godhead, to remain those 'angels of sex' as Norman Mailer described Marilyn Monroe in his biography of her? Whether by coincidence or destiny, the prior contender to Marilyn's crown of love queen, to her sex-angel's title, also died young. Her name was Jean Harlow and she too was blonde, sexy, beautiful and unhappy. But let us start with Rudolph Valentino, the gorgeous, strangely moving and faintly ridiculous male angel of sex (if angels have a sex), who died over half a century ago, yet whose myth is still vital enough for a film to have been made of his life in 1976 by Ken Russell, with another Rudolph and another legend – Rudolf Nureyev – in the title role.

VALENTINO

Rudolph Valentino was born in 1895 in Castellenata, a small town in southern Italy, to a respectable middle-class family. He did poorly at school, not from lack of brains so much as from a lack of interest and application. He got into minor scrapes and deliberately tried to shock his elders and betters by wearing flamboyant cravats or walking arm in arm down the main street with a 'loose' woman, not from any inherent delinquency but from sheer boredom and the need to stand out. He spent a great deal of time daydreaming about becoming a bigshot somewhere in the golden world of promise that lay outside the frontiers of Castellenata. Rudy was not very different from most, but he did happen to be better-looking, and more determined than many to escape the cramped existence that lay in store for him if he remained at home in Castellenata. He proved his determination and his powers of seductive persuasion by convincing his family, even his all-powerful and adoring *mama,* to allow him to go and try his luck in America, as so many other Italians were doing at the time. Thus, aged only eighteen, Valentino set off on his own. He arrived, full of dreams but without an overcoat, in the freezing New York winter of 1913, not speaking a word of English and carrying all his belongings in a battered suitcase. Only the most menial jobs were available for someone in his situation, and he did them all: messenger, refuse collector, dishwasher, laundry assistant and undergardener. There was plenty of time to dream of future glory. Even more time when, out of work, having pawned all he possessed and been thrown out of his $1.50 a week room, he wandered the streets aimlessly, eating out of restaurant dustbins and sleeping on benches. The man who was to own 1,000 pairs of socks, 300 ties and 40 suits then had

to use discarded newspapers for underwear. The man who later owned eight cars could not afford a subway ride and walked the streets of New York until, at his lowest point, he walked across the East River bridge and thought of drowning himself. But worse than the poverty was the contempt: the doorman chasing him out of the hotel where he had tried to sneak in to write a letter to his mother on the hotel stationery; the burly Irishman who lorded over him at work and bullied him because he belonged to an even more despised immigrant group; the police who might arrest him on charges of vagrancy; the haughty New York girls who would not cast a glance in the direction of a handsome but shabby alien.

But Valentino was too attractive and too determined to go on in this way for very long. It is unlikely that at this stage he was thinking of a film actor's career; his ambition did not relate to a specific occupation so much as to achieving a financial state that would allow him to wear silk shirts, to smell delicious and to drink champagne in the company of classy ladies. He might have become a gangster, a common way for Italian immigrants in New York to attain such a goal, but his character was not suitable for crime and, in his way, he was a man of principle. He became a nightclub dancer instead, paid by the club which employed him to ask single ladies to dance, something he learned to do with matchless grace. It may be that he was also paid by those same ladies to perform other acrobatics in more intimate surroundings but with equally matchless grace. Rudy was an instant success as a professional male dancer, and the clubs where he worked quickly became more elegant. Just as James Dean's future success with the 'kids' was foreshadowed by young audience reaction to his early TV appearances, so Rudy's later delirious film success with 'mature' women was foreshadowed by the

swathe he cut during his days as a young gigolo. Riper ladies thrilled to his suave, old world manners, to the way he bowed and clicked his heels as he asked them for the next dance. Their hearts fluttered at the smouldering way he looked into their eyes when he danced the waltz or the tango with them. They relished the discreet elegance with which he took the fat tips they slipped into his hand when the dance was over. For several years Rudy, who by now spoke perfect English, was one of the most fashionable and sought-after nightclub dancers in New York. Would his ambition have stopped there, now that he had plenty of money, wore silk shirts and drank champagne nightly in luxurious surroundings? It was not to be. Fate intervened as it must, or at least it should, in the person of a beautiful woman. She was a dark, passionate Latin American lady called Bianca de Saulles, whom he met on the dance floor and it was love at first tango. Unfortunately, she happened to be married to a prominent gangster and, in the drama which unfolded as a result of her affair with Rudy, she murdered her husband in an argument. The scandal and the court case which ensued made things uncomfortable and dangerous enough for Rudy to flee New York and to end up in 1918, in Los Angeles, ostensibly to take up farming. But there his career as nightclub dancer began again, and it was inevitable that he should start forming other ambitions in the capital of the film world.

Rudy soon became friendly with people connected with the film business: an actor called Norman Kerry and the director Emmett Flynn. Both urged him to try his luck in the movies and Valentino was only too willing to follow their advice, but his distinctively Latin looks were a handicap in getting lead roles at that time. Over the next three years, Valentino played a variety of small film parts, portraying villains and miscellaneous other unsavoury characters. There is a tendency to think

of Valentino as an overnight sensation, so it comes as something of a shock to realize that he had already appeared in seventeen films before *The Four Horsemen of the Apocalypse*, which propelled him to stardom in 1921. June Mathis, an MGM writer, had seen him in a movie called *Eyes of Youth* (1919) and had decided he would be perfect for the lead in *Four Horsemen*, an adaption of the famous Blasco Ibanez novel about a carefree Latin American aristocrat who goes out to fight for France during the First World War. June Mathis persuaded the reluctant MGM to try out the almost unknown Italian and his fantastic popular success in the part can be compared to the one James Dean was to have in *East of Eden*.

Valentino went on to make a succession of box-office hits for MGM, Paramount and his own independent production company: including *The Sheik* (1921), *Blood and Sand* (1922), *The Young Rajah* (1922), *Monsieur Beaucaire* (1924), *Cobra* (1925) and *The Son of the Sheik* (1926). The films themselves varied in quality but this no longer mattered; the fans went to see Rudolph Valentino films not to judge the picture's worth, nor even to judge the leading actor's real merits. They were so taken with Rudy's appearance and sex appeal that they hardly cared about his other qualities as an actor and a human being. In fact, Valentino could

be a good actor, could project emotion with absolute sincerity, could convey gentleness as well as passion, obviously had a sense of humour about everything including himself and had tremendous athletic abilities.

Why did it have to be Rudolph Valentino? What was his secret? He was wonderfully photogenic, he moved with feline grace and he projected sexual passion, but others too have done as much. Yet Valentino did more. In his films, he never merely portrays a sexy cad. He is also brave and chivalrous, fights bulls in *Blood and Sand*, takes risks to save a woman's reputation in *The Sheik* and enlists to fight a war in *The Four Horsemen of the Apocalypse*. Even when his morals leave something to be desired, finer qualities are always present. Though he retains the more seductive characteristics of the film villain – the suavity, the sophistication, the sexual menace – he sheds the villain's more unpleasant traits such as cruelty, deceit and cowardice. In his love scenes, his manner is the opposite of crass: he is sexually threatening not because, like a true villain, he would rape a woman, but because he would take advantage of her inability to resist his charm. In *The Sheik*, it was seduction and not violation which got the better of the heroine's resistance. This was made quite clear in the original novel by Edith Maud Winstanley, alias E. M. Hull, a farmer's wife from the North of England: ' "Come," he whispered hoarsely, his passionate eyes devouring her. She fought against the fascination with which they dominated her . . .,' but lost, of course, for who could resist Rudy? The sheik did not have to throw the heroine to the floor; she fell there of her own accord, overcome by the 'strange fear that the man himself awakened in her, which had driven her at last moaning to her knees'. It is the eyes which devour far more than the arms which grab, and a woman has to fight against herself rather than against her seducer when that seducer happens to be Rudy.

In the early days of the screen, it was common for a film to have two male leads: a hero and a villain. The old-fashioned hero has been described as 'silent, kind, noble, generous, patriotic, pious, slow to anger yet quick to avenge his honour, and horse-loving'. These are admirable qualities but they are not particularly erotic ones. Early screen heroes like Carlyle Blackwell, King Baggott and Harold Lockwood looked as though sex was the last thing on their minds as they puffed on their manly pipes, looked pious and patted their horses. The old-style film villain has been defined by Ben Hecht as someone who could 'lay anybody he wants, have as much fun as he wants, cheating and stealing, getting rich and whipping the servants. But you have to shoot him in the end.' The villain was slick, suave and usually

foreign-looking; provincial film audiences could project their phobias on him, their fear of foreigners, their distrust of aristocratic panache and their envious contempt for anyone who came from the Big City. But they could also indulge through the villain in 'their own secret desires for luxury, skullduggery and unlimited illicit sex'. By the time Valentino appeared on the screen, morals had grown laxer and audiences more sophisticated. The novel combination of heroic and villainous traits helped to turn Valentino into the fantasy lover of every woman and the envy of every man. In *The Four Horsemen of the Apocalypse,* his first big part, he was foreign and aristocratic and lived in sinful Paris just like a villain might; yet he was noble, generous and ready to die for his adopted country as a hero should. In his most famous role as the Sheik, he was both hero and villain in all the most traditional aspects of both parts: the unprincipled Arab sensualist who took advantage of the virtuous maiden in his power, and the shining knight who eventually saved her from her predicament as a seduced woman by marrying her and turning out to be a well-born Britisher in the end.

Valentino exuded style and *savoir faire,* qualities many of his American female admirers probably found sadly lacking in their real-life sweethearts or husbands. He was infinitely Continental and obviously madly experienced in the arts of love. Each of his screen loves was a *grande passion* and his concentrated expression of tender lust potently combined sensuality and romantic emotion. Over the last fifty years, our taste in male sex appeal has changed. The trend is more towards

sweaty T-shirts and torn jeans than to dinner-jackets and brilliantined hair. Valentino may not excite today's girls and he may even strike them as a bit ridiculous; yet anyone who sees a Valentino film or just a series of stills from his pictures is struck by the actor's suave yet virile charm, by the flesh appeal, the aura of sexuality which never seems effeminate despite the powdered wigs of *Monsieur Beaucaire* or the strings of pearls he wore in *The Young Rajah.* Lustful yet sensitive, Valentino could sweep you off your feet, but he wouldn't let you fall flat on your face either; your fantasy of True Romance coupled with sexual fulfilment was safe in his hands.

Valentino's private life was full of material comforts and ego gratification, but it was not always happy; yet it was perhaps less catastrophically unhappy than seekers after sensation and lovers of paradox have maintained. There is nothing to support any evidence that Valentino was impotent or that he was masochistically attracted only to domineering women, though both claims were often made. His second wife, Natacha Rambova, was strong-willed indeed and she influenced him, not always wisely, in his career. But her past career as assistant to the great Russian actress Nazimova entitled her to assume that Rudolph would value her artistic judgement, and she possessed a good deal more than a domineering character; she also happened to be an extremely beautiful woman and, in many respects, she was interesting and original. Natacha's real name was Winifred Hudnut, and she was the stepdaughter of Richard Hudnut, a millionaire manufacturer of perfumes. The couple married in 1923 and were very happy for at least some of the time they were together. A great deal of foolishness has been said about Rudy's ill-fated first marriage to a pretty young actress named Jean Acker whom he had met in Hollywood before his days of stardom. Actually the facts of this marriage, or non-marriage as it should be termed, cast no discredit on Valentino nor raise any special doubts concerning his potency. The whole painful story of his wedding-night with Jean Acker would come out later when he had become a star and was thus supremely newsworthy. Arrested on technical charges of bigamy when he married Natacha without being properly divorced from Jean Acker, Rudy was forced to prove in the trial that ensued that his first marriage had never been consummated. Jean Acker, who was a lesbian and who claimed to have married him 'out of pity', had changed her mind at the crucial moment and had ordered her newly-wedded husband out of the bedroom. A group of horrified friends had overheard Jean screaming at Rudy that the thought of his body close to hers was nauseating and that she would rather die than let him touch her. Short of raping her, there was nothing he could do but leave. The whole episode would have been disagreeable and humiliating for anyone to live through, but it was Valentino's misfortune that it should be made public and that, naturally, it made him the target of endless cruel jokes since his entire reputation was founded on his powers of seduction.

The five brief years of Valentino's glory were much like those of many another superstar. He made a great deal of money, yet spent so much that he was always in and out of debt and was all but insolvent at the time of his death. He basked in the adulation of his fans yet came to dread their frenzy. He relished being welcomed like royalty wherever he went in America and Europe, yet yearned to walk the steets undisturbed like any other man. He chafed against his studios and felt both underrated and underpaid, yet fared no better when he set up independently. He quarrelled continuously with his beautiful wife until a point of no return was reached. So was Valentino happy? Unlike many superstars, Valentino gives the impression of having been a very normal man, but the abnormality of his position was beginning to take its toll on his psyche by 1926, the year of his death.

His marriage to Natacha Rambova was over; whatever its shortcomings, she had been the great love of his life and it had been intended to last forever, to be the nucleus of the family he craved, a real Italian home with lots of children. The drawbacks of so much celebrity, once the delight in it had worn off, were only too apparent. If he grew a beard, as he did for *The Eagle*, the American Master Barbers' Association launched a campaign against him because the male population would all grow beards as a result and the barbers would go bankrupt. If, on his arrival in England in 1923, he politely said that he intended to get a few suits 'because there's nowhere in the world like London for men's clothes', this aroused storms of protest on the part of American tailors. When Natacha gave him a platinum slave-bracelet for Christmas and he promised her that it would never leave his wrist, he was sneered at in the press; it was said that his wife led him by the nose and that Rudy must be a pansy for wearing a bracelet. Success meant that he had to hide as assiduously as if he were an outlaw. When in London he was asked to say a few words about his latest film, *The Eagle*, Valentino could not just walk from the royal box to the stage like anyone else because he would be mobbed by his fans. On thatoccasion he had to disappear up flights of steps, across the cinema roof, down an iron ladder, back into the building, down more stairs, then through a concrete cellar under the stage. Outside in the streets, it was far worse; wherever he ventured he was in physical danger. Here is a description of Valentino's arrival at the opening of *The Eagle*: 'The severely-tested police could cope no longer. Screaming women broke through the cordon and surrounded the star, grabbing at his coat, his arms, his hair. Those who could not get near enough shrieked his name again and again in a chilling, monotonous litany. Others, clambering to get a better view, pulled down advertisement boards, whose glass shattered and broke. With police shoving and pulling hysterical girls from him, Valentino shouldered his way into the

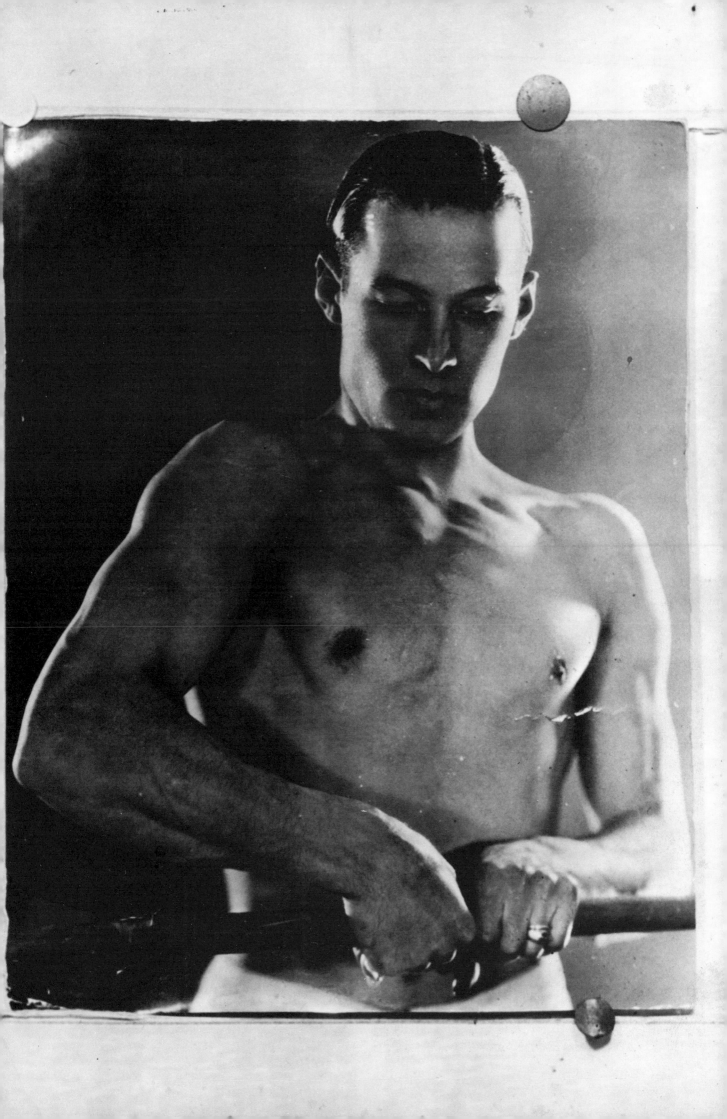

Valentino's early death evoked world-wide
hysteria. On the day of his funeral over 100,000
people lined the streets to pay homage to his
funeral cortege. Below centre: Valentino lying-in-
state in a Broadway funeral parlour, 1926.

cinema, where attendants struggled to close the doors
against the surging mass battling to keep them open'.

Yet other assaults on the love god were even more
distressing for they were born of hatred and envy rather
than of love and admiration. Verbal attacks left permanent wounds on Valentino's spirit. In 1926, that last
hot summer of Rudy's life, an editorial appeared in the
Chicago Tribune concerning an event which seemed
wholly unconnected with the Great Lover: the men's
washroom in a new public ballroom had been equipped
with a slot machine dispensing talc via pink powder
puffs. The author of the editorial attributed this so-
called proof of the effeminization of American males
to Valentino's influence, wailing: 'Why didn't someone
drown Rudolph Gugliemo, alias Valentino, years ago?'
Valentino, who was good-natured and not usually vin-
dictive about attacks on him in the papers, was overcome with wrath and wounded pride when he read the
article. He wrote an open letter to its author declaring:
'You slur my Italian ancestry; you cast ridicule on my
Italian name; you cast doubt upon my manhood.' He
wanted to challenge his anonymous attacker to a duel,
but as this was illegal he was ready to settle for a boxing
or a wrestling match 'to prove in typically American
fashion (for I am an American citizen) which of us is
more a man'. Valentino started training for the pro-
posed contest immediately and was anxious for it to
take place in private so that it would not seem to be a
publicity stunt.

The challenge was not taken up and the whole
affair petered out, but it continued to prey on Valentino's mind. He became so obsessed by the slight which
he could neither forget nor avenge that he decided to
consult a well-known journalist, H. L. Mencken, to ask
him how he could best deal with the pink powder puff
taunt. Mencken told him to forget the whole business
but Valentino was reluctant to follow the suggestion.
They met and talked it over, getting nowhere, until as
Mencken recalls, 'it suddenly dawned on me . . . that
what we were talking about was not really what we
were talking about at all . . . He began by talking of his
home, his people, his early youth. His words were simple
and yet somehow very eloquent. I could still see the
mime before me, but now and then, briefly and darkly,
there was a flash of something else. That something else,
I concluded, was what is commonly called, for want of a
better name, a gentleman. In brief, Valentino's agony
was the agony of a man of relatively civilized feelings
thrown into a situation of intolerable vulgarity, destructive alike to his peace and to his dignity – nay, into a
whole series of such situations. It was not that trifling
Chicago episode that was riding him; it was the whole
grotesque futility of his life . . . Had he achieved, out of
nothing, a vast dizzy success? Then that success was hol-
low as well as vast – a colossal and preposterous nothing.
Was he acclaimed by the yelling multitudes? Then every

time the multitudes yelled, he felt himself blushing inside.' This poignant account is probably the best sum-
ming up of Valentino's predicament and state of mind
at the height of his career. A few days after the meeting
with Mencken, Valentino fell gravely ill. After an emergency operation for appendicitis and gastric ulcers, his
first words upon opening his eyes were: 'Well then, did
I behave like a pink powder puff or like a man?' He
died a few days later, his heart poisoned by septoen-
docarditis.

Most people who know next to nothing about Valentino's life and who have never seen him in a film know
about the riots unleashed by his death. Yet the actual
story sounds almost too preposterous to be true:
imagine a young man, dead at only thirty-one, lying in
state in a bronze coffin inside a Broadway funeral chapel,
his face and shoulders exposed to view. His face is
serene, the atmosphere dignified and melancholy. Then
imagine about 15,000 people standing outside the
chapel in the pouring rain, blocking every street, with
policemen trying to hold them back. The crowd grows
restive and angry; as they surge towards the funeral

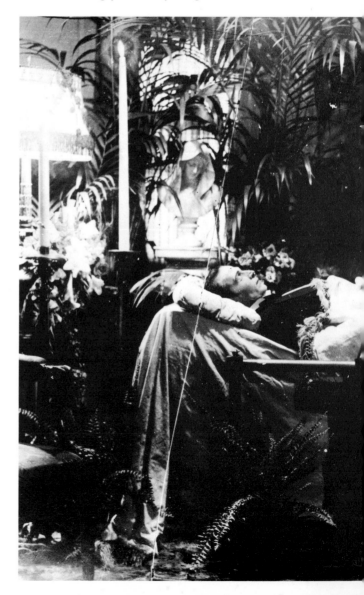

chapel, its huge plate-glass window shatters, showering everyone with splinters. The crowd panics and turns into a mob on the rampage. Mounted policemen begin charging into the crowd to break it up and to prevent it from destroying the chapel. Everyone starts screaming and struggling as the horses' hooves trample women and children underfoot. People faint and scream. Scores are injured and a room in the mortuary is hastily turned into an emergency hospital. When the doors of the funeral parlour finally open, the mob surges forward, pushing and kicking everything in its path. Still shouting, screaming and swearing, it invades the Gold Room where Valentino lies. Within moments, the Gold Room is a shambles, the crowd has to be beaten back and the body is hastily removed to another room on the second floor. All the streets outside are littered with torn clothing, shoes and battered hats. Eventually things are organized and, on the first day alone, 40,000 people are ushered past Valentino's coffin. They are entitled only to a two-second glance at the body before being rushed out again. Sobbing women are roughly hurried on when they try to kiss the glass case that protects their idol. An atmosphere of scandal prevails: the doctor appointed chief physician to help the injured turns out to be a former con-man cashing in on the proceedings. The guard of honour, black-shirted members of the Fascisti League who were supposedly placed there at Mussolini's personal request, turn out to have been hired by a funeral parlour press-agent as a stunt; a violent scuffle ensues between the black-shirts and a group of militant anti-Fascists, with more kicking, swearing and shattered windows. Rumours run as wild as the crowd outside the funeral parlour: Valentino has been stabbed by a jealous rival, no he has been shot, no he is really alive and that is only a wax effigy lying in the coffin. The hysteria reaches its apogee when the Polish film star, Pola Negri, Rudy's last love, appears in widow's weeds which are said to have cost $13,000. Weeping and supported by her maid, she screams and falls into a faint before the admiring multitude. Throngs of mourners line the streets as Valentino's body is taken to the railway station to make its last journey back to California where he is to be buried. At every city where the trains stops, crowds will turn out to look at the train which is carrying the screen's greatest idol to his final resting place.

After the funeral, Valentino's personal belongings were auctioned off; his handkerchiefs, ties and garters became sought-after relics for the shrines to his memory that sprung up all over America. Yet even 1,000 pairs of

socks were not enough to satisfy popular demand. The vault where he lay was regularly hacked to bits and the chips were sold as souvenirs. Five men were discovered trying to break into the vault itself; they were reported to be 'ghouls planning to steal the body of Valentino for commercial purposes'. Not until the death of James Dean would there again be such a morbid love-after-death cult. Women claimed to have communicated with Rudy's spirit, others said he was the father of their child, several committed suicide, and one sued for divorce on the grounds that her husband would not allow her to live near Valentino's tomb. Pola Negri was hounded by men who claimed that Rudolph's spirit had entered their bodies and that if she married them she would be reunited with her lover. A mystery woman, veiled and dressed all in black, continued to bring red roses to Valentino's tomb on each aniversary of his death until 1951. Love had brought Rudy fame, fortune and doubtless some happiness during his lifetime, but it had also, even in death, brought with it the 'intolerable vulgarity' of which Mencken had spoken.

In the days when Marilyn Monroe was still only a little girl growing up in a foster home, Jean Harlow was the reigning queen of Hollywood. Though her legend has

HARLOW

dimmed, her contemporary impact was huge, her films averaging fifteen or twenty million tickets in the United States, out of a total population of one hundred and twenty five million people. Parties of tourists were escorted past her house, described as a magic, orgiastic temple 'where champagne flows and anything goes'. She was almost as popular as Marilyn was to become, and there are many parallels to be drawn between the careers, the lives and

the 'blonde bombshell' image of the two stars. Like Marilyn, Harlow in real life was 'full of apprehensions, shy and puzzled'. She was nicknamed 'the Baby' by everyone, and that childish, uncertain quality showed through her *femme fatale* image and probably contributed as much to her success as it later did to Marilyn's. Harlow's basic film character has been defined as 'a wise-cracking prostitute whose cynical exterior disguises a tender, affectionate nature'; that redeeming quality of niceness and tenderness could not be faked on screen, it had to be there in the real Harlow. It shone out of her baby-blue eyes and lingered in her quizzical smile. In a sense, Jean Harlow was the precursor of the Monroe myth. She more or less invented the stereotype of the gorgeous blonde, the dim but glamorous dummy who represented a democratic ideal since her image was a common denominator of average male erotic fantasy, and her sexual appeal lay within the reach of all imaginations.

When Monroe began her acting career, ten years after Jean Harlow died, many people were struck by her resemblance to Harlow. Ben Lyon, the casting director at 20th Century Fox, exclaimed: 'It's Jean Harlow all over again!' and Billy Wilder compared the two in terms of that famous flesh appeal which he said he had never found in anyone else except for Clara Bow and Rita Hayworth. It is probable that Marilyn, consciously or unconsciously, was influenced by Harlow's image when she was casting about for her own, bleaching her hair from light brown to silvery blonde like Harlow's, plucking her eyebrows into high, thin arcs, wearing black or white satin to set off her creamy skin. It often happens that today's unknown starts off by imitating an established star, adding his own unique characteristics until he becomes a celebrity in his own right, sometimes outshining the orginal. James Dean emulated Marlon Brando and Montgomery Clift, Cliff

Jean Harlow became an overnight star as the two-timing heroine in Hell's Angels *(1930). Left: With the producer and director, Howard Hughes and below, with her co-stars, Ben Lyon and James*

Richard copied Elvis Presley. It was inevitable that Marilyn should eventually be asked to impersonate the dead actress she resembled in a screen biography of Harlow. She might have grabbed at the chance early in her career, but by the time she was offered it, she was already a star and the idea of imitating another famous blonde was out of the question. She found the whole idea distasteful, anyway, and said, 'I hope they won't do that to me when I'm gone.' (But they did, in a film made in 1975 called *Goodbye, Norma Jean*, starring the unknown Misty Rowe.)

The parallels between Jean Harlow and Marilyn are not limited to their physical appearance or their screen image. Their lives and characters had much in common. Both were extremely precocious in their development, as though sexual maturity was seen as an escape from an unsatisfactory childhood situation. Both were married for the first time at the age of sixteen and were to have three husbands. Both seemed to be looking for spiritual father substitutes in men who would love them for their inner self rather than for their bodily charms. Yet both were too narcissistic about those same bodily

charms not to resent the very men who attached less importance to appearance than to spiritual beauty. Both became profoundly dissatisfied with the 'gorgeous broad' stereotype which they assiduously cultivated at first and which catapulted them to stardom. Both had a fatal gift for making their private lives miserable despite all their official good fortune; somewhere inside them lay a self-destructive streak. And both, by a strange coincidence, had Clark Gable as their leading man in the last film they were to make before they died.

But of course there are differences as well as resemblances between Harlow and Marilyn. Jean Harlow had a surfeit rather than a shortage of family life. She was born in Kansas in 1911, the daughter of a dentist named Montclair Carpentier, and named Harlean. Her parents were divorced when she was nine years old and she and her mother went to live with her grandparents. Harlean's childhood and adolescence were dominated by her rigid, authoritarian grandfather. He had complete control over her after her mother remarried an Italian named Marino Bello, when Harlean was eleven. It may have been partly to escape from the tyranny of her relations that Harlean eloped at barely sixteen years with a Chicago college student named Charles McGrew.

Harlean had been sent to a smart school which she hated; her mother wanted her to leave but her grandfather would not hear of it. The elopement was obviously a desperate gesture, which paid off since she was naturally expelled from the school.

Harlow was quickly taken back into the family. Her grandfather managed to obtain a divorce for her without the couple ever meeting again; the McGrew family were just as glad that the marriage could be brought to an end without fuss. Not long afterwards, Harlean moved to Los Angeles with her mother and stepfather; she would live with them and they would live off her for most of the remaining years of her life. Like any exceptionally pretty girl in Hollywood who dreamed of becoming a movie star, she had begun to work as a film extra at the age of seventeen, changing her name to Jean Harlow (in fact her mother's maiden name). As Marilyn Monroe would do later, she knocked about for a year or two, landing the odd part, including the joke sexy blonde in Laurel and Hardy shorts like *Double Whoopee,* just as Marilyn would play the sexy blonde in a Marx Brothers comedy decades later.

Jean Harlow's basic image was always that of an ordinary, gum-chewing American girl. Her near vul-

garity turned out to be one of her biggest assets. There were plenty of classy, expensive-looking ladies in the film world, but Jean was refreshingly down to earth. As her biographer, Irving Shulman, put it: 'A man didn't have time to think of money when he dreamed of Harlow, so desirable, so willing, so available; she might be found in commonplace settings, perhaps behind the counter of a cigar stand, or at the coffee urn of a luncheonette, or offering to wait on him in a dime store, or standing next to him in an elevator, or taking the seat next to him in a bus.' *The New York Times* described her as 'the gold digger type; the sort of under-educated, utilitarian, quick-tongued, slightly unaware female then in vogue among cartoonists'. Stan Laurel perhaps noted this quality when he decided to point her out to agent Arthur Landau. Landau himself noted something else: 'It was the girl's platinum hair that made me look twice.'

Thus Jean Harlow, the Platinum Blonde, was born. It was Landau who suggested her for her first major role in Howard Hughes' First World War film *Hell's Angels* (1930). Originally scheduled as a silent film, Norwegian-born Greta Nissen was cast in the lead, but with the advent of sound the film was re-scheduled as a talkie, and Miss Nissen's pronounced accent was not suitable. Jean was given a screen test. Cameraman Gaetano Gaudio recalled its inauspicious beginning: 'The poor thing was sent back to make-up after she first appeared on the set. Her dress was all wrong, too, and that had to be changed.' Somehow she got through it however, and Hughes was prepared to take the risk, especially as Harlow seemed to be the epitome of the 'combination good kid and slut' which the *Hell's Angels* character required.

When the film opened in 1930 Harlow was an over-

night sensation. The famous line from the film, 'Do you
mind if I slip into something comfortable?', became a
catchphrase just as well-known as Mae West's 'Come
up and see me sometime'. Her career as star and sex
symbol was assured and in 1931 she appeared in no less
than five different films. At first Jean did not care about
the fact that no one considered her a 'real' actress, that
she was just a blonde bombshell, a platinum Venus. 'If
audiences like you, you don't have to be an actress,' she
answered triumphantly to charges that she could not
act. In fact, she had considerable talent as a comedienne,
but people almost deliberately overlooked her gift and
Jean herself, when she began to have artistic yearnings,
was less interested in developing her flair for comic
delivery than in trying to get the parts of polished
ladies which were usually reserved for actresses like
Myrna Loy. Her studio, MGM, was adamant about
refusing to change her image. It wanted 'Jean Harlow
as the public *liked* Jean Harlow; the dumb blonde with a
heart of gold'. In her five short years of stardom, Jean
Harlow played that role over and over again. After
Hell's Angels her best known films were *Public Enemy*
(1930), *Red Dust* (1932), *Bombshell* (1933), *Reckless*

(1934), *China Seas* (1935) and *Saratoga* (1937). There
was nothing fatal about the temptresses she played, even
though they radiated 'self-conscious allure'. As Irving
Shulman put it, Harlow 'was the woman who first typi-
fied the distinctive, unique American type of beauty . . .
basically it is gay and carefree, healthy and athletic,
wholesomely sexual without being furtive or dirty'.

Jean Harlow may have impersonated gay and carefree characters on the screen but her own personal life
was fraught with complications and dramas throughout these years. She struggled to break free of her
parents but never succeeded, and much of her earnings
were spent keeping mother and stepfather in the style
to which they had become accustomed. Her gifts to
them ranged from luxurious villas to solid gold sock
suspenders for Marino Bello. Her second marriage in
1932 to Paul Bern, a respected MGM executive, ended
in tragedy and scandal after only two months when
Bern committed suicide. It was revealed in the court
enquiry which followed that Bern had sadistically beaten
his bride on their wedding night, that the marriage had
never been consummated because Bern was completely
impotent and that Jean had fled the house on that first
occasion, screaming and sobbing, her body covered with
weals and bruises. Her third marriage in 1934 to a
cameraman named Hal Rosson ended less dramatically
than her marriage to Bern, but its failure, which was
largely due to her family's interference, affected Jean
deeply. She later became involved with William Powell
and was probably hoping that he would eventually
became her first Mr Right. It is interesting that all
Jean's partnerships were with much older men. It seems
that she was constantly searching for the sort of warm

'father-daughter' relationship that she had been deprived of as a child. By all accounts she was beginning to find this with Powell, when her sudden death in 1937 put an end to all her plans and aspirations.

The death of Jean Harlow at only twenty-six came as a shock to the world, which had not even registered the fact that she was ill. Her death was officially attributed to a cerebral oedema, but in the scandal-laden atmosphere of Hollywood it was unofficially attributed to an amazing variety of causes, including a botched abortion, heavy drinking, kidney damage resulting from Paul Bern's beatings and even rape by a gorilla! In fact, whatever illness killed Jean Harlow might well have been avoided had it not been for her mother's last and most catastrophic interference. Mrs Bello was a convinced Christian Scientist and therefore refused to let her daughter have any medical treatment or to be taken to hospital for emergency surgery until it was too late.

Harlow's funeral was almost as much of a tasteless, Hollywood super-production as Valentino's had been a few years earlier. It was attended by two hundred celebrities and crowds of sightseers. The coffin was smothered under gardenias and lilies of the valley and an airplane dropping white gardenias almost drowned out the service. It flew so low at one point that the assembled stars quailed and one reporter wisecracked: 'If that plane comes much closer, they won't ever have to hold another funeral in this town.' Jeanette MacDonald sang 'Indian Love Call', Harlow's favourite song. Nelson Eddy sang 'Ah, Sweet Mystery of Life', while everyone wept; several mourners became hysterical or fainted and had to be ushered from the church. As soon as it was over, thousands of fans invaded the Wee Kirk and stripped bare the $15,000 worth of floral tributes. Though her admirers were distraught, Harlow's death did not set off the frenzied displays of grief that had attended Valentino's demise. MGM quietly cashed in on the publicity by quickly releasing her last film, *Saratoga*. It was a great success but her last: Harlow would never prove to be as popular in death as she had been in life. Yet something of the Harlow myth has endured and her face is well-known even to many who have never seen her in a film: the high arches of her pencilled eyebrows, the fine oval of her face, the round chin with its little cleft, the good-humoured, thin-lipped smile and of course the famous platinum hair.

Marilyn Monroe needs no introduction. Like James Dean or Elvis Presley, she is a universal celebrity. Hers is the Cinderella story of the poor little girl who made it to

MONROE

the ball, but did not live happily ever after. The details of her life are sad enough, but they are perhaps less grim than her admirers, her chroniclers and Marilyn herself have made them out to be. It was in Marilyn's somewhat disturbed nature to colour the past in its darkest hue, as it is in the public's nature to want tragedy to be even more tragic than the facts warrant. Many of those who were personally involved with Marilyn from her earliest days would step forward to give the lie to her more extreme descriptions of her childhood traumas, but the public was reluctant to give up its myths and listen to, say, her first husband, Jim Dougherty, who swore that Marilyn was a virgin when he married her, though Marilyn claimed to have been raped at the age of six. To some extent, Marilyn may have distorted the facts of her life knowingly during her early career because it made better copy, such as her declarations that she was an orphan when she knew that both her parents were alive. But in all likelihood most of her falsifications were not deliberate; it was just that her subjective recollections of early abandonment and later victimization seemed like God's truth to her, though the objective reality was often less dramatic.

She was born Norma Jean Baker on June 1st, 1926, in Los Angeles. As Norman Mailer put it, 'she has no roots but illegitimacy on one side and a full pedigree of insanity on the other'. Both her maternal grandparents were committed to asylums and died there, while her mother, Gladys Baker, also lived out much of her later

life in an asylum. An uncle of Marilyn's had committed suicide. It was never known for sure who her father was, but it is generally assumed that he was Stanley Gifford, an employee of Consolidated Film Industries who worked with her mother. Gifford refused to have anything to do with his presumed daughter even when, in later life, she became famous and tried to get in touch with him.

These were inauspicious enough circumstances for Norma Jean, yet she was not an unwanted child and her mother never disowned her or gave her up for adoption. Gladys Baker worked hard to support them both and left her baby in the care of a respectable, strict, but kindly couple called the Bolanders who lived across the street. Gladys would spend the weekends with her child and would sometimes take her to the film laboratory where she worked. By the time Norma Jean was seven, Gladys had scraped enough money together for the down-payment on a house where she went to live with her daughter. At last Marilyn had a real home, but disaster soon struck: only a few months later, Gladys went mad and had to go into an asylum. Norma Jean's troubles now really began; she was taken in by various friends and neighbours who were well-meaning and concerned for her future, but who could not keep her forever. By the time she was eleven, there was nowhere for her to go and she was taken to an orphanage, a traumatic enough experience in itself, though by all accounts the institution was far from being as Dickensian as Marilyn later described it. After two years in the orphanage she spent two more years in foster homes and then got married.

Marilyn was just sixteen; her husband was a young Irishman named Jim Dougherty. Though they were not

unhappy together, Marilyn was soon bored and restless with her life as a working-class housewife. It was wartime. Jim was away in the Navy and Marilyn went to work in a parachute factory where she was 'discovered' by a photographer who asked her to model for him. Marilyn also discovered something that had long lain dormant within herself: the irresistible need to please as many people as possible with her face and body, to draw attention to herself, to become successful and, why not, famous. She became a professional photographer's model and, like most models in Los Angeles, she started dreaming of making it in the movies. Her marriage came to an end and her real career began. It was in 1946 and she was twenty years old.

Norma Jean landed a modest seventy-five dollars a week contract with Twentieth Century Fox, changed her name to Marilyn Monroe and, for the next few years, lived the life of any starlet: taking studio classes, making up to the right people (it is said that, when she got her first big film contract she declared to her lawyer: 'Well, that's the last cock *I* have to suck'), appearing under studio orders at conventions and a-top floats in parades, and, more occasionally, getting into films for a few seconds at a time. Helped on by two successive lovers, the first an old Fox executive called Joe Schenck, the second her influential agent, Johnny Hyde, but helped on most of all by her own drive and beauty, Marilyn began to get bigger and better parts: in *Love Happy* (1950) with Groucho Marx, in *All About Eve* (1950), in *The Asphalt Jungle* (1950). Her progress to the top was gradual but steady chiefly because, as with all true superstars, the public liked her and demanded more of her and her studio had to concede that what the public liked was what the public had to get. By 1950, Marilyn was a blonde to be reckoned with, almost a national celebrity. By 1952, her name got the most prominent billing on the marquee in *Clash by Night*, though she only had fourth lead. Her romance and eventual marriage in 1954 to Joe DiMaggio, one of America's top baseball stars, consecrated her fame and her popularity. With the making of *Gentlemen Prefer Blondes* in 1953 Marilyn became Hollywood's leading young female star.

Marilyn Monroe was to make over thirty films for her studio and for the independent film company she set up. Her good fortune was that at least half a dozen of the films she starred in were fine enough examples of their *genre* to become classics in their own right and not just because she appeared in them. *Gentlemen Prefer Blondes* (1953), *How to Marry a Millionaire* (1953), *Bus Stop* (1956), *The Seven Year Itch* (1955), *Some Like It Hot* (1959) and *The Misfits* (1961) deserve their enduring popularity. But for Marilyn addicts, even films of lesser worth are treats because of her unique 'misty radiance' which illuminates their relative mediocrity. Films like *River of No Return* (1954), *Niagara*

(1953), *The Prince and The Showgirl* (1957) and *Let's Make Love* (1960) are still cherished by the millions who firmly believe, more than fifteen years after Marilyn's death, that she was the greatest love goddess that ever appeared in the movies.

What goes into making a love goddess? In many ways Marilyn was the exact feminine counterpart of Valentino. She projected pure sexiness and the unabashed determination to bowl over every man who crossed her path, yet she never appeared bitchy or vamp-like in the process. In most of her screen roles, she was basically a 'sweet young thing'. When she played a straight *femme fatale* in *Niagara*, a 100 per cent wicked woman who drove her poor husband crazy with jealousy then tried to get him bumped off by her lover, she was not convincing because she just seemed too nice to do that sort of thing. Even when she was out to marry money in *How to Marry a Millionaire* and *Gentlemen Prefer Blondes,* she did not seem like a gold-digger. True love always proved to be her strength and when the supposed millionaire in *Some Like It Hot* turned out to be a penniless musician, it did not matter a bit. She dreamt of having a mink coat in *Bus Stop,* but was quite ready to settle for an old rabbit fur when she fell in love with a simple cowboy. There is something hard and threatening about a beautiful woman deliberately using her charms to attract men for mercenary purposes, but in Marilyn it was all soft, innocent and basically an act. She was a beautiful, simple creature in the body of a bombshell. Thus a male fan could desire her flashy beauty, drool over its availability as she flaunted it in every variety of skin-tight dress and flowing undress; yet in his fantasy of a relationship with her he remained secure in the knowledge that Marilyn would prove to be a honey and would not use her charms to crush a fellow or get the better of him. He knew Marilyn was a little girl looking for a daddy and her naivety was a guarantee that she would not get the upper hand. Her need for protection would be the ultimate flattery for his ego. She was amoral, which made her so exciting, but hers was the amorality of innocence, not that of vice.

Much has been written about the quality of innocence in Marilyn; it was an innocence that in no way impaired her ability to convey raw sex, but on the contrary enhanced it. In one of her earliest films, *Monkey Business,* Cary Grant fondly excused her by saying that she was 'half child'. 'Not the visible half', Ginger Rogers replied bitterly. The schema is simplistic, yet it was the key ingredient in Marilyn's vast success.

This brings us to another characteristic which has been worked to death in connection with Marilyn's appeal: vulnerability. That was Marilyn's secret weapon, giving her the edge over all her dumb siren rivals. In a eulogy at Marilyn's funeral, the famous theatre coach, Lee Strasberg, described it as 'that luminous quality – a combination of wistfulness, radiance and yearning –

to set her apart and yet make everyone wish to be a part of it.' 'Wistfulness? Yearning?' might have said the lusty GIs who cheered her in Korea when she went to entertain the troops there in 1953. 'Sucks to that! All we're interested in are the figures: 37-22-35. Ya-hoo!' Yet even when Marilyn was only a little starlet, before any East Coast intellectual had ever heard of her or theorized about her appeal, soul was a part of Marilyn's power. The famous nude shot of her on a 1949 calendar was entitled 'Miss Golden Dreams', a somewhat too poetic title for a pin-up destined to be tacked on the walls of barrack-rooms. He might not have formulated it in the words of someone like Lee Strasberg, but even the huskiest lunk-head of an American male wanted a golden dream. And part of a golden dream is radiance, wistfulness and, yes, a form of spirituality, a something which says: 'I am worthy of your attentions, not just my magnificent boobs, my fabulous fanny, but the whole of me'. The goddess of love can never be just a beautiful body or something would be lacking in the ideal of love, however physical. Botticelli's Venus has the same dreamy, nostalgic look, the fuzzy dewiness which we consistently find in Marilyn's expression even when she gives the standard Hollywood grin; it comes across despite the jazzy red lipstick she usually wore, the flutter of her false eye-

lashes and the harsh black eyeliner which outlined her childlike blue eyes.

Like Valentino, Marilyn's style is a bit *passé* today even though her seductiveness is timeless. Apart from the fact that she never wore a bra, there is too little of the liberated woman in her for the taste of the seventies. Her image belonged to her times; she was a typical fifties lady, super-feminine, whispery-voiced, deferring to male supremacy by hiding her brains even when she was being clever, rejecting any apparel such as glasses, comfortable clothing, and no-nonsense footwear which might make her seem serious or purposeful. In her films, she was always vague, scatter-brained, impractical and unpunctual. The shrewd, clever features of an actress like Katharine Hepburn, the cool, wise-cracking manner of Lauren Bacall, the tough-babe charms of Bette Davis are more in keeping with our present-day notion of how a woman ought to be: self-reliant and independent as well as a sex-object, honest rather than full of feminine wiles, someone who would be a challenge not only erotically but also intellectually. Yet as a love-symbol, Marilyn has never been surpassed; she still fascinates, still seems the embodiment of love, the Miss Golden Dreams of all time, ageless, delectable, indestructible. She is the myth of total love, unhampered by concepts of duty, companionship or responsibility. She incarnates

CINEMASCOPE brings you the world's most beautiful women in the most glamorous entertainment of your lifetime!

20th CENTURY-FOX presents

MARILYN MONROE · BETTY GRABLE · LAUREN BACALL

How To Marry A Millionaire

DAVID WAYNE · RORY CALHOUN · CAMERON MITCHELL and WILLIAM POWELL

with ALEX D'ARCY · FRED CLARK

TECHNICOLOR

CinemaScope's amazing Anamorphic Lens engulfs you in the dazzling world of Manhattan penthouses, Maine ski slopes, fabulous fashion promenades...as the screen's most beautiful women go after the world's richest men. A glittering extravaganza on the Miracle Mirror Screen...a wonder of wit in Stereophonic Sound!

Produced by NUNNALLY JOHNSON · Directed by JEAN NEGULESCO · Screen Play by NUNNALLY JOHNSON

SIGNATURE

the primeval emotion before it was split up into various components such as spiritual love versus physical love, chaste love versus unchaste love, romantic love versus sexual love. Marilyn is a goddess and thus holy; even the most vapid of her flutters, the most sultry of her bump-and-grind routines has the quality of a sacred rite.

By 1955, Marilyn was at the peak of her career. Beautiful, adored, rich and famous, she should have been happy but of course she was not. She felt misunderstood and victimized both in her private and her professional life. Her marriage to DiMaggio was coming to an end. She felt that her studio was underpaying her and not giving her good enough roles. She felt that the press and the public were being unkind because they refused to take her seriously when she revealed growing aspirations to becoming a 'real' actress and mocked her gently but unfairly for wanting to play Grushenka in *The Brothers Karamazov*. In fact she would have been perfect for the part but people found it funny to think of their favourite blonde even speaking of someone as highbrow as Dostoievsky. Marilyn resented the pressure of her image and yearned, as Jean Harlow had, to break out of the prison of her film stereotype. She dreamt of finding an environment and a man who would really appreciate her true worth and, with admirable determination, she set out to look for both. In 1955, she made a great decision. She left her studio, set up her own film company, moved to New York, started taking lessons in method acting with Lee Strasberg at the Actors Studio and began an affair with Arthur Miller, one of America's most serious and respected play-

Below: Marilyn and her husband Arthur Miller.
*Bottom left: Leaving a New York hospital after
she has undergone an operation following a*

wrights. Not bad for a supposedly dumb blonde who had
never finished high school and who was meant to have
asked where the headlights could be turned on when she
rode a horse at dusk.

Yet Marilyn was doomed to suffer disaster. Her
marriage to Miller, which caused a sensation in 1956,
would turn out to be even unhappier than her previous
two. The filming of her first independent production,

The Prince and the Showgirl, co-starring and directed
by the prestigious English actor, Laurence Olivier, was
fraught with tensions and quarrels, and the final product
was not even very good. What started out as the
happiest years of Marilyn's existence rapidly degener-
ated into a period of growing stress and inner turmoil
which would finally break her. Over the next few years,
she became increasingly neurotic, sleepless, pill-ridden
and unreliable in her film work. Though she herself was
wonderful in all her later films, her personal triumph
as an actress was achieved at a cost that no one involved
in the making of those films is likely to forget. Night
after night she would lose count of the sleeping pills
she took in her fruitless quest for sleep. Morning after
morning, everyone on the set played the exhausting
game of guessing if Marilyn would be three hours late
that day, if she would show up in the afternoon or not
at all. When she finally got to work she would fluff
the simplest lines from sheer nervousness and inability
to concentrate. During the shooting of one scene of
Some Like It Hot Tony Curtis had to nibble forty-two
chicken legs through forty-two takes because Marilyn
could not get her lines right. He can almost be forgiven
for declaring afterwards that he would have preferred
to kiss Hitler in person than Marilyn. Things went a
little better during the shooting of *Let's Make Love*
because Marilyn had fallen in love with her French co-
star, Yves Montand, and was trying to please him. But
they went even worse during the filming of *The Misfits*,

miscarriage. Below right: With director John
Huston and Clark Gable during the shooting of
The Misfits *(1961), the last film she completed.*
Bottom right: With Laurence Olivier in The Prince
and the Showgirl.

which spelled the end of Marilyn's marriage to Miller,
the end of her film career, the end of Montgomery Clift's
career and the end of Clark Gable's life. The disasters,
rivalries, hatreds and despairs born of those weeks spent
on location in the burning desert for *The Misfits* were
rich enough in drama to be chronicled in a full-length
book by James Goode. As many noted at the time, the
film could not have been more aptly named. Marilyn's
final attempt to pull herself together was equally aptly
entitled: *Something's Got To Give.* Divorced for the
third time, living alone in Los Angeles, surviving on pills
and visits to her psychoanalyst, she tried to make a
comeback, but the 'something which had to give' was
Marilyn. During a month and a half of shooting in June
1962, Marilyn made it to the set only six times. The
film was finally suspended (it was never completed),
Marilyn was fired by her studio and, a few weeks later,
the Angel of Sex was dead, two months after her thirty-
sixth birthday.

After Marilyn died, a friend of hers, the poet Norman
Rosten, wrote a poem called 'Who Killed Norma Jean?'
It was later set to music and sung by Pete Seeger. In it,
the blame for Marilyn's death was laid on her fans, her
lovers, her agents and the press. When a person kills
himself, those who knew him or her always feel guilty,
seeking explanations and blaming themselves or others.
But was anyone really guilty for Marilyn's death except
Marilyn herself? Hers is the only recorded case of
suicide among those who died young; a coroner's report

called it 'probably suicide'. There is no doubt that
Marilyn had often wanted to die, especially during her
last years. She had made previous suicide attempts and
after one of these she had declared to some friends:
'There is too much pain in life. When they brought me

back to life after my suicide attempts, I was very angry. People have no right to make you live when you don't want to.' In a poem she wrote, she conveyed her anguished fear of life, her yearning for oblivion:

> Help! Help!
> Help! I feel life coming back
> When all I want is to die.

On the last night of her life in July 1962, having already taken the Nembutals which would kill her, she telephoned a friend. Marilyn's friend was out and she spoke to someone on an answering service. She was found dead in her bed a few hours later by her house-keeper, the phone still clutched in her hand. Yet this does not prove that Marilyn wanted to survive and hoped at the last minute that someone would save her. It was a habit of hers to phone close friends in the middle of the night when she felt lonely and frightened, just to hear a friendly voice. But it is unlikely that she would have been grateful to have been saved once again on that occasion, and all too likely that she would have tried again until she succeeded.

Was it stardom which killed Marilyn? It was once said of Janis Joplin that she lacked 'the necessary degree of honest cynicism needed to survive an all-media assault', and this was probably even more true of

3. WINNERS CAN BE LOSERS

Why should one talk of Carole Lombard and Gérard Philipe in the same breath? Why not put Carole Lombard, one of the golden ladies of the Hollywood screen, with Jean Harlow and Marilyn Monroe, two other golden ladies who died young? Why not put Gérard Philipe in the Dean-Clift-Cybulski class of post-war anti-heroes which he often portrayed in his films? Perhaps because neither Lombard nor Philipe were born losers. There was no tragic streak of unhappiness or self-destruction in their natures, as there was in Harlow, Marilyn, Clift or Dean, and therefore no sense of inevitability about their early end. Their early deaths were no more than dreadful accidents of fate which killed two of the most positive and life-loving characters of the entertainment world. It is certain that both Carole Lombard and Gérard Philipe would have continued to grow and develop as actors, and their art would have given others pleasure for many more years if they had survived. There is a flagrant injustice about their death at the peak of their careers and their personal fulfilment as human beings. Unlike the other people in this book, they were extraordinarily happy and successful in their private lives as well as in their careers.

Physically, Carole Lombard and Gérard Philipe were two of the most ideally handsome people ever to appear on the screen, where so many handsome faces have stirred our imaginations. Theirs was not a strongly-typed beauty, one moulded by the mature, fully-formed personality, as were the magnificent looks of Greta Garbo, Marlene Dietrich or Clark Gable. It lay, rather, in a perfection of features which reminds us of the angels and madonnas in Italian masterpieces of the Renaissance. Not that there was anything characterless or bland about their faces; but they were like smooth, flawless mirrors reflecting all the human qualities we yearn to possess. Lombard and Philipe project an image of perfection that not many can attain and which we know to have been not only skin-deep; by all accounts, both were not merely exquisite to look at but marvellous individuals as well, and this too enters into the charm of their legends. It is customary to praise the dead, to extol their characters and to gloss over their failings, but it is most unusual to come across two stars about whom no one could find anything to criticize while they were still alive, before an early death could sanctify their merits and place them beyond the reach of disparagement. It is reassuring to know that positive natures can still appeal to the imagination as strongly as the negative ones we so often cherish in our pessimistic age. Carole Lombard and Gérard Philipe are anachronisms: in an era of general doubt, they make us believe in the redeemable side of human nature. They are two of the most genuine heroes we have left in this age of anti-heroes.

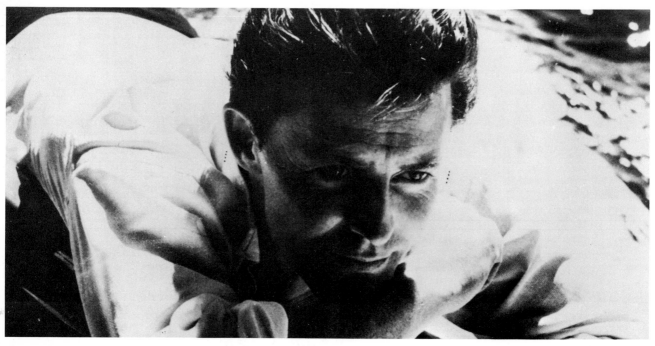

Carole Lombard's real name was Alice Jane Peters, a matter of fact, unpretentious name which probably suited her real personality better than the screen name

LOMBARD

she adopted. She was born in 1908 and lived in Los Angeles. The tow-headed tomboy Alice attracted the attention of a film director who saw her playing baseball with her two brothers in the suburb where she lived. Already, little Alice Jane Peters possessed that combination of cheery, out of doors high-spiritedness coupled with strikingly glamorous looks which would make her famous. She therefore began her film career at the age of twelve, but fortunately for her, she did not turn into that coy and synthetic Hollywood product known as a child star.

After her film debut, Lombard played in a few more movies but she remained an ordinary American girl who led the life of a typical teenager. Then, something happened which seemed to spell an end to any ambitions about becoming a real film actress: while she was out on a date with a boyfriend, she was involved in a car accident which slightly disfigured her. Discouraged and depressed, she assumed her film career was over, but her face healed quickly and soon there was only a faint scar on her cheek. In 1928, she was signed on as a Mack Sennett bathing beauty, a job where a curvaceous figure mattered more than having a perfect face. Over the next two years she played in thirteen Sennett

comedies. Having custard pies thrown in her face or being doused with buckets of water offered little scope for development as an actress, but it did teach Alice Peters, as she was still called, an excellent sense of comic timing and a flair for sensing what would come over as funny on the screen. In real life, Lombard loved playing practical jokes on her friends, and her humour made her a natural comedienne. In 1930, she joined Paramount and acquired her new name along with her definitive image: from now on, she would be Carole Lombard, the glamorous yet funny heroine of the zany comedies so popular in the thirties. She rapidly became one of Paramount's top stars and was soon making as many as five films a year.

Audiences took to Carole Lombard as a screen character and as an individual. They avidly read the gossip about her private life, the dazzling parties she gave, her romantic involvement with some of Hollywood's most eligible males. She eventually married another star, the urbane William Powell; the marriage ended in a friendly divorce on grounds of mutual incompatibility only two years later. William Powell would later become Jean Harlow's closest companion; in this way the lives of Harlow and Lombard were interwoven as well as in another: in a number of her films Harlow was teamed up with Clark Gable who was to become the great love of Lombard's life. By the mid-thirties, Lombard's fans were fascinated by the tantalizing rumours of her amours with Gable, the reigning King of Hollywood, who was unfortunately already married. The Lombard-Gable affair was an open secret for many months and, despite the hypocritical conven-

ing as those of her attending a film premiere or sitting in a fashionable restaurant. Here was a sexy girl who would never double-cross you, a funny girl who would know when to be serious, a girl who could vamp and wiggle with the best of them, then cheerfully kick off her dancing shoes to go on a cross-country trek with her man when he got tired of the effete nightclub atmosphere.

To understand the scope of Carole Lombard's appeal in the thirties, we must turn back to earlier ideals of femininity on the screen. The female stars of the silent screen represented a type of womanhood which was still very close to the nineteenth century ideal; they were physically fragile, diminutive and child-like. They might be morally courageous, but they were also helpless and dependent on male protection. They were invariably pure and virginal, or they would not have been heroine material. Mary Pickford, with her golden ringlets and her simper, was the queen of them all and her hand-maidens were the delicate Lillian Gish and Mae Marsh. A tough, sexually-liberated woman could only be wicked and untrustworthy by definition, and a man would have to be either immoral or a fool to fall into the snares of a vamp like Theda Bara. A less puritanical feminine ideal began to emerge, however, reflecting the changing morals of society. Good-bad girls began to steal the scene from the old-fashioned heroines by in-

tion that film stars should be sexually explosive on the screen but paragons of virtue in real life, the popularity of neither star was affected by their irregular situation; they made such an irresistible couple, the fair willowy Carole and the dark, suave Clark. When Gable finally got a divorce and married Lombard, it seemed an ideal marriage. Carole Lombard's fans were ecstatic: their golden girl had been as successful in her private life as in her film career. Indeed, unlike so many Hollywood marriages supposedly made in Heaven but in fact lived out in Hell, the Gable-Lombard marriage turned out to be a perfect match and the couple lived exceedingly happily together until death parted them five years later.

Many today have not seen any of Carole Lombard's films, so that they can only speculate on the nature of her unique appeal, however vivid her beauty is in photographs. But in her films, Carole Lombard's very special charm is obvious. She had everything a man could ask for in a woman and yet other women could like her too. Her appeal was probably less potent than the radiant, nakedly sexual one of Jean Harlow and Marilyn, yet it was also broader. Women admired Harlow and Monroe, but they also felt threatened by their blonde and blatant sexuality. The fact that Lombard was the perfect wife to Gable in real life confirmed the authenticity of her image. Gable once said: 'You can trust that little screwball with your life or your hopes and she wouldn't even know how to think about letting you down.' Gable liked the simple, outdoor life so Lombard made herself like it too. He enjoyed going fishing and hunting so Lombard made those her hobbies as well. The photographs of them feeding their chickens or riding in the desert show us a Lombard just as appeal-

'You can trust that little screwball with your life and she wouldn't even know how to think about letting you down'. A perfect match, Gable and Lombard were parted only by her death aged 39 in 1941.

and the huge Tabernacle pipe organ. This was to be her final public appearance. The last impression Americans were to have of Carole Lombard was that of a beautiful, dedicated woman in a black, strapless evening dress, weeping as she sang her country's national anthem along with the audience, against a backdrop of flags and banners urging all to 'Sacrifice, Save and Serve'. It was perfectly in keeping with the image which Lombard had projected in her films and that which she had in real life. On her way back from Utah to California, she and her mother were killed in a plane crash along with fifteen army pilots. The plane, seven miles off course, had crashed into Table Rock Mountain, a few minutes out from Las Vegas, and had burst into flames. There were no survivors.

Carole Lombard's death was treated as a national tragedy, but Clarke Gable refused to allow her funeral to become the same kind of hysterical spectacle that had marred Jean Harlow's. Both Lombard and Gable had been present on that occasion, and Carole, deeply shocked, had apparently expressed a hope that nothing like that would happen at *her* funeral. Accordingly Gable and MGM made sure that Carole's funeral was a simple, private service with only close friends present. Gable himself felt personally guilty about Carole's

death for many years afterwards, having quarrelled violently with her just before the trip. The close relationship had not been entirely free of marital problems, which had erupted again at that point over Lana Turner, but the couple had made up by telephone. It was Carole's anxiety to get home to her husband which made her insist on taking up seats on the plane which had been requisitioned for three officers at an Albuquerque stopover.

Lombard's status instantly changed from that of film-star to heroine. President Roosevelt awarded her a posthumous medal as 'the first woman to be killed in action in the defense of her country in its war against the Axis powers'. A Navy air squadron decided to call itself 'The Lombardiers' in her honour, and used her profile on its insignia. A Liberty ship was named the *Carole Lombard*. The myth of Lombard was finally consecrated by Gable's sudden decision to enlist in the Army, where he served until the end of the war, because it was something that Carole had been urging him to do from the start of America's entry into the war. The story of the golden girl of the silver screen had now become a legend of virtue and valour; perhaps the only way for the public to compensate for the tragic death of such a likeable personality.

PHILIPE

Gérard Philipe was an intellectual, cultured, sensitive and somewhat withdrawn, whereas Carole Lombard had been none of those; Lombard was intelligent but not highly educated, sensitive with people but also an extrovert. Yet there were similarities in their positive and hopeful attitudes towards life. Both were decidedly optimistic, not because they couldn't see the darker side of things but because they felt the darkness had to be overcome, that it would be wrong to give in to it. As a friend once said of Lombard: 'Her philosophy was laughter. She had known black despair and heartbreak. She believed that you had to win through them and presume that good would triumph, and thus that laughter was an outward sign of grace.' This belief in the ultimate triumph of good over evil, if one really set one's heart on working for the good, was characteristic of Gérard Philipe as well. In real life, as in most of his roles on stage and in films, Philipe was a rebel *with* a cause, and even if his cause were to prove futile he would find other, better causes to defend. This basic faith in human nature, in the rightness of the final outcome, which shone through the existential despondency of the characters Philipe sometimes portrayed was a reflection of Philipe's own fundamental optimism. Temporary despair over the present wretched state of the world was the only consequence of being idealistic, compassionate and honest; but the despair was not to be allowed to crystallize into neurosis and defeatism. In his roles as in his life Philipe conveyed not despair but 'the disgust, the indignation of the young, their contempt for those modern myths called money, power, wheeling and dealing; and even though it grows harder and harder to believe, he says that everything is still possible in a world gone astray'. This was how Maurice Perisset described Philipe in the angel's role which first brought the young actor to prominence.

Gérard Philipe was born on 4th December, 1922 in Cannes. His family was well-off and politically right-wing. In fact, at the time of the Liberation of France, in 1944, his father would be sentenced to death *in absentia* for collaborating with the Germans. As is traditional in conservative and affluent French families, the young Gérard was educated in a private religious school and was very pious in his youth, which did not prevent him from loving jazz and enjoying the existence of a handsome, privileged boy living on the French Riviera and being looked after by a doting mother. Very early, Philipe showed a keen interest in the theatre and a special gift for reciting poetry. A film director, Marc Allegret, who knew him in his teens, later described his early impression of the adolescent: 'Gérard impressed me by a kind of violence he contained and which one always felt ready to come to the surface. Withdrawn and reserved, like all very sensitive people, he restrained his enthusiasm and his tenderness'.

Gérard Philipe obviously had an artistic temperament, but his father wanted him to study law. He soon gave up law, however, to start studying acting, first in Nice, then in Cannes. In 1943, he went to Paris and it was in the capital that his career really got started. Though he was particularly good-looking, there was something too intellectual and serious about his manner and appearance, his 'melancholy grace' as the film director René Clair described it, to suggest the makings of a conventional matinée idol or a box-office star. But the climate of romantic melancholia which prevailed in the concluding years of the war and just afterwards would give Philipe the chance to impose his unusual, pensive style.

After a few tiny parts in films and plays, he got his first real opportunity playing the angel in a play by Giraudoux about the destruction of Sodom and Gomorrah. In it, he denounced the state of the world in terms that must have seemed strikingly appropriate to young Frenchmen who were still living through the German Occupation. Philipe, as the angel, compared the earth to 'a corpse, from which all things that can fly have fled'. In the play, the angel speaks eloquently of the corruption and the despair he had found on Earth, the hideousness of human society and his grief over its damnation. But the ugliness and horror the angel had witnessed made him seem even more untainted and

For over a decade, Philipe enjoyed great fame.
*Left: In 1955 his political sympathies led him to
the Soviet Union where he was besieged by crowds*

intact by comparison. Maurice Perisset has described
the electrifying impact this new actor made on the
young people who saw him: 'Someone now represented
them, gave them a reason not to lose hope . . . they
identified with this new being who was untouched, pure
and fiery as a sword, who made no concessions. The
angel told them that Love is always possible, that there
is more hope in a single blade of grass than in all the
decadence of an adult society.' Overnight Philipe became
'the chosen brother, the one who could not deceive you,
the one who understood everything and who expressed
the truth of everyone'. From that moment, his career
was meteoric and the cinema soon turned him into an
international youth hero. Yet Philipe's appeal was not
limited to the young; unlike many other youth heroes,
his image was not founded on a total rejection of established values. He might criticize the society that had
been created by adults, but he remained on the side of
all those who were in good faith and who were ready to
work at making the world a better place, whatever their
age might be.

Growing popular and critical acclaim did not
spoil Philipe. He continued his acting studies at the
Conservatoire de Paris for a time and never gave up his
stage career even when he had become an international
film star. He refused tempting Hollywood contracts,
preferring to play in high quality French films and

simultaneously acting in the best kind of French drama,
both classical and *avant-garde*. His best-known stage
roles included the ultra-modern play, *Caligula* (1945)
by Albert Camus and Corneille's seventeenth century
tragedy of *Le Cid* (1951). He repeatedly went on world
tours with the Théatre Nationale de Paris, a prestigious
theatre company, and so contributed a great deal to
making French culture better known abroad. But it was
through his films that he became internationally known
to foreign audiences. *Fanfan La Tulipe* (1952) was to
play in fifty countries, a record for a French film.

For over a decade, Philipe was one of the world's
best known Frenchmen; he was besieged by crowds of
admirers wherever he travelled, whether in a Moscow
bus, walking down Broadway or hiking to a little village
in Japan. Yet he avoided all the traps of stardom. He
remained simple and unaffected, always ready to stand
and chat with the people waiting for him outside
theatres. He was invariably courteous and affable with
everyone but firmly refused to let adulation and flattery
go to his head. He did however go to great lengths to
guard the privacy of his personal life. In 1951, he married. His remarkable young wife had been the first European woman to follow the Marco Polo Trail on foot from
China to India, and has since become a well-known

writer under the name of Anne Philipe. It was characteristic of Philipe to find his wife outside the film profession and a woman of considerable accomplishments in her own right. The Philipes were exceptionally happy together and had two children whom they carefully shielded from all publicity. Like Carole Lombard, Philipe loved outdoor life and took refuge from the world of the actor by fleeing to the country at every opportunity; he was never so happy as when he could spend days on his country estate driving a tractor or weeding the garden.

Philipe made good use of his fame by putting it at the service of his convictions. He regularly attended peace marches and meetings against the Atom bomb; he demonstrated in a wide variety of ways his belief in the need for each individual to make an effort at improving the state of the world. Though he was very patriotic, he openly expressed his disapproval of the war the French were then waging in Indochina. He was always ready to sign petitions and make speeches on behalf of his ideals. He liked to act for workers' organizations and to help young actors personally. Eventually, he became the active head of the French Actors' Union. His Leftist leanings led him to visit the Soviet Union in 1955, China in 1957 and Cuba in 1959,

long before it was common for Westerners to go to these countries. But Philipe's political outlook was basically humanitarian rather than Marxist and he was a natural champion of any good liberal cause. In all these ways his real-life personality reflected the warmth and concern of his stage and screen characters: the enthusiast, the idealist, the defender of the weak and the wronged, the redresser of injustices, the outspoken critic of persecution in any guise. In real life as in his roles, Philipe would know moments of discouragement, of scepticism, even of despair at the sheer magnitude of the task, but it was not true existential despair, born of hopelessness and a sense of futility. That sort of despair paralyzes the urge to act or react, while Philipe's would spur him on to ever greater effort.

Philipe played basically the same character over and over again, though his great talent made each portrayal subtly different from the rest. He played a troubled adolescent in love with an older woman in *Le Diable au Corps* (1946). He played the simple, saintly Prince Myshkin who laughs so charmingly along with those who are making fun of him in *The Idiot* (1947). In his best-known film, *Fanfan La Tulipe* (1952), he played a romping yet chivalrous young blade whose impulse to set wrongs right was not very far removed from the more serious Myshkin's efforts to help all those in trouble. Even when Philipe later started playing more complex adult roles, his fresh, youthful magic still had a way of shining through. When he portrayed Modigliani in a film called *Montparnasse 19* (1957), the alcoholism and tragic end of the painter did not greatly modify the character of Philipe's appeal, since the uncompromising, eager dedication of the young artist to his work was well in keeping with the actor's idealistic image. When he played another alcoholic, the doctor in *Les Orgeuilleux* (1953), hope and 'the triumph of good' still won out, since Philipe was finally redeemed by his commitment to the medical profession and by the love of a good woman (played by Michele Morgan). Youth and hope always seemed to be Philipe's basic message even when he played negative characters. In *Le Rouge et Le Noir,* he made the hero Julien Sorel's ambition seem no more than the outcome of young pride and the laudable impulse to better himself. Sorel's bitter, envious contempt for society came across as a rejection of corrupt values when Philipe played the part. He became the most lovable and unsatanic Mephistopheles in the history of the cinema when he played the role in René Clair's version of the Faust legend. The film was appropriately entitled *La Beauté du Diable,* for in French 'the devil's beauty' in no way conveys a sense of evil but means a combination of the lively vigour and attractiveness which Philipe-Mephistopheles had and which Michel Simon, playing the old Faust, craved to possess. In Clair's version, Faust sold his soul in order to exchange bodies with Mephistopheles, and when one sees

63

Left: In Le Diable au Corps *with Micheline Presle who was indirectly responsible for making him world famous; France's biggest star had chosen Philipe as her leading man. Right: With Joan Greenwood in* Knave Of Hearts *(1954).*

Philipe in the part one can understand why. Indeed, when Philipe first met René Clair, he asked the director playfully: 'And why shouldn't Faust *want* to be damned?' It was only in *Les Liaisons Dangereuses* (1959), considered an extremely risqué film at the time of its release, that one sees Philipe in a more ambiguous role, where evil is not alleviated by humour and leads to inevitable tragedy.

Philipe's health had never been particularly robust, but his end was appallingly sudden. He had felt extremely tired during the shooting in Mexico of his last film, Luis Buñuel's *La Fièvre Monte à El Pao* (1959). On his return to France, it was discovered that he had a rare form of cancer, though Philipe himself was not told. A few weeks later he died in his sleep at the age of thirty-seven. As his wife said in the book she wrote about their last days together: 'I knew that between your beautiful and brief destiny and a long, mediocre existence, you would not have hesitated. But why this choice? Are there two races of men and did you belong to the one which speeds through life like a shooting star in a summer sky?' Philipe's funeral was, like his private life, a totally private affair; his body was taken to be buried at Ramatuelle, in the South of France, where he had a house. However, the news of his death engendered a flurry of articles, eulogies and tributes from around the world. None were overtly political, although the French Left pointed out that Philipe was a strong sympathiser and tried to make capital of his leftist activities and past allegiances. But Philipe was, above all, an artist and an idealist rather than any sort of 'party' man.

Gérard Philipe was both more and less than the other celebrities described in this book. More, because he was a completely serious and creative actor and director; less, because his sheer popular appeal was never as far-reaching. His image was too subtle; he was too 'uncommercial' to become the darling of an unsophisticated public, to set off the delirious screams of teeny-boppers round the globe. If he could come to life again, the friend of Camus, the interpreter of classical and *avante-garde* drama might be shocked to find himself in the company of Rudolph Valentino or Jimi Hendrix, though others in this book like Garfield, Clift and Cybulski were also serious stage actors as well as screen idols. Yet Philipe has his place in any work about mythical young heroes. He must be included in all attempts to define the process of audience identification and projection which makes an entertainer seem legendary both in his lifetime and afterwards. His magnetism on the screen has just been compared to that of James Dean, and indeed to Valentino's, by one writer who stressed that Philipe's romantic appeal 'lay in his presence rather than in his roles – and in the dreams of his audience. He exerted on the public the same spell he cast over the heroines of his films'. The mark of the

true superstar lies in that ability to be a *presence* rather than in the way he acts, however brilliant. He fascinates not just because he plays well or looks great but because he is *there* and his presence has the power to make us dream. This is as true for Philipe as it is for Valentino or Jean Harlow.

Gérard Philipe also had the screen idol's capacity of transcending national and cultural barriers. His image belonged to everybody who chose to identify with it anywhere in the world. He incarnated youth to all those who were young or had been young and the symbol has been durable; Philipe has remained a youth hero. After his death, when his loss was being mourned all over the world, the French poet, Louis Aragon, made this very point: 'He could not grow old. His eyes have closed before he became different from himself . . . Gérard Philipe leaves only the image of Springtime behind him, and we must, however bitterly, envy him for it. Heroes like him will never grow wrinkled. He will forever be himself.' Gérard Philipe represented the ideal romantic hero but without any of the *clichés* and the sentimentality usually inherent in the Romantic image. He symbolized eternal youth and died before age could give the lie to that image.

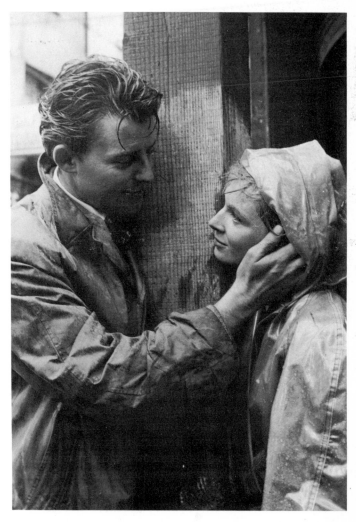

4. BORN TO LOSE

There is one category of heroes who had a genius for personifying the self-doubts and the scepticism of twentieth century man, his disillusions, his bitterness, his despair and yet his yearning quest for an ideal. These heroes are sometimes described as being born losers and are a variant of the rebel hero. The rebel hero, the tough guy with a vulnerable core, was a well-established cinematic type by the early thirties; he was the forerunner of the loser type and had many of his features. The early rebel hero might be a gangster, a convict, or an ordinary man who committed a crime almost by accident. He was often shot down at the end of the film, or he might be executed, but his death was completely different from that of traditional cinema villains in so far as audiences were invited to sympathize with his plight and to identify with his tragedy. No one was expected to rejoice, as they would have done in early screen dramas when the stereotyped villain fell off a cliff or was justly killed by the hero. The rebel hero has our sympathy: society usually had to eliminate him because he was a menace, but he was also the victim of circumstance or misunderstanding, and he was usually an attractive, likeable personality underneath. Perhaps he had been deprived of love, or he had encountered injustice. If life had treated him more fairly, he would have been redeemed. What had set him on the wrong course was a cruel father, a sadistic prison guard, a two-timing girlfriend. His understandable indignation and wish for retribution was often what led him down the fatal path of crime and revenge.

James Cagney, Paul Muni, Clark Gable, James Mason, Humphrey Bogart and Jean Gabin, among many others, all played the roles of anti-social men who, deep down, were embittered idealists. They also portrayed tough cynical cops, journalists or private detectives who knew what a rotten place the world was, yet still had good instincts and lived by them. The continuing popularity of rebel hero actors and the vogue for films starring good-bad criminals or good-bad cops indicates how strong the impulse is to identify with a social outcast, a man who does not fit in with the pre-ordained pattern of normal existence. The whole world loves a winner, but the whole world also loves a loser, at least when that loser happens to be young, virile and sexually attractive.

The original screen rebel hero was an iconoclast who lashed out at hypocrisy and conventions. But at the same time, he was successful in a way most people could rarely be, not only in his private life off-screen, but also in his film persona. Maybe he is killed or defeated at the end of the movie, but he will have displayed superhuman courage and style before they finally get him. He will have fought and won against muscular opponents, and often courted and won extraordinarily beautiful women. We could never hope to emulate the *savoir-faire* with which Bogart lit a cigarette or pulled down the brim of his battered felt hat, or how Gabin huddled up against the rain in his crumpled mackintosh or how Cagney tossed off a wisecrack even as he lay dying. The

rebel hero truly exemplifies the definition of the hero as 'a man beyond us yet ourselves'. He is a winner in the guise of a loser, even though he may be defeated in whatever personal battle he has waged against society.

There are important differences, however, between this type of rebel, who is nevertheless a born winner, and the anti-hero who is basically a born loser. This latter type is too confused in his mind, too deeply scarred by his ordeals, too much of a misfit ever to get by even if his films have a seemingly happy ending. He may be courageous in his way, but he certainly isn't tough. He is at war with his *milieu,* but he is even more at war with himself. The winner talks tough because he doesn't care to reveal his vulnerable core. He has fashioned for himself a shell of hardness and cynicism which he tries to wear at all times because he knows from experience how dangerous it is to let the mask slip. But the true film loser is not so resourceful or disciplined, although he is nonetheless a hero; he may also try to wear a mask of toughness but he usually fails to convince. He is inarticulate, not because he deliberately chooses to disguise his inner feelings, but because he is too emotionally confused and scared to try to communicate with others. When he does try, he usually fails and the anticipation of failure lends an air of defeatism to his words, his gestures, his facial expressions. He wants to explain to his parents, his girl, his brother, the cops, how he really feels, but at the same time he resists telling them because their lack of comprehension will hurt him even more. He wants to be loved and understood, yet he assumes he won't be, so he strives to give the impression that he doesn't care if he is disliked and misunderstood. This basic ambivalence is characteristic of the 'born to lose' hero; it is easy to see why the best known representative of the type, James Dean, wanted to play the part of Hamlet, the great hesitator, torn between his need to hate and his desire to love, in conflict with himself as well as with those around him.

In his book *The Rebel Hero,* Joe Morella describes the typical stance of the loser as 'the vulnerable man who cares so very deeply that he must pretend not to care at all, and this is epitomized by the mumble and the inarticulate response, the hooded eye to shield the hungry heart, the hunched shoulder to hide the sensitivity of soul'. And of course, once these gestures and mannerisms become recognizable to audiences, the loser reveals himself by the very actions he tried to hide behind. Joe Morella's definition however could never apply to the classic rebel heroes of the screen like Cagney, Paul Muni or Bogart. They always appeared positive and self-assured, even if it was only a façade. It was not really until the late thirties and the forties that a different kind of rebel hero emerged with John Garfield, followed in the fifties by Montgomery Clift, Marlon Brando and James Dean and, in Europe, by France's Jean-Paul Belmondo and the Polish film actor Zbigniew Cybulski.

The type is not an absolute one, either, since Brando and Belmondo could also personify winners with ease. Other actors, like Gérard Philipe, could play both winners and losers convincingly.

The 'born to lose' rebel came into his own during and after the war, a product of the method school of acting, of post-war disillusion and of Existentialist despair; his emergence also coincided with a generalized acceptance of psycho-analytical concepts in popular culture. After the double trauma of world economic depression and world war, audiences were prepared to accept a non-linear, more complex and self-searching character than before, a man full of contradictions and unresolved inner conflicts. It does not seem surprising, then, that four of the greatest exponents of this loser type also experienced conflict in their private lives, that they personally found many of the problems of identity which were common to their screen images, and that all four died, more or less young, and in violent or tragic circumstances.

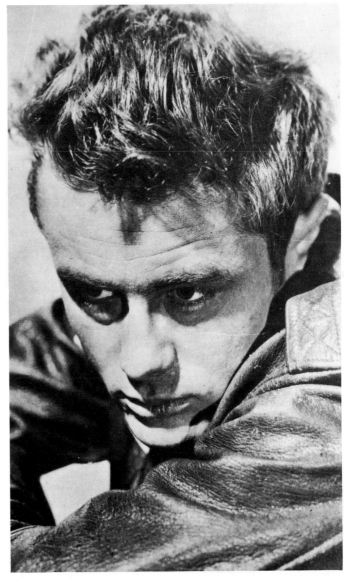

GARFIELD

John Garfield was the first real loser of the film world. His early life reads like a classic rags-to-riches Hollywood story: New York Jewish upbringing, astonishing success in his teens on the stage and an overnight sensation in his first film, at the age of 24. But even then it seemed that the disillusioned character he portrayed on the screen ('Fate's whipping boy' as one critic described him) was already reflecting the incipient bitterness of his private life.

Garfield does not represent the type of mass cult figure that James Dean has become, although his appeal was similar during his lifetime, but he is greatly admired by actors like Warren Beatty, Jack Nicholson and Al Pacino. These actors owe much to Garfield's original anti-hero image which preceded that of the better-known Brando and Dean. Yet Garfield himself would have been mystified by this lasting fascination, as his biographer Larry Swindell has pointed out: 'Above all he wanted to be a great actor, but his instinct as well as his most intimate critics told him this was not possible. Yet he was a great symbol and he barely appreciated that. Neither accepting nor understanding his own significance, he died unaware that he had been the prophet of the new actor in America . . . Prototype and archetype he was the first of the rebels.'

So who was Garfield? What was there about him that led him to become the original born to lose rebel? He was born on March 4th 1913, the first son of first generation American Jews, Hannah and David Garfinkle. Named Jacob, Julius was later added as a middle name – soon shortened to Julie, the name by which he would always be known off-screen. Julie was a small child and would always be less than average height, a physical trait he shared with James Dean. Like Dean also, his mother died in 1920 while Julie was still a child, and the positive influence in his early life disappeared. The seven-year-old Julie and his two-year-old brother Max were left to be brought up by their sad and rather fatalistic father. Julie never acknowledged his step-mother Dinah, whom David Garfinkle married three years later. She was by Garfield's own admission 'the woman my old man was living with'. Three years of being farmed out to various relatives around the Bronx had toughened the boy: 'Not having a mother,' he said later, 'I could stay out late, I didn't have to eat regularly or drink my milk at four o'clock. I could sleep out and run away, which I did a lot of.'

Julie Garfinkle was an outgoing, extrovert character, at home in the streets, but inevitably he spent most of his early adolescence in trouble with the juvenile authorities. But he had a lucky break when he began attending school run by a pioneering psychiatrist, Dr. Angelo Patri, who specialized in the rehabilitation of problem youngsters. Garfield said of him, 'For reaching

into the garbage pail and pulling me out, I owe him everything'. Dr. Patri noticed that Julie expressed himself very well. He encouraged the boy so effectively that Garfield eventually won an elocution prize and discovered a vocation for acting. Almost overnight, the young delinquent was transformed into a young man with a goal in life. As he was fond of saying, 'If I hadn't become an actor, I might have become Public Enemy Number One'.

Julie did not really want to continue his education in high school, but Angelo Patri arranged for him to enrol in one and pulled strings as well to obtain a dramatic scholarship for him with the Heckscher Foundation. Julie thrived on his acting classes but failed at his lessons. It was after his success in a Heckscher Foundation play that he first met Jacob Ben-Ami, one of the star actors of the Jewish Art Theatre, who recommended him as a pupil at the American Laboratory Theatre. Julie was still only sixteen years old but his ambition was constant and unerring: he was determined to make acting his career.

The American Laboratory Theatre was run by Richard Boleslavsky, a pupil of Stanislavsky who had left the Soviet Union in 1920. Julie was the youngest student at the 'Lab' and stayed a year, in spite of his father's opposition. Angelo Patri paid his tuition fees, but Julie also took a variety of menial jobs to finance himself while training, so that he could give his father something towards his keep. The 'Lab' was aggressively anti-Hollywood until the 1929 crash wiped Boleslavsky out, forcing him to recoup his losses on the West Coast, and brought the Theatre Guild, which had set up the

Criminal (1939), a remake of *20,000 Years in Sing-Sing*. He relished his success but suffered from the stereotyping which left him no opportunity to grow and develop as an actor. 'Please parole me!' he groaned when Warners asked him to play yet another jailbird. He would have liked to try his hand at comedy, but the studio wouldn't hear of it – their star had an image to preserve and he had to stick to it. Losing was the key to his popularity and it made money for everyone, so what more did he want? And in a way they were right; Garfield could moan, 'I've made eight or nine pictures and I haven't cracked a joke yet', but at the same time he revelled in his new-found fame.

Garfield's thirst for movie fame was in conflict with his desire for intellectual acceptance among his political and East Coast theatrical acquaintances, and it began to affect his marriage as well, since Robbie was undoubtedly the more serious of the two and was not keen on the limelight. Hollywood's seamier side made its mark on Julie: 'I was in Hollywood a week before I got laid,' he said. 'Julie does all the things Errol Flynn says *he* does,' someone at Warners noted, although Julie's exploits were less public than Flynn's. While by his own admission, he gave Robbie reason 'to despise the whole business and town', he seemed to be trying to live up in reality to his virile but tragic screen image. In the event, the marriage lasted at least on the surface almost to the end of his life.

The public continued to love Garfield but the critics who had first acclaimed his performance soon wearied of his limitations as a stock film character. The Second World War gave him ample opportunity to play the standard part of the one in the crew with the chip on his shoulder in a succession of war films, as well as starring in *The Sea Wolf* (1941) and *Tortilla Flat* (1942), on loan to MGM. His popularity remained steady and he was among the first Hollywood stars to entertain the troops, but underneath he was smarting with disappointment from his 4-F rating by the Army. He tried to keep the result a secret: the medics had found a heart murmur and he was only 29. In fact he did suffer a mild heart attack two years later, which again he tried to keep secret.

After the war Garfield broke with Warners and during the forties made what many have felt to be his

finest pictures, including, at last, some comedies. One of the most notable films was *Body and Soul* (1947), in which his portrayal of the doomed boxer perfectly encapsulated his loser image. The film, directed by Robert Rossen, has been interpreted by Clifford Odets as an allegory of Garfield's own life, in which the fight game symbolized the movie business and the two female roles symbolized Julie's lasting relationship with Robbie and his constant straying with other women. Polonsky directed him later in *Force of Evil* (1949), arguably his best film but by then the atmosphere in Hollywood had soured and the film was only given B-picture status. Julie had been moving into the superstar bracket, on a par with Humphrey Bogart. He was being directed by other big names, like Elia Kazan (*Gentleman's Agreemen,* 1948) and John Huston (*We Were Strangers,* 1948). But then came Senator Joseph McCarthy and his Committee dealing with 'un-American' activities.

The advent of the Cold War between America and Russia had created an atmosphere of dislike and dis-

trust in the USA for anything that seemed related to left-wing causes. Garfield was a natural victim of this new development. Not only had he been associated with a number of liberal leftist causes throughout his career, but his screen persona was the embodiment of thirties' radicalism: the have-not son of the people who has never been given a break and who points an accusing finger at the selfishness, greed and hardness of the ruling classes. He was bound to suffer when McCarthy's right-wing House Un-American Activities Committee was set up to weed out and persecute suspected 'Reds' in the movie business. 'Friendly' witnesses were persuaded to name names, accusation and innuendo took the place of evidence, and established careers were ruined. Abraham Polonsky, for instance, did not make another film after *Force of Evil* for over twenty years.

While HUAC was beginning its work on breaking down old Hollywood loyalties, Julie made the ironically titled *The Breaking Point* (1950), a literal adaptation of Hemingway's *To Have and Have Not*. As Larry Swindell says, the early Bogart version had a happy ending, but the new version retained the original tragic element: 'Bogart was a winner – and Hemingway's Harry Morgan was a loser. So Warners summoned John Garfield.' Once again the screen image was being reflected in real life. Garfield was one of the first film personalities to be denounced as a possible Communist, especially with his past association with the Group Theatre. He denied the charge vehemently, and pro-

Below: As the 'tough guy' in the highly successful
Body and Soul *(1947); it was his story and he was*
nominated for an Academy Award as best actor.
Right: In We Were Strangers *(1949).*

claimed his attachment to the democratic way of life, but HUAC was not convinced by his testimony. The prevailing ambiance of fear and suspicion which resulted from these political witch-hunts made it hard for Garfield to get work in the last couple of years of his life. Worse still, it put an intolerable strain on his relationship with the politically committed Robbie. He resisted the Committee's probings when he came before them, but even so his career suffered. Garfield sought to save his career after a frustrating year by preparing a sixteen page 'manifesto' for *Look* magazine about his left-wing activities and contacts, but it was the end of his marriage. During the spring of 1952 he had met Iris Whitney, an ex-actress, who seemed to be a possible replacement for Robbie, rather than just another affair. But Garfield did not actually move out of the family home until a couple of weeks before his death, and the political 'about face' was more probably the reason than his latest affair. Garfield completed his confession on May 18th, 1952. After three days of sleepless nights wandering from friend to friend he finally died of a heart attack after a quiet evening with Iris Whitney.

Garfield's sudden death at the early age of thirty-nine consecrated the image he had created on the screen. He was an embittered and disillusioned man who had suffered harassment at the hands of established society in the form of the U.S. government. In a sense, dust *had*

been his destiny. At the end of his life, he had gone full circle back to the early days of his youth when he had been another sort of social outcast, a delinquent kid whose poverty and ethnic background cut him off from the prosperous American mainstream. Those who had known him were quick to make the parallel. Abraham Polonsky said after the actor's death: 'He defended his street boy's honour and they killed him for it.' Who were 'they'? In Garfield's case 'they' were middle America and its elected representatives, the smug, conformist and prejudiced society which the young loner had denounced in his life and in so many of his films. Though Garfield was a fading star by the time he died, he was by no means forgotten. 10,000 loyal fans turned up at his funeral and an article in *Newsweek* claimed that 'not since the death of screen idol Rudolf Valentino has there been such a public display of grief over a film personality'. The tough softy, the fatalistic interloper who dared not let himself believe in anything, had made a lasting impact on his contemporary audiences, an impact which was to echo through the next twenty years. Unfortunately for his posthumous glory, few of his films have become screen classics, and are rarely shown despite Garfield's powerful presence in them. Yet he has remained a legendary figure in the world of serious film-goers and his myth, though dormant, has never been laid to rest.

All four of the great screen 'losers' began their careers in the theatre. But of the four, Montgomery Clift's reputation was the most solidly established as a stage actor be-

CLIFT

fore he started in movies at 27. His successful theatre career had begun in his early teens. James Dean once said, 'Acting is the most logical way for people's neuroses to manifest themselves in the great need we all have to express ourselves'. If this was true of Dean, it was probably even more true for Clift.

Edward Montgomery Clift was born a twin on October 17th, 1920. His family was privileged and aristocratic, his father coming from an old Southern family. But his parents lived apart most of the time and he was completely ruled by his beautiful, cultured, charming but possessive mother Ethel, whom he both adored and hated. When he and his twin sister Roberta were still barely a year old Ethel Clift began the series of extended trips which eventually became a way of life, and which kept the children away from their father in New York for most of the year. Educated by a series of private tutors in Europe, Bermuda and various locations in America, Monty's childhood was as rootless and solitary as a little prince in exile. Hypersensitive and physically delicate, this 'hobgoblin existence' as he later called it, took its toll on his developing personality.

The 1929 crash and subsequent Depression put a stop to Ethel Clift's travelling; in 1933 the family were temporarily immobilized at Sarasota, Florida. Monty was thirteen – it was here that his acting career began, although he had shown an interest in the theatre from the age of eight. He persuaded his reluctant parents to let him start playing juvenile roles in amateur productions, culminating in his first professional role in *Fly Away Home*. The family had moved again, to Connecticut, the play was in rehearsal at a new theatre in

Stockbridge, and a juvenile member of the cast had just dropped out, so Monty stepped into the part. Ironically, when the play transferred to Broadway in January 1935, Ethel Clift moved back permanently into an apartment with her husband for the first time since Monty was a year old.

Because of his constrained upbringing and his own secretive, introverted temperament, Monty was unable to express and thus work out his private conflicts: his growing resentment of his parents, especially of his mother, his sense of estrangement from others, his alienation from his environment wherever he happened to be, his propensity for depression and above all, his dawning homosexuality which he could neither come to terms with nor overcome. Though barely in his teens, the theatre was already his escape route, his refuge, his safety valve. It was a means of extricating himself from his mother's influence, of giving vent to emotions on stage which he was too controlled to express otherwise; it was a milieu which might accept him as he was, where his homosexual and neurotic tendencies would be judged leniently; it even provided him with the first real stability he had ever known.

Those who worked with Monty in the mid-thirties in *Fly Away Home* and *Jubilee* were impressed and disturbed by the seriousness and intensity of the slight, handsome boy. Once, at a cast party, someone referred to the serious fourteen-year-old as 'the oldest person in this room'. Though Monty would become a youth symbol through his acting and his juvenile good looks, it was never the carefree, spontaneous or dynamic sides of youth which he portrayed. It was rather the anxious, self-questioning, vulnerable nature of very young men, their sacrificed innocence, their reluctance to leave the dreams of childhood behind them and to step into the ugly tormented world of adults. By the time he was nineteen, his basic personality type was established. In a play by Robert Sherwood called *There Shall Be No Night* Monty played a patriotic youth who overrides the objections of his pacifist father to go and fight the Russians when they invade his native Finland. During the Second World War Monty, whose health was too precarious for real army duty, would often take the part of boy soldiers senselessly killed or maimed in a war not of their making. Either the young man would get killed in combat, or he would survive with his spirit irrevocably damaged by the suffering and horror he had experienced. The morally wounded casualty of circumstance was a part Monty was already playing in his late teens and early twenties in plays like *The Searching Wind* and *Foxhole in the Parlour*, just as he would play the part in his forties when he was cast as a Jew castrated by the Nazis in *Judgment at Nuremberg* (1960). He would play other roles, of course, in the course of a twenty-five-year career; but basically he was best at personifying the born victim who may con-

sent to the necessity of his destruction, physical or emotional, but who remains lucid, who clearly sees what is being done to him and who therefore sits in judgement of the evil all around him. This character was not necessarily passive or spineless; he often had surprising moral strength and courage based on a quiet awareness of what was right and the determination to stick to that despite inferior strength or a shaky ego.

During the early years of his Broadway success, Clift continued to live at home and appeared to enjoy, even to need, his mother's company and approval of all his activities. Meanwhile the cult following began – from his opening night in *The Mother* in 1939 Clift's appeal transcended ordinary recognition of talent and his admirers turned into hysterical fans. This special appeal barred him from landing a part in *Life With Father*, but also meant that he was free in 1940 to do *There Shall Be No Night* with the legendary Alfred Lunt. Lunt had a lasting influence on Clift's acting style, touring as he did for two years with Lunt's company. At the same time Monty was influenced, like John Garfield, in the acting method developed by the Group Theatre which, although decimated by defections to Hollywood, had left its legacy on Broadway in the forties. He was befriended by Elia Kazan, and even moved away from home and his mother during these years, although he continued to manifest

his need for a mother figure through his attachments with older women, many of whom were actresses.

Although, like Garfield before him, Clift was ambivalent in his attitude towards Hollywood, it was clear that it would only be a matter of time before he appeared in movies. But unlike Garfield he was able to hold off tempting offers from the big studios until the right part and the right deal was presented to him. Once in Hollywood in 1946 his established theatre image was developed further. In his first film, Howard Hawks' *Red River* (1948), Monty played the cowboy son of an overpowering, ruthless father, played by John Wayne, the he-man of all time. Though withdrawn and fragile, no match for Wayne in build or temperament, Monty convincingly portrayed a weaker man who refuses to be bullied and reluctantly accepts an all-out confrontation with his father when no other course is left open to his conscience. In his most famous role as Prewitt, the ex-boxer army bugler in *From Here to Eternity* (1953) Clift summed up the credo of the loser who stubbornly clings to his personal code of honour: 'If a man doesn't go his way he's nothin'.' Prewitt is emotionally destroyed by his brutalized environment and by the memory of a man he accidentally killed while he was a boxer. He rejects violence, refuses to conform and is persecuted by his army comrades; but his inner weak-

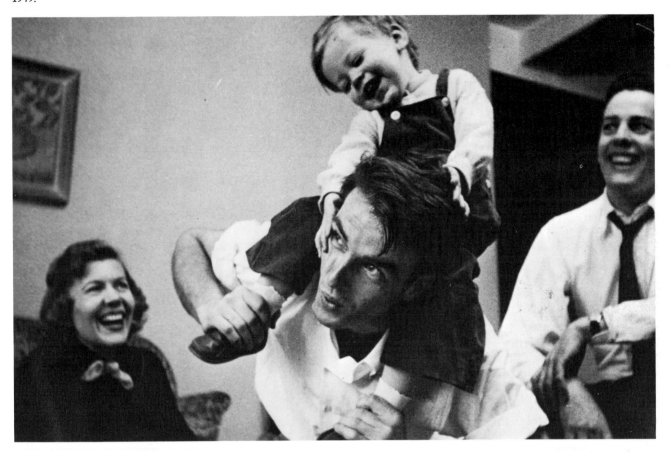

pretty revolting: all that touching and pinching and groping about . . . With me and Montgomery, it wasn't that way at all. Love with him would be long, langourous sighs, pressing close against his manly chest and telling each other those secrets we had never told anybody, gazing eyeball to eyeball, and he wouldn't think of putting his hand on my thigh.'

Montgomery Clift was not only the golden boy of the film critics and the darling of young girls; he also seemed the personification of youthful rebellion, the searching young man who refused easy answers and rejected the authority of his father or society if their values didn't make sense to him. He so completely identified with the image of the rebel hero that he was naturally offered the role of Terry Malloy in *On The Waterfront* and of Cal Trask in *East of Eden*; but he turned them both down and the roles went to the lesser-known Marlon Brando and the then unknown James Dean. In 1949 Monty had made *A Place in the Sun* (released in 1951), a story about a poor, ambitious young man who falls in love with an heiress. The way Clift played the part of the hero struck a deep chord in young Americans of the post-war years. Here was a true anti-hero, brooding, misled by the false values of society, aspiring to something better and paying for his mistakes with his life. As Joe Morella wrote, '*A Place in the Sun* was tremendously relevant to the youth of the early fifties. A new generation of soul-searchers reacted to the tormented hero portrayed by Clift . . . He was a man rebelling against his fate without knowing how and questioning why. He was a rebel hero of the day'.

In his private life, Clift soon developed the various symptoms of self-destructive behaviour which were dictated by his oversensitive, neurotic disposition. It took a genuine misfit to play a misfit so well, just as the root of Garfield's talent at portraying a character with a permanent chip on his shoulder lay in his deep-seated inferiority complex, and Dean's genius at conveying rebelliousness stemmed from his own compulsive need to rebel against all restraint and convention. Clift was by nature distrustful and brooding, every bit as strange and detached as the hero of *A Place in the Sun*. As his popularity on the screen grew, so did his neurosis, insecurity and manic-depressive tendencies. When he was with people, he hunched his shoulders as though he were afraid they would hit him. Many of those who met him were struck by his way of talking 'as though he wanted to tell you something and at the same time didn't want to tell you'. He had odd, infantile habits like insisting on eating from others' plates and crawling around on the floor in company. Even more disconcertingly, he would suddenly hop out of a room and hang from the window ledge by his fingertips thirteen floors above street level; or he would astound friends by climbing down from their roofs and suddenly appearing head downward outside their windows. La Guardia suggests that these death-defying pranks were really bids for help, Clift symbolically crying out 'Please rescue me!'.

By the time Clift reached Hollywood, he already had a severe drinking problem and what made the habit worse was that he usually mixed various barbiturate and opiate-based drugs into his liquor. From the time of an acute attack of amoebic dysentery in 1939, Clift had become obsessed with drugs and never travelled without an entire trunk full of pills. There is an anecdote about him which would be amusing if it were not also tragic. As a joke, his doctor-psychiatrist in Hollywood once presented him with an enormous card on his birthday with the words HAPPY BIRTHDAY MONTY spelled out in pills of every shape and colour: 'Monty was ecstatic. He knew the identity of every pill just by the colour and shape and started picking them off the card like pieces of candy'. He sometimes carried a thermos flask of liquor mixed with 'downers' from which he took swigs throughout the day. The result was that he was often drunk on set and would periodically black out or collapse while shooting. This made it increasingly hazardous to employ him on a picture and, despite his prestige, many directors were reluctant to work with him.

A car accident in 1956 temporarily disfigured Monty, then 36 years old, and the shock further plunged him into depression and alcoholism. Though he scored a number of successes after *From Here to Eternity* in films like *The Young Lions* (1958) and *Suddenly Last Summer* (1959), the deterioration in his physical and mental condition began to affect his performances. By the time he made *The Misfits* in 1960, the cowboy he played was totally different from his role in *Red River*; he no longer seemed a tormented boy but a man utterly wrecked by life. His co-star, Marilyn Monroe, said when she met him, 'He's the only one I know who's even worse off than I am'. Her own death was only a year away at the time. There were many temperamental similarities between Marilyn and Monty. Both had a child-like dependence on the few people they trusted. They had to have their private drama coach on set throughout a picture, more for reassurance and approval than for actual guidance in their acting. Like Marilyn, Monty would call up friends at all hours of the night just to hear a friendly

voice. Or he would call them for advice on trivial subjects like whether to allow his dentist to work on a lower molar. Friendship with Monty meant taking care of him, holding his hand while he drank himself into a stupor or cried for hours, as he often did; it meant not trying to reform him but looking on helplessly and sympathetically as he proceeded to destroy himself.

By the mid-sixties, Monty had accomplished the task of wrecking his life, his health and his talent. Constant bouts of illness were exacerbated by his own refusal or inability to regulate his life accordingly. His gait was slow and halting and his weight was down to a hundred pounds. A glazed, blank look of mute misery never left his eyes. When Ralph Zucker saw him in 1964, he was appalled: 'He seemed as if he were in a trance, as if he were no longer with us, as if his overwhelming personal isolation were irremediable. And I remember thinking: he's a dead man.' Zucker was right; Monty died of a heart attack a few months later, on July 22, 1966. Though he was only forty-five at the time of his death, he had long lost his mystique as youth symbol and rebel hero. One hundred and fifty people attended his funeral, but the large crowd of onlookers outside the church had come to see the living celebrities, not to mourn the dead star. Others had taken his place and yet the myth of Montgomery Clift had survived. Millions still treasure the memory of the thin, quiet, intense young man who conveyed an independence of spirit and a kind of rectitude in the face of insuperable odds.

When James Dean appeared on the screen – angry, dishevelled, hurt – youth's response was immediate. In East of Eden *(1955) (left) and (below), and* Rebel Without a Cause *(1956) (right).*

DEAN

'I think there's only one true form of greatness for a man. If a man can bridge the gap between life and death – I mean, if he can live on after he's died, then maybe he was a great man.' So said the legendary James Dean, who has himself been adored since his early death more than he ever was during his short life and even shorter period of stardom.

James Dean only made three major films, two of which were released posthumously. So there was little to give substance to the myth of rebellious youth that he came to represent. But it was the fact that he didn't live to maturity that made him such a potent symbol for the adolescents of his own and of subsequent generations. Children never really believe they will grow into adults, but adolescents are only too conscious that the passage is imminent. Most of them feel furiously resentful of their parents because they see their own destiny mapped out on the faces of their elders. They know their precious, short-lived youth is doomed, just as Jim Stark, the hero of *Rebel Without a Cause,* senses that in a few years' time he could become like his submissive, compromising father. Most of Dean's fans have remained faithful to his memory because Dean is their totem, their Peter Pan, the one that got away, the proof that they too were young once. In *The Stars,* Edgar Morin wrote 'The adult of our middle-class society is the man who agrees to live only a little in order not to die a great deal. But the secret of adolescence is that living *means* risking death; that the rage to live *means* the impossibility of living. James Dean has lived this contradiction and authenticated it by his death.' Though James Dean did not commit suicide he felt a compulsion to gamble with

his own life until he finally lost it, and by losing it won not only posthumous glory but the privilege of never growing up, of never becoming 'one of them', of never betraying the youth he personified by joining the ranks of adulthood.

James Dean made films not only about how difficult it is to be young but also how difficult it is to be anything else. The heroes he portrayed strive to take on responsibility, but their intentions are misunderstood by the world of real adults and so they take refuge in the behaviour of childhood once again. In *East of Eden* (1955) Cal Trask bursts into tears and runs away when his father rejects the money he has made to try to save the family fortunes. In *Rebel Without a Cause* (1955), Jim Stark takes on the difficult and paternal responsibility of attempting to disarm young Plato. But his premature 'fatherhood' fails when Plato is gunned down, and Jim takes refuge from the intolerable idea that it was his fault by acting like an infant once again. Thus, by a synthesis of his film characterisations and his actual life and death, James Dean became the heroic representative of the transition from adolescence to adulthood. He is the personification of an idealized, eternal teenage in which manhood and responsibility is forever postponed.

James Dean's face is so well-known that it is surprising to realize that behind the familiar expressions of anguished frustrations or gauche good humour, there is an average, almost ordinary, handsome face: blond, blue-eyed, square-jawed and clean cut. This quality of physical averageness is also important in an appraisal of Dean's incredible popularity with teenagers. It made him one of them as well as one apart. Not surprisingly, one of the features of the James Dean death cult was a regularly-held contest to find the boy who looked most like Dean. Thousands felt they resembled him enough to

come forward and enter the competition. They found it easy to imitate his slouch, his rumpled hair, his mannerisms, his way of dressing which was the standard uniform of teenagers anyway and has remained their favourite style: jeans, a white T-shirt and a zip-up windcheater. The effortlessness with which so many youths could impersonate Jimmy made identification with him easy, natural: they could feel like Jimmy, look like Jimmy, be Jimmy in a way that would have been impossible if Dean's features had been particularly unusual and distinctive. Boys felt they *were* Jimmy, just as Jimmy *was* them. As David Dalton said in his biography of Dean: 'In America, greasers, college students, transvestites and punks all identified with James Dean in the conviction that the self he projected was what they really wanted to be. Although Jimmy invented few of the attributes associated with him, he had created from his many impersonations a composite image that was universally applicable.' The Dean legend rests on the universal applicability of that composite image. Not only college students and punks felt that Dean's image was their own, so did office workers, factory hands and farm labourers; the only common denominator was their youth. As we know, man creates gods in his own image and Dean has come as close to god-like status as it is possible for any human being in the twentieth century. Jimmy did not have to invent the attributes associated with him because some of those attributes were already present in the Westernized youth culture of the fifties and others were present in every youth culture. All he had to do was to embody them, to personify youth so that he would become its mirror reflection.

Even Dean's early life was quite uneventful; it has a quality of averageness which makes much of it sound like the typical story of an American boy. It contains no dark tales of illegitimacy and orphanages like Marilyn's, no saga of emigration like Valentino's, no childhood poverty like Elvis Presley's, no juvenile delinquency like Garfield's. He was born on February 8th, 1931, in a small town about fifty miles from Indianapolis and he was named James Byron Dean. His middle name, chosen by his mother Mildred, reflects her cultural preoccupations, and she brought up her only son to appreciate literature, music and art. The family moved to Los Angeles, but unfortunately Mildred Dean died of cancer in 1940 when James was nine, and although his father had tried to prepare him for the shock, the boy was undoubtedly profoundly affected. However, the tragedy was more than cushioned by the fact that James was sent back to live on the family farm in Fairmount, Indiana. There it was his good fortune to find a stable, readymade home with his grandparents, uncle and loving aunt, who did all she could to become his substitute mother. Between the ages of nine and eighteen, Jimmy Dean led a pleasant, uneventful existence on the farm, helping with chores, shooting rabbits and keeping pets. At school, he was well-adjusted, got good grades and was a sports enthusiast. So far there was nothing to suggest that he would one day become identified with adolescent rebelliousness, in conflict with his family, the authorities and his peers. The only hint of future disturbance and revolt could be found in Jimmy's early passion for speed and physical risk: dare-devil trick-riding on his motorcycle, trying out foolhardy stunts on a trapeze until he fell and broke his front teeth, always swinging a tractor through a gate with the smallest possible margin. But at the same time this was only seen as the natural high spirits of a healthy teenage boy. Jimmy's relations have always insisted on his complete normality. 'I've said it until I'm sick of saying it,' his uncle once complained. 'Jimmy was just like any other kid who grew up in this town.'

The first sign that Jimmy was in any way different from other country boys was his burgeoning acting talent. While still at high school, his obvious gift was noticeable and he won a state recitation contest with 'The Madman' by Charles Dickens, beginning his monologue with a blood-curdling scream. But it wasn't until he went back to California to live with his father and go to college that he began seriously to think about becoming an actor. Jimmy wanted to study dramatic arts at U.C.L.A. but his father disapproved, persuading his son to take a physical education course at Santa Monica instead. It was only a year before Jimmy actually got his own way but in the meantime an immovable wedge had been driven between father and son. His uneasy

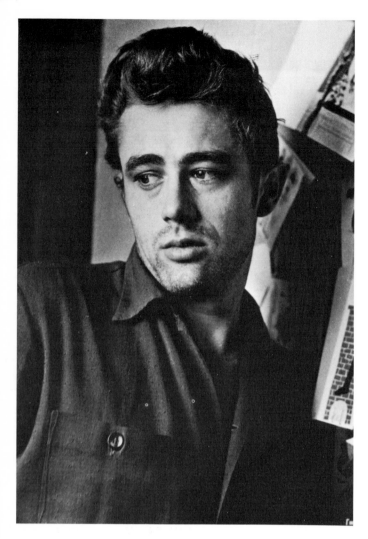

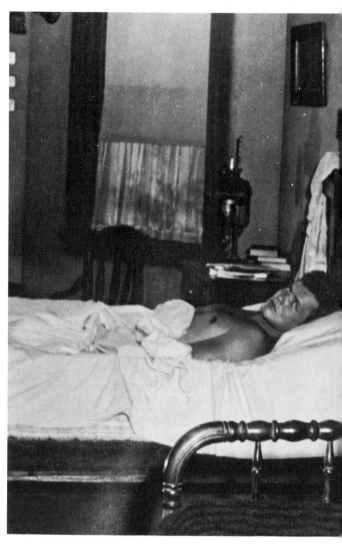

Left: Jimmy at home: West 68th Street, New York.
Below centre: With Richard Davalos (Aron Trask)
in a cut scene from East of Eden. Kazan suggested
that they shared accommodation during prepar-

relationship with his father, whom he had hardly seen in the previous nine years, may well have laid the groundwork for his later portrayals of misunderstood youth, although outwardly their relationship was civil, if formal. Even when he enrolled at U.C.L.A. he didn't really fit in either with the academic requirements of the course or the fraternity with which he lived, who contemptuously nick-named him 'the ploughboy'.

By 1951 he had dropped out of college but he stayed on in Los Angeles for a time to try his luck as an actor. He did not get anywhere beyond appearing in a Pepsi Cola commercial and doing a little work as a film extra. Hollywood may have been the movie capital of the world, but New York was the Mecca which beckoned anyone with aspirations to serious acting, with its promise of actors' studios and quality plays on and off Broadway. When he was twenty years old, Dean left Los Angeles and went to seek his fortune in the Big Apple. It was there that he found himself truly alone for the first time. Before then he had indeed been something of a loner within the crowd, but the crowd had been ready to include him if he would make the effort to leave his shell. But during the early months of his stay in New York, his isolation was complete and the experience jolted him badly. The awful loneliness and inner confusion of this period would later help him to portray

lonely, confused young men. At first, his attempts to get work as an actor were as fruitless or frustrating as they had been in Los Angeles. The only acting jobs he got, if they could be called acting, were being a stooge for the TV programme *Beat the Clock* and a few TV walk-on parts. The rest of the time he survived on loans and odd jobs. Most of his life during the winter of 1951-52 was spent going to casting sessions and being turned down, or waiting for offers of work which never came.

Yet Jimmy's talent was so real and so evident that this lean period could not last for very long. He was taken on by agent Jane Deacy who worked behind the scenes to get him suitable roles, especially the many TV dramas in which he appeared. He even managed to get into the select Actors' Studio, after being chosen from 150 applicants, although he rarely attended the sessions. It was there he met Elia Kazan who would eventually choose him to play in *East of Eden*. (Elia Kazan figures in the lives of Garfield, Clift and Dean and his influence on all three in various ways was uncannily profound.) Dean's career was served not only by his natural talent but by his tremendous drive. His admirers have tended to assume that his real character matched his film image

exactly, but there were facets of his personality that had nothing to do with the aloof dreamer he portrayed on stage and screen. Success did not just happen to James Dean by accident, nor was stardom thrust on him; he knew exactly where he was going and was determined to get there. Everything about his conduct during his years in New York shows that he was ambitious and success-orientated and he was not above pulling strings or doing a little manoeuvring to steer his career on the right course; he cultivated a friendship with the producer Lemuel Ayers, for example, without breathing a word about his hopes for a stage career until the relationship was sufficiently consolidated for him to confess that he was a budding actor and coveted the leading role in Ayers' next play, *See The Jaguar*. He got the part and though the play folded after only six days, he personally received such good reviews that it led to bigger and better parts in 'live' television dramas.

Most of Dean's TV performances have not survived; in those days, even if a print existed it was soon lost or destroyed by the TV studios. But it was in these plays, made in 1952, 1953 and 1954, that Jimmy developed his unique image of the teenage rebel. His expressive face

and neurotic acting style lent themselves perfectly to the character of 'a terribly upset, psyched-out kid, a precursor to the hooked generation of the sixties, the type that became part of the drug/rock culture', as Rod Serling, the writer of one of those dramas, described it. These roles not only revealed Dean's genius for portraying 'psyched-out kids'; they also gave a foretaste of the sort of audience identification the young actor could arouse. After each Dean appearance, the TV studios would get 'rave letters from young girls, brotherly letters from young boys', which more than hinted at the madness to come.

By 1953, Dean was an established TV star who, like Monty Clift, could afford to turn down film offers until the right role should come along. Elia Kazan, who was equally at home in the film and the theatre world, was looking for someone to play the pivotal part of Caleb Trask in his next film, *East of Eden*. He had disliked Dean's manner when he had met him at the Actors' Studio, but he was shrewd enough to see that the very things he disliked about the young actor would make him a perfect Cal. The screen tests of Jimmy confirmed this, and it was obvious from the start that Dean would probably become a major new film star. But no one quite anticipated what an incredible hit he would turn out to be with the young. As Elia Kazan recalled, at a Hollywood preview: 'The balcony was full of kids who had never seen Jimmy before and the moment he came on the screen they began to screech, they began to holler and yell and the balcony was coming down like a waterfall.'

Before *East of Eden*, Dean had been a successful actor. After *East of Eden*, he was at once a legend, a superstar, an international youth hero. There has always been some controversy as to whether Dean relished the switchover or whether it infuriated him, and the truth probably lies somewhere in between. Dean's fans have always revelled in their hero's proudly aloof, non-conformist image, conveniently forgetting

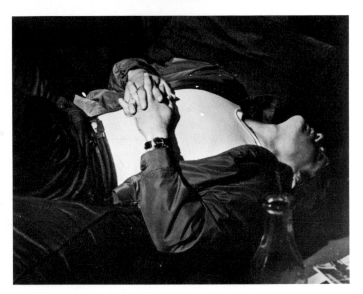

that the image was cultivated and perfected by Jimmy himself, who realized he had much to gain from seeming somehow different, unconventional and original. While he had been a struggling actor, Dean had had to toe the line to an extent, to stomach injustices, to put a brave face on defeats or humiliations. So it must have been a sweet revenge to be rude, unco-operative and arrogant whenever the fancy took him. 'Ahhhh,

they love it!' he could laugh after being particularly obnoxious to a journalist or a film executive. Whether they loved it or not, his growing reputation of eccentricity and rebelliousness only served his youth hero image, as did his surliness and scruffy way of dressing. Montgomery Clift and Marlon Brando before him had discovered that snarling their way through interviews and wearing loafers, jeans and tee-shirts were useful badges of distinction in a world of grinning conformists and squares in dinner jackets. Those who scoffed that such attitudes were mere gimmicks to get extra publicity were wrong too, however: a bohemian life-style and a certain contempt for conventional behaviour came naturally to these young actors, fresh from the world of the New York theatre and cast adrift in the technicolor artificiality of Hollywood life.

Yet in fact Dean's existence in Hollywood after *East of Eden* did not differ radically from that of other film stars. He enjoyed all the privileges of stardom and had no objections to dating pretty starlets, escorting them to the most fashionable restaurants or nightclubs in expensive sportscars. During his first months in Hollywood, he was ready to play the game right through: though he proclaimed his utter scorn for actors who tried to get favourable publicity, he deliberately courted the influential gossip columnist

cowboy. Right: Fated lovers: Jimmy and Pier Angeli. 'For better or for worse, I'm going to spend the rest of my days with her.' But she married Vic Damone the next year and died herself aged 39 in 1971.

Hedda Hopper, charming her into becoming his defender and champion.

This apparent time-serving is understandable in the circumstances. Dean wanted to ensure that his career would get as far as it possibly could and was far more ambivalent and self-contradictory in this and other respects than his worshippers have wished to believe in their quest for an ideal hero, though ambivalence and conflicting aspirations seem natural enough in someone as young and complex as Dean. He both wanted to climb to the top and to continue feeling like an underdog. He wanted to remain a serious *avant-garde* actor, appreciated by the discriminating few, and also to be a popular star admired by the maximum number of people. He wanted to be left alone, yet he also wanted people to talk about him. He felt intuitive suspicion and even dislike for the gilded privileges of life at the top, yet he was also curious to savour the fruits of success. On a visit to his hometown, after *East of Eden* had brought him fame, he complained bitterly and no doubt sincerely to his first acting teacher, Adeline Nall, about what he called 'the Hollywood commotion'. She tried to point out to him: 'This is what *you* chose. *You* wanted to be an actor.' But Dean was not prepared to listen, to come to terms with his own mixed feelings about fame and success.

Both on screen and in real life Dean seemed unable to push revolt to its logical conclusion: the true rebel turns his back on what he has rejected and proudly accepts the outcast's role he has elected by being different from the rest and true to himself. Dean could never quite make the break; he was someone who craved affection, interest and acceptance from the very people he had criticized and wished to shock. His last role in *Giant* (1956) is like a parable of the real Dean's inner contradictions. The traditional Western cowboy outcast freely chooses isolation, leaving behind those who can never understand him. But in *Giant,* the misfit cowboy played by Dean stays put and builds a rival ranch just on the outskirts of the Benedict ranch where he used to work. He will try to force people's respect by growing rich and successful within full view of those who once scorned him, because he cannot quite bring himself to make a complete break with the past and with the only established society he knows. Perhaps Dean himself would eventually have turned his back on the system if he had lived, refusing the movie-god status which undeniably made him feel uncomfortable; maybe the pressure would have led him to drop out of films altogether. Or he might finally have become integrated into the system, settling by degrees for the 'sell-out' as some of his young fans would have construed it, the cushy life of a Hollywood prince churning out box-office moneymakers. At the time of his death, however, he had not yet opted for one or the other and was still, as he had always been, hesitant, restless, experimental, excited and depressed.

There is also something mysterious, even unfathomable, about the emotional life of James Dean, who has been love's young dream to so many millions of adolescent girls. While in New York he showed that he was

capable of long-term attachments in his relationships first with Elizabeth ('Dizzy') Sheridan, and then with another young actress called Barbara Glenn; this latter affair was the longest lasting and did not come to an end when he left for California; long after he had become a national idol, he was still writing to Barbara and telling her how desperately he missed her. Later in Hollywood he fell in love with the young Italian actress, Pier Angeli. But he lost each of the girls in turn when they married other men and in both cases he seems to have been genuinely and deeply upset. Though Pier Angeli later compared her romance with Dean to that of Romeo and Juliet, the actual barriers that kept the lovers apart seem flimsy now: Pier's mother disapproved of Dean, while his agent felt that marriage would not be good for his career. In fact, there was also something in Dean's nature which made him fearful of emotional commitment. Perhaps John Howlett was right to say in his biography of Dean that this reluctance lay rooted in Jimmy's early loss of his mother, a loss which made him feel all deep attachments were too risky because they would cause intolerable grief if they were severed. He preferred to remain somewhat disengaged in his relationships with women. (There has even been some conjecture about his heterosexuality. Indeed the appeal of Dean to fans of both sexes may be rooted in his own bisexuality, which has been hinted at but never clearly corroborated.)

Dean's attitude to women may or may not have 'made life hell for any girl who gave him her affection', as one of his few detractors was to write after his death, but James Dean was by all accounts someone difficult to love. Kazan played on his moodiness and outrageous-

ness to heighten the tensions between the actors on the set of East of Eden so that they were projected into the characters. It was only through Julie Harris's patient friendship that both Jimmy and Richard Davalos (who played Cal's twin brother Aron) could keep on an even keel in the highly charged emotional atmosphere. But Nicholas Ray, director of Rebel Without a Cause, developed a good working relationship with Dean and although the film was viewed with apprehension by Warner Brothers during the shooting, it was clear from the early rushes that both Dean and Natalie Wood were giving exceptional dramatic performances; and besides, after The Wild One (1954) and Blackboard Jungle (1955), teenage movies were now big box office.

Meanwhile there was Giant. George Stevens' epic of Texan oil tycoons had been in preparation while Dean was making East of Eden and Dean had been promised the part of Jett Rink in 1955. It was fortuitous that shooting had to be delayed on Giant to allow Elizabeth Taylor time to have a baby otherwise Rebel might never have been made. The shooting of Giant was not a particularly happy time for Jimmy – George Stevens was not an actors' director, while both Kazan and Ray were, in their different ways. In addition, under his contract Jimmy was banned from road racing, his self-confessed safety valve for all the frustrations and conflicts of Hollywood life.

James Dean was well-served by the three films he made during those sixteen short months of stardom before he died. He was a mythological American hero in all of them, as well as encapsulating the preoccupations of youth both in the fifties and later. As William Zinsser, critic for the New York Herald Tribune, des-

*Below left: As Plato is shot dead by the police,
Jim Stark is screaming; 'But I-got-the-bullets!'
Bottom: Jett Rink and the Reata Ranch – the*

scribed him in *East of Eden,* 'Everything about Dean suggests the lonely, misunderstood nineteen-year-old. Even from a distance you know a lot about him by the way he walks – with his hands in his pockets and his head down, slinking like a dog waiting for a bone. When he talks, he stammers and pauses, uncertain of what he is trying to say. When he listens, he is full of restless energy – he stretches, a small boy impatient with his elders' chatter.' Uncertainty, restless energy and impatience with elders' chatter are all qualities which will help the rebel hero in his typically American quest for

self-betterment. As Jim Stark in *Rebel Without a Cause,* he is in revolt against the alienation of middle-class life and the fatal path of criminality represented by the delinquent gang he encounters, and against the dehumanized brutality of organized society, represented by the cops who senselessly shoot down a sick, frightened boy. In *Giant,* he stars as the heroic archetype of the independent cowboy who starts out with only his lassoo and his Stetson hat to call his own but ends up a multi-millionaire through his own resourcefulness and tenacity, though he becomes embittered and disillusioned in the process.

The nature of Dean's impact on the screen can never be satisfyingly put into words. It is too visual, too emotional. Those who want to understand its mystery must see his films and draw their own conclusions. But it is like love at first sight: either you feel it or you don't. At the time some, particularly older people, couldn't see it at all. They felt nothing but distaste for 'the loutish and malicious petulance which present-day teenagers profess to admire', as a reviewer, Courtland Phipps described it. They maintained that nobody as churlish as Jett Rink in *Giant* could possibly have interested Leslie Benedict (played by Elizabeth Taylor) even for a moment. Some critics dismissed Dean as a second rate actor, others charged him with slavishly imitating Brando. But his detractors were in a minority. Most people recognized star material when they saw it and even if the Dean virus did not contaminate them they weren't going to make fools of themselves by scoffing at the new wonderboy.

When he died at the wheel of his sports car on his

image that captured the spirit of Texas. Right: Jimmy in his new Porsche, a few days before his death on September 30th, 1955. Below right: A fan's shrine.

way to a race meeting on September 30th, 1955, James Dean became a mythological hero. He was twenty-four. Edgar Morin wrote: 'Death fulfils the destiny of every mythological hero by fulfilling his double nature: human and divine. It fulfils his profound humanity, which is to struggle heroically against the world, to confront heroically a death which ultimately overwhelms him. At the same time, death fulfils the superhuman nature of the hero: it divinizes him by opening wide the gates of immortality.' The quest for the absolute must logically end in death since it means always taxing one's endurance further, always striving to overcome one's human limitations.

The cult of James Dean which came into being after his death began slowly but soon gained momentum. *Rebel Without a Cause* opened just four days after the crash and Jack Warner soon discovered how wrong he had been in his assumption that Dean's two unreleased movies would flop because 'no one will go to see a corpse'. On the contrary, the success of this film and subsequently of *Giant* was guaranteed by Jimmy's death and all three of Dean's films continue to make money for his studio a quarter of a century later. One post-office worker in London has claimed to have seen *Rebel* over four hundred times. Indeed, Dean's fans would have paid a fortune to see his real corpse. As it was, a great many paid 25 cents just to look at the wreck of his Porsche Spyder and 50 cents to sit in the driver's seat where he had died. They were ready to pay good money for chewing-gum envelopes supposedly from gum chewed by Dean. Three thousand people attended the funeral in Fairmount, Indiana. While in sheer numbers this may not compare with Valentino's previously or Presley's subsequently, it was an immense tribute to an

actor who at the time had only been seen in one major film, and who was still being described as a 'newcomer'. It was after *Rebel* and *Giant* had reached mass audiences that the posthumous hero worship reached vast and often bizarre proportions. At one point, 3,800,000 people in the United States alone were paying members of Dean fan-clubs created after his death and given such titles as 'Lest We Forget', 'Dedicated Deans' and 'Dean's Teens'. Records like *Jimmy Dean's First Christmas in Heaven, The Ballad of James Dean* and *His Name Was Dean* all did excellent business. Even the patently fabricated account of Dean's spirit life, *Jimmy Dean Returns,* which purported to be 'His own words from the Beyond', sold half a million copies, so great was the hunger for anything touching on the dead star's memory.

Why this frenzied cult of love after death? David Dalton may supply the key when he says about Dean's young mourners: 'An inconsolable sense of loss was intensified by identification with Jimmy. His death became their death, and romantic fantasies about their own immortality overlapped with his.' Just as the young had felt that the living Jimmy was part of *them* and vice versa, so the dead Jimmy was also them; the need to feel that death is not the end, a need felt particularly keenly by young people, made them keep Jimmy alive in the only ways they could: by going to clubs to discuss his memory, by attempts at spiritual communication with him, by look-alike competitions and by collecting photographs, articles and flesh-coloured rubber masks of their idol. Another way of keeping Jimmy alive was

to pretend he wasn't really dead. Many youngsters persuaded themselves that he had only been disfigured in the crash and was hiding somewhere. Hundreds of thousands wrote to him as if he were still alive. During the three years following his death, letters addressed to Dean continued to outnumber the fan mail of any living star.

What of the Jimmy Dean legend more than twenty years on? It is doing very well though the initial hysteria has calmed down. Perhaps Dean has more fans now than he did at the time of his death, for it would seem that love at first sight is also enduring. People don't 'outgrow' Jimmy Dean the way they may outgrow other movie idols of their teens. Once a Deanager, always a Deanager, so that his ardent admirers now cover an age group of fifteen to fifty. The influence of his image on the popular culture of the sixties and on nearly all its most famous representatives has ensured Dean's survival as myth and legend well into the seventies. People have not yet grown tired of Dean's face. In a poem about Dean, written in 1958, the American author, John Dos Passos, described

> 'the resentful hair
> the deep eyes floating in lonesomeness
> the bitter beat look
> the scorn on the lip.'

This is the imagery of revolt, of disillusion, of frustration. This is the image of James Dean, in Andy Warhol's words, the image of 'the damaged but beautiful soul of our time'.

CYBULSKI

Those who were inconsolable over the loss of James Dean looked for a worthy successor and many felt they had found one in the late fifties. He had a name they could not pronounce. There was something halting yet eloquent about the way he spoke in the soft, liquid tongue no one understood; his face, full of childish pain and adult intelligence, was so riveting that one could hardly bring oneself to leave it for a second to read the subtitles below. Not that it really mattered: he had already conveyed his every nuance of meaning with his expression and his mannerisms. He was known in the West as the Polish James Dean and his name was Zbigniew Cybulski. Although Cybulski's film career began a year earlier than Dean's audiences outside Poland only discovered him in 1958 with Wajda's *Ashes and Diamonds,* and by then any rebel hero could hardly escape comparisons with the great James Dean. Indeed the image of Maciek, created by Wajda and Cybulski, deliberately aped that of Brando and Dean.

Cybulski's similarities with Dean were quite striking, even in their private lives and backgrounds. Cybulski was of the same generation as Dean, had lived through the same times and had studied similar acting methods; this more than accounted for certain similarities between the two, apart from the fact that they had a superficial physical resemblance and, apparently, a temperamental one. What various people who met Cybulski said about him could also have applied to Dean. They spoke of Cybulski's 'painful, almost Dostoyevskian sensibility', of his 'ambiguity' which made him difficult to define, always seeming to want to say more than the actual words he spoke. His gestures, deliberately unfinished, 'drew arabesques in the air which always seemed to hide some mystery'. Not surprisingly, the two actors projected in a similar fashion when they acted similar parts. Maciek in *Ashes and Diamonds* is a rebel who has lost faith in his cause, a close cousin to Jim Stark who never had a cause in the first place. Except in the tougher, more uncompromising Polish film world, Maciek could be allowed to die, while Stark survived.

Dean and Cybulski were also much closer in type than were, say, Brando and Dean. They both conveyed a shrinking nature, a soul that is forlorn, immature and ill-equipped for life. There is an incredible, though perhaps coincidental, similarity between the opening shot of Dean's most famous film, *Rebel Without a Cause,* and the end of Cybulski's best known film, *Ashes and Diamonds.* The poignancy of both these scenes perfectly illustrates the nature of their heroes' appeal. In *Rebel Without a Cause,* we see the drunk Jim Stark, left alone for the evening by his parents and thus symbolically abandoned; he has staggered and fallen in an empty street full of alien litter and greasy papers. At the end of *Ashes and Diamonds,* Cybulski alias Maciek knows that

he will be killed for not being able to shoot a man he was under orders to execute. He starts to run through a no-man's land of rubble and garbage, a kind of urban desert full of menace and despair which can neither hide nor shield him. We feel the emotion again: this wonderful young man alone in a hostile world with nowhere to go. A shot rings out, Maciek staggers, falls dying and curls up on the barren filth which is to be his last resting place.

Cybulski and Dean were both orphaned seekers after the truth; their faces and stance suggested the various ages of man: the doubtful, hurt child, the anxious adolescent on the threshold of manhood, the adult ready to face the consequences of his acts, even the wizened old man bowed down with the woes of the world. The rich complexity of their natures, the infinite variety of expressions which flitted across their sensitive faces explain their impact on our sensibilities. Yet there were also vital differences between them which would emerge in their screen persona. Cybulski was a European who had lived through the horrors and privations of the Second World War in Poland, perhaps the country most devastated by that war. Born in 1927, he was only twelve when the Germans invaded.

Educated in secret during the occupation he was destined for journalism, but at the end of the war gave this up in favour of the Cracow Theatre School. After a spell in provincial repertory he founded the student theatre Bim Bom in Cracow, in association with

ZBIGNIEW CYBULSKI

98

Left and right: Cybulski as Maciek in Ashes and
Diamonds. *A rebel who has lost faith in his
cause, a close cousin to Jim Stark who never had
a cause in the first place. Except in the tougher
more uncompromising Polish film world, Maciek*

Bogumul Kobiela. This *avant-garde* company gained considerable fame and influence, and led to his first film roles and his first association with Andrzej Wajda, with a brief role in *A Generation* (1954) the first of Wajda's trilogy on the Polish resistance.

Cybulski was eighteen when the war ended and Poland was plunged into bitter civil war with the advent of Communism. This followed the Nazi invasion, occupation, genocide, bombardments and blood-drenched uprisings, and it was these events which Wajda chronicled. Cybulski also readily acknowledged the traumatic impact of these gruelling years on himself and on all those of his generation. He was conscious that his personal trauma was a collective one, that his entire generation had been sacrificed, irreparably damaged during its formative years. This awareness led him to hope that other generations would be more fortunate and more 'whole' because the circumstances of their childhood and youth would be different. He once expressed this conviction in the following terms: 'I belong to the war generation . . . but new men will come along who will not be neurotic, the way we are.' He could take comfort in this belief and its basic optimism coloured even his portrayals of despair.

Cybulski played in several films before *Ashes and Diamonds* brought him international star status. The

idea of the 'Hamlet in windcheater and dark glasses', as David Robinson called him, was to stay with Cybulski for the rest of his life. *Ashes and Diamonds* was one of the most successful films ever made in Poland, and it is for the role of Maciek that Cybulski is chiefly remembered. However, unlike some of the anti-heroes of the West, his whole concept of the anti-hero was influenced by the Marxist view that a man is a product of his circumstances and that human nature is perfectible. He once defined his approach to the anti-hero rebels he played on stage and on screen in the following terms: 'At a workers' club I run I was asked if I was afraid the public would stop liking me if I played a negative hero . . . There is no fundamentally good or bad individual . . . conditions of life make individuals good or evil.'

Though Cybulski was always involved in *avant-garde* theatre and experimental cinema, he never came into open conflict with the Polish state and its strict ideological control of culture. He was a non-conformist in the way he lived, dressed and worked, yet he was not a rebel in the true sense of the word: a man persecuted by society for being different. He was sophisticated and articulate, and his intellectual approach was reflected in more than forty films such as *The Eighth Day of the Week* (1957), *The Innocent Sorcerers* (1959), *The Saragossa Manuscript* (1964) and *See You Tomorrow* (1960).

is allowed to die, while Jim Stark survived.
Cybulski died in mysterious circumstances in
1967. His death, suicidal or accidental, was true
to the death of the romantic rebel.

But, like many other stars whose most famous roles are fixed in the minds of their admirers, Cybulski's later achievements are rarely seen or remembered outside the 'art film' circuit, at least in the West. Cybulski became a national hero but like many others before him, he seemed unable to stand the strain, and friends watched helplessly as he put on weight, drank to excess and pursued an endless round of promiscuity.

Cybulski's mysterious death in January, 1967, while trying to board a late-night train, confirmed the aura of doom and pathos he had so poignantly projected as Maciek. Was his death an accident? Was it suicide? His end was as ambiguous as his image. At any event, it seems that many of his friends were unsurprised by the suddenness of his death at age 39. Like Garfield before him, and Elvis Presley later, the Cybulski which the public mourned was not the paunchy 'faded matinée idol' he was apparently turning into but the youthful hesitator, caught in the uncertainties of the immediate post-war years, that he had portrayed as Maciek. Who really *was* Maciek-Cybulski? A hero of the new order or a victim of the old? A man full of faith or one who secretly doubted? A despairing optimist or a pessimistic idealist? What secret did he hide and reveal behind those shadowy glasses and those half-finished arabesques he drew in the air? Andrzej Wajda had deepened the mystery in the semi-biographical film *Everything for Sale* (1968) which was inspired by Cybulski's death, and in which complicated personal conflicts were hinted at involving Cybulski, Wajda himself, and his wife. His death, accidental or suicidal, was true to the death of the romantic rebel.

5. THE BOY NEXT DOOR & THE KING

Buddy Holly and Elvis Presley, two of the greatest stars of rock and roll to come out of the fifties, both died young, yet neither died quite at the best moment of his career as far as his posthumous legend was concerned. Buddy Holly, who died in a plane crash in 1959 at twenty-two, was still too young for the good of his

myth, while Elvis Presley, who died of a heart attack in 1977, aged forty-two, was already too old. Buddy died before his personal image had made its full impact on the world, while Elvis lived long enough to give the lie to his original image of untamed youth. It is some measure of both singers' talent and originality that, despite the handicap of dying either too soon or too late, both the Holly and Presley cults are thriving.

It is not always enough to be a youth hero and to die relatively young; one also has to die at the right moment which means that, like many of the cult figures discussed in this book, one must die at the very zenith of one's career. Jimi Hendrix and Janis Joplin, for example, would still have been fine people and great performers at thirty-five, but would they have maintained their hold on their youthful fans? Unless they had been able to develop fantastically in new directions (and why should they be expected to?) would not their style have started to seem a bit stale, already *passé* after several more years? Their very originality as performers would have told against them in the long run, their acts would have seemed like a pastiche of their early selves, a form of self-parody, an accusation which has often been levelled at the later Jagger and Presley performances. Janis Joplin at twenty-seven already found her singing manner restricting just because it was so special. Hendrix chafed at the Hendrix-stereotype he could not break out of; he would yell at his audiences: 'I'm not a jukebox, you know!' when they demanded his earliest hits and wanted them performed in exactly the way that had originally rocketed him to fame. Five or ten years later, these two stars would have found it even more deadening to keep true to their early style, yet if they had altered it they would have risked losing their popularity. Film and pop music fans are unfair; they expect an entertainer to remain true to the image they have of him, yet are quick to scoff at him for 'never doing anything different'. Alternatively fans outgrow their stars by growing up themselves and are quickly replaced by a new generation of younger fans which wants new heroes. Even a superstar who dies relatively young may live well beyond the peak of his career, so that his death will not trigger off the lamentation that helps to transform his memory into a myth.

HOLLY

Ironically, youth heroes can also die *too* young for the good of their myth. Buddy Holly is one who did. He built up a reputation and success during his extremely brief career; many of the records he made have become classics, sounding as fresh today as when they were first issued. Not only that, but Holly's actual influence on subsequent rock and roll musicians was tremendous; many of the later 'greats' of rock owed his style something and the greatest of greats – singers like Bob Dylan, the Beatles, the Rolling Stones, and John Denver – have willingly acknowledged that debt. Much has been written about Holly's musical originality and the innovations which were widely imitated: he experimented with double-tracking; he featured the then unusual lead/rhythm/bass/drums line-up, without keyboards or brass; he was one of the first to use almost entirely his own material, and to move away from the conventional twelve-bar and sixteen-bar forms. All this has ensured that his music is still popular twenty years after his death, and Holly has a well-deserved reputation as a cult figure, but the personality of Buddy himself remains nebulous; there is too little in it of the stuff that myths are made of, and part of the reason is simply that he died too young, before a clearly-defined image of him as an individual could become well-established.

PEGGY SUE

Words & Music by JERRY ALLISON & NORMAN PETTY

2/-

Recorded by
BUDDY HOLLY
on
VOGUE-CORAL Q 72293

Although Buddy Holly's plain college-boy face with its dark-rimmed glasses is very well-known, there is something oddly static about all the photographs of him which does not feed the curiosity we ought to feel about him as a person. What gives a depth to our awareness of the personality of stars like Hendrix, Joplin or James Dean is the extraordinary mobility of their expression. Their familiar features remain the same, but each expression captured by the still camera seems to reveal a new facet of their complex natures, helping us to build up an overall impression of them which is full of variety and nuances. Buddy Holly's face is sweet and bland; it reflects the eager innocence of his singing style, the almost childish playfulness of his songs, their adolescent earnestness. In photographs, whether he wears a sweatshirt or a conventional suit, whether his dark hair is tousled or slicked back, he always makes the same rather neutral impression: that of a proper, clean-cut boy of the fifties. If Buddy had lived into the sixties, he might well have grown his hair longer and joined the counter-culture. But even if he had not, his maturer personality would almost surely have been projected in a more striking fashion.

The bare facts of Buddy's life do not make very exciting reading. He was born in 1936 as Charles Hardin Holley and grew up in Lubbock, Texas, at the centre of a cotton-growing area. In his studious way, he was almost as far removed from the stereotype of the brash, rangy typical Texan as was Janis Joplin, who also came from the Lone Star state. His family were fundamentalist Baptists, and Buddy was quite religious, 'coming to know the Lord' and being baptized at the age of fourteen. Buddy was the youngest of four children and was apparently rather spoilt as a child. He led the conventional existence of a small-town boy, but didn't show a great interest in music until he started playing the

guitar in 1948. At high school, he teamed up with a friend, Bob Montgomery, who wrote most of the songs they played together. Their main influence at the time was the County and Western music they picked up from radio stations in Nashville, Shreveport and Dallas and from various locations in Louisiana. One of their earliest heroes was Hank Williams, whose music was intensely personal. (Ironically, Williams' hard life, which lent a romantic tinge to his music, also led inevitably to his early death in 1953, at thirty.) The boys also listened to black rhythm and blues from another Shreveport station. (Segregation was pretty complete in Lubbock so the boys never heard it locally.) They were so successful when they performed at high school dances and at various functions that they were given a regular 'Buddy and Bob' programme on a Lubbock radio station. During this period, they made a group of recordings, all plaintive, country music with a dash of Mexican and Hawaiian influence in the guitar style. In 1956, Buddy got a recording contract with Decca and cut sixteen tracks of Presley-type rock and roll music. Though Buddy imitated the wildly popular Elvis, his manner was very different from the King's. It has been described as 'playful rather than sensual; it is a wink not a snarl'.

By 1957, he was being managed by a musician-turned-producer named Norman Petty and had assembled a band named the Crickets. In the autumn of 1957, they scored the first big hit with *That'll Be The Day*. They had other successes that year, including *Peggy Sue* (named after drummer Jerry Allison's girl-friend) and *Rave On*, and by the time they went on a tour of Britain their music was already well known. However, it was not always welcomed by the English critics even if the fans were delirious. The Bradford *Telegraph and Argus* wailed, 'Where on earth is show business heading?' But he had to acknowledge their expertise grudgingly: 'The tragedy often is that many of the performers, like the trio last night, have a basic talent which they distort in order to win an audience's

favour.' But Keith Goodwin's review in the *New Musical Express* hints at the flavour of the Crickets' live performance – and gives the lie to Buddy's general clean-cut image: 'If enthusiasm, drive, and down-to-earth abandon are the ingredients necessary for success in the rock'n'roll field, then Buddy Holly and the Crickets are all set for a long and eventful run of popularity! They rocked their way through a tremendous, belting twenty-five minute act without letting up for one moment. . . . How these boys manage to make such a big sound with their limited instrumentation baffles me!'

In 1958, there were many more hits: *Early In The Morning* and *It's So Easy* among them. But as always in the music business things were not running as smoothly as they appeared on the surface. Buddy Holly, though barely turned twenty, was obviously mature beyond his years and took a keen interest in the business side. He was also very conscious of his image. But he and the Crickets were inexperienced, and there were

famous Alan Freed Holiday of Stars Show. Right:
Buddy and Maria-Elena at their wedding on 15th
August, 1958.

frictions between them and their manager Norman
Petty, and even on occasion among themselves. (Holly
didn't like the boys to drink or smoke, at least to excess,
and wasn't afraid to say so.) Norman Petty was tight
with money, and also claimed authorship of many of the
songs – for instance, *Peggy Sue* was attributed to Jerry
Allison and Norman Petty, and it was only after Holly's
death that Allison, stricken with remorse, acknowledged Holly's hand in the writing and assigned most of
his royalties to the Holly estate.

Things were exacerbated when Buddy got married
in 1958. His wife, Maria Elena Santiago, was born in
Puerto Rico, but lived in New York, and there was
something of the magic of *West Side Story* in their 'love
at first sight' romance. Unlike the Maria of *West Side
Story*, however, Buddy's Maria was not poor; her aunt
was head of Southern Music's Latin American division
and it was while Maria was working as receptionist for
Southern Music that she met Buddy. The Crickets

arranged for her to come out to lunch with them and
during the meal, Buddy monopolised her. 'You see this
girl,' he told his friends, 'I'm going to marry her. And
I'm going to get her to agree in the next two days,
before we leave New York.' He was right. But there was
tension in both families. Maria's aunt had to be persuaded that Buddy was not just another dissolute entertainer; while in Lubbock, the Holley family would have
to contend with the possibility of hostility on two
counts. As John Goldrosen wrote in his biography *Buddy
Holly*, 'racial and (especially) religious inter-marriage
was opposed by many of the Holleys' fundamentalist
Baptist brethren for reasons that mixed prejudice and
principle', and it meant that the couple could not set up
house in Lubbock – as a New Yorker Maria could not
stomach the discrimination of the South.

Buddy's father ended up approving the marriage,
but Mrs Holley was less sure. Buddy as youngest had
always been her favourite. According to Goldrosen Mr
Holley told Maria: 'You're the best thing that's ever
happened to Buddy. You've cut his umbilical cords.
When he was younger, he was tied to his mother; then
he was tied to Norman Petty; but now he's come into
his own – he's finally a *man*.' Buddy was twenty-one,
Maria a couple of years older. She apparently gave
Buddy the self-confidence he had lacked previously, an
insecurity so often reflected in his song lyrics, and she
was obviously an important influence on the development of his career, with her inside knowledge of the
music business and her New York independence. She
even persuaded Buddy to take acting lessons at the Lee
Strasberg Actors' Studio with a view to breaking into
the movies. Norman Petty recognized her as a threat
to his management.

Like most show business managers, Norman Petty

the Crickets. Petty believed Holly's success as a rock'n'roller would be short-lived – two years at the most. In one, tragic, way he was right, but in another he was completely wrong, for Holly's reputation and prestige have never ceased to grow.

Buddy and the Crickets drifted apart when Buddy finally broke with Petty, for the latter persuaded the Crickets to stay with him. In early 1959, Buddy joined a package show on tour called 'The Winter Dance Party'. Its cast included the Platters, an ex-disc jockey turned singer known as the Big Bopper, and Ritchie Valens who had already quite a name in the world of rock though he was only seventeen. The show played in Iowa on 2nd February; Holly chartered a four-seater plane to take him to the show's next date in North Dakota and the spare seats were taken by Valens and the Big Bopper. Buddy was tired from touring – he already had a stomach ulcer – and his insistence on putting across a professional image made him anxious to get to Moorhead, Minnesota, in time to spruce up their crumpled clothing. The plane crashed minutes after take-off, killing everyone on board. It seems that the young pilot, though qualified, may not have been familiar with this particular plane's controls system, and the weather conditions were very bad at the time.

Buddy Holly was buried in his home town of Lubbock on 7th February 1959. A thousand people attended the funeral at the Tabernacle Baptist Church, and tributes poured in from all over the world, including a telegram from Elvis Presley who was then in Germany serving his time as a G.I. Pallbearers included some of Buddy's oldest friends and musical companions, among them Bob Montgomery, Jerry Allison and Phil Everly. The burial place with its flat headstone carved with a representation of Buddy's electric guitar has been a place of pilgrimage for thousands of fans from all over the world since that time.

has had a bad press, and it is sometimes difficult to disentangle the conflicting stories when so many different interests are at stake. But it is undoubtedly true that Petty was instrumental in getting Holly and the Crickets national and international recognition. It was he also who suggested that Buddy should record ballads with string backing in his own name, hoping to build up the singer's individual reputation as well as with

New York Paramount in September, 1957. Right:
Buddy Holly rehearsing with Jerry Lee Lewis on
their successful Australian tour in 1958.

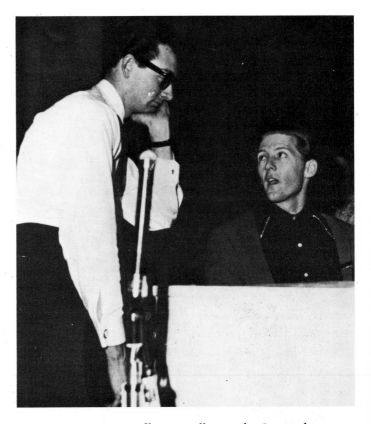

Unlike almost every other rock and roll star of the fifties and sixties, Buddy Holly never appeared in films, although he had plans to. This fact alone is enough to prevent present-day fans from forming a vivid picture of him as a person although now a fictionalized movie of his life has attempted to do just that. The little mannerisms of a performer, the way he nervously touches his lips or cocks his head to one side as he answers an interviewer's question often do more to convey a sense of his unique personality than even seeing him live on stage. The combination of filmed performance and private glimpses produces a coherent, well-rounded picture. Today, a well-known singer is invariably also something of a film or television personality; his legend is propagated by these media almost as much as by his recordings. It was not until Elvis Presley and the Beatles started appearing in films that people really got to know them as charismatic individuals outside their music. Full-length documentaries about Bob Dylan, the Rolling Stones, Janis Joplin and Jimi Hendrix have spread their legend wider and made it sink far deeper into the popular consciousness than records and photographs alone could ever have done. If there were enough footage on Buddy to make a feature documentary about him, the real Holly 'myth' would undoubtedly have far more substance. The contrast between his off-stage personality, sweet and retiring, and his on-stage performances in which he came across as self-assured and something of a 'frenetic raver', as he has been described, would give dimensions of complexity and depth to his image that are impossible to sense with only stills and descriptions to go by. As one of his high school teachers later admitted, 'to be honest, it was only after the news was in the papers about his death that I remembered he had been in my class. He was a quiet kid – wasn't any great student, but didn't cause any trouble either, you understand. So I really don't remember anything about him'. Apparently Buddy did not think of himself as a particularly fascinating person either, let alone a romantic misfit. He wrote the following about himself in a school essay: 'My life has been what you might call an uneventful one, and it seems there is not much of interest to tell.' He listed his hobbies as hunting, fishing, leatherwork, reading, painting, and, only last, playing western music. He did add that he was thinking of making a career out of western music, but cautiously qualified this ambition with the words: 'If I am good enough, but I will just have to wait to see how that turns out.'

That very quality was probably his hidden asset, the key to his instantaneous success when, still at high school, he began playing professionally. For, as has been said of Buddy, 'he looked like the boy next door and his songs were what the boy next door would have chosen to write and sing if he only had the talent'. There were millions of boys-next-door just like Buddy (even his name has the right boy-next-door sound), growing up in conservative small towns all over the States that were identical to Lubbock. And there were also millions of girls-next-door ready to buy Holly's records when he started cutting them. Those girls were looking for a boyfriend who would sing and court them with words like the ones in Buddy's songs and in that tone of voice: tender, unthreatening, sincere and cheerful. Songs like *I Wanna Play House With You, Take Your Time* ('and take mine too/I can't wait'), *Think It Over* and *I'm Looking For Someone to Love*, all contained the reassuring message of 'true-romance-love is for keeps' and 'I won't-rush-or-rape-you' which very young girls wanted to hear. When he was eighteen, Buddy had seven of the Top Forty hits in the United States. The fact that his records are still so popular in the blasé seventies is partly due to the musical and vocal originality which has kept Holly's songs from sounding stale or dated, but also to the fact that people continue to relate to the idea of a simple, uncomplicated love which would be 'so rare and so true', of finding a partner who would be ready to 'Go with me through/Times till all times end'. The cynical one-night-stand approach to sex of many later rock songs has never completely replaced the gentle, courteous hesitant appeal of a Holly song. It has guaranteed him a posterity which does indeed give him legendary status. Buddy's is the myth of the average teenager who happened to have a sort of genius for conveying the sincerity and idealism as well as the insecurity and naivety of teenage love. He was not a complex person or an 'oddball', yet his music, his dark-rimmed glasses, his strange little hiccup, his vocal glides from bass to falsetto and back again, have left their distinctive mark on popular culture.

If Buddy Holly was nipped in the bud, Elvis Presley was something of an overblown rose by the time he died in August, 1977. He was only forty-two, quite a young man

PRESLEY

really, but many claimed that Elvis had gone to seed during his last years. Was he 'just a forty-two-year-old crooner, shuffling off in a haze of pills, powder and half-remembered glories'? Was he truly 'a sick, obese, tortured hulk, dying lonely, miserable, dope-raddled'? Was his ex-wife, Priscilla Beaulieu, right in saying after his death: 'It's sad, but perhaps it's better that it ended now. If he had gone on much longer, he'd have ended up as a vegetable'? Had he really 'napalmed his brain with smack and cocaine' during his last years? The very people who had most fervently idolized the young Elvis often turned out to be the most severe in their descriptions of the older Elvis and the life he led. One early Presley worshipper, Charles Murray, wrote in *New Musical Express* after the singer's death, 'he became a monster: first a young, beautiful and awesome monster, then a bland, castrated monster and finally a hideous, pitiful monster who inspired a mixture of pity and derision and, maybe, a shudder of mortality, a frisson of decay – Dorian Gray for Our Generation'.

The key to this severe attitude towards the last years of the King of Rock and Roll obviously lies in the notion of Elvis serving as Dorian Gray for his generation. The disappointment he caused his most fanatical fans when he started changing and, yes, decaying as the years

passed was some measure of their earlier expectations: they had wanted Elvis to remain the symbol of their flaming fifties youth. They had wanted him never to age physically or morally, as they would have to, to always remain the sexy, wild young greaser he had been and which they felt they had been too. They had wanted him to go on shocking the older generation forever, to defy the establishment long after he (and they) had become a part of the older generation and the establishment. In short, they wanted the middle-aged multi-millionaire who had enjoyed every goody money and fame could buy for over two decades to go on looking and acting exactly like the nineteen-year-old truck driver, the 'have-not' Southern white who had been born and brought up in the poorest area of America during the worst economic depression of its history.

Elvis had a tantalizing way of turning the clock back to his best days. It all depended, quite literally, on the shape he was in. In the late sixties and early seventies, you would occasionally catch a photograph of him looking bloated, listless and middle-aged, and you would think that this time he was through. Or you would hear a song on the radio so tame and conventional that you would do a double-take when the disc jockey announced whose latest it was 'What? Is that Elvis? He's really through!' Then, the next thing you would know, Elvis would make a comeback. There he would be on television, slim, leather-jacketed, dynamic and looking about nineteen. He would give the old snarl and growl: 'If you're looking for trouble, you've come to the right place!' Then he'd launch into one of his fabled numbers with unchanged fury and gusto. As someone put it, Elvis was 'preserved like the great woolly mammoth in a block of ice' at such moments, so much did the singer seem like a symbol from another era. So what if, by then, his dazzling white teeth were capped and his jet-black hair was dyed? The illusion was intact and that was what counted. So what if some sneered about self-parody and pastiche? How else can you go on being your teen-

His performances may have seemed a declaration of war on the older generation, but to the young they were more like a declaration of independence. Elvis was their leader in the guerilla war against their colonialist elders. Marlon Brando in *The Wild One* and James Dean in *Rebel Without a Cause* had been the two John the Baptists of the cause, but they could never have outraged the senior members of society like this new messiah of teenage revolt. For Elvis expressed revolt more stridently than Brando and Dean had done. Gone were the rebel heroes without a cause. Elvis did not care about trying to understand whatever values he was rejecting. His was a purely intuitive rebellion – unsubtle, unselfconscious and unabashed. He did not have to study method acting to convey the revolt of youth against its elders; something about his manner made him a natural vehicle for expressing the message of youth rebellion. As Richard Williams puts it: 'He represented not sophisticated or even specific emotions, but a simple projection of adolescence – arriving at that point not by design and skill, as had James Dean, but through some chance genetic factor.' Someone else compared his 'twitchy juvenility' in the first film he made, *Love Me Tender* (1956) to that of 'some wired-up, untutored James Dean'.

Elvis was untutored; like his music, he was rough and raw and that was why he seemed so authentic and sexy. Presley's earthy sexuality could not be swept under the carpet: 'Elvis had animal magnetism. He was even sexy to guys. I can't imagine what the chicks used to think.' Indeed, long before he hit the big time, Elvis's performances at local shows had driven prim little teenagers into orgasmic bouts of screaming and shaking. Not that his songs were obscene; their imagery of poor butterflies and invocations to be his teddy-bear (' 'cos tigers are too rough') were a long way from the 'Cocksucker Blues' of the later Rolling Stones or the earlier explicitness of some black songs ('I'm going to squeeze your lemon till the juice runs down your leg'). It was just the way that Elvis sang. As Mae West, another expert at raunchy innuendo had once declared, 'It's not what I sing, it's the way that Ah sing it.' It was also the way Elvis looked and behaved on stage. Tony Palmer has described the young Elvis's impact in the following terms: 'He came on leering and twitching, his hair all down his eyes, his grin lopsided. The moment the music started, he went berserk. Spasms rocked his body as if it had been plugged into the same electrical source as his guitar. His hips began to grind, his legs vibrated like power drills. He pouted and humped and walked as if he were sneering with his legs.' It is one of life's more charming ironies that the very gyrations which so outraged the more puritanical elements of American society when they first became acquainted with 'Elvis the Pelvis' should have been copied from the twitches of the evangelist preachers Elvis had seen as a child when they

age self for twenty-five years? In one 1968 TV special in particular, Elvis proved that he could still be what his generation wanted him to be. He also showed the younger generation what all the fuss had been about, though the teenagers of the late sixties would never quite be able to grasp his shock value when he had first hit the scene nearly fifteen years earlier.

For if Buddy Holly had seemed like the boy next door in those days, Elvis had seemed to come from the dark side of the moon. He was the one parents did not want their teenage daughters to date, the one whose musky voice and curled-back lip snarled threats of rape in the back seat, the one whose mocking leer warned that he would plough the old jalopy into a brick wall on the way back from the school prom, where he would have been taking illicit swigs of whisky from a hip flask all evening. In his prime, Elvis was declared 'morally insane' by a Baptist pastor in Des Moines. He was charged with obscenity in Miami (the start of a bizarre tradition in the State of Florida). What he did with his hips and pelvis while he sang was considered so lewd that some TV sponsors refused to allow him to appear on television except from the waist up. A Communist paper in East Germany declared that he was 'a weapon of the American psychological war aimed at infecting a part of the population with a new philosophical outlook of inhumanity'. When he first appeared on the fifties scene, Elvis seemed like the ultimate subversive. He blew the lid sky-high off the kettle of complacency. He let every cat out of the bag of convention: sex, rage and defiance.

exhorted their congregations at sermons and revival meetings in the deep South. Elvis described the impression they had made on him in his usual laconic way, but perhaps also with tongue in cheek: 'Then there was the preachers and they cut up all over the place, jumpin' on the piano, movin' ever' which way. The audience liked 'em. I guess I learned from them.'

Elvis was indeed the anti-Holly of the mid-fifties. Even though Buddy Holly imitated a few of the Presley gyrations on stage (and who did not?), his could never have matched the crude suggestiveness of Presley's. Buddy actually admired Elvis, and considered him a great star a year before he had been recognized nationally in the United States. In fact, when Elvis played at Lubbock's Cotton Club in 1955 for the princely sum of thirty-five dollars, Buddy Holly and Bob Montgomery went there to see him. And there really was not much difference between the boys then – Elvis was seen as a Country singer, not a rock'n'roller – and the manager of the Club recalled that 'Elvis didn't

even smoke or drink when I knew him then. Between sets that night he just sat in a corner, drinking a Coke . . . Later Buddy said to me, "You know, he's a real nice, friendly fellow".' But once Elvis had achieved national notoriety, teenagers were faced with the choice: in the light of parental disapproval, it was either conform or rebel.

The problem was not new; adolescents always have been and always will be of two minds over the issue. Only a few will opt for open rebellion or for total conformity. Most will do a little of one and a bit of the other until the pressures of life and adult responsibility take over and they become the older generation. The impulse to break out of conventional mores was, if anything, even stronger in the fifties, than in subsequent decades, for restrictions on teenage freedom were far more stringent than they are today. For example, it was out of the question for nice girls and boys to experiment with sex beyond a bit of necking. It was lethal to dress extravagantly at school or at home. It was an absolute scandal to smoke pot, and even cigarette-smoking and drinking were very strictly limited. Parents had far more of a say in their kids' affairs than they do now. Childhood conditioning goes deep and social pressure is effective; most fifties teenagers conformed to the behaviour expected of them. They did not question the fundamental validity of rules and precepts about premarital chastity, tasteful clothing and proper behaviour. Sometimes they chafed at restrictions, but it was *their* morality too and this was why they could also relate to the nice-boy ethics of someone like Buddy Holly.

But Elvis stood for what parents abhorred and that, too, was a reason for kids to love him. The Rolling Stones later and the Punk rockers now were to owe much of their success to the same principle: if so many adults find them revolting, they can't be *all* bad. To love Elvis, to play his records full-blast for hours on end, to imitate his manner of dressing were effective ways of expressing resentment against adults in control without taking the risks of open rebellion. Elvis was a fifties' teenager too, so he knew how it felt and how to express the sense of discontent the young felt at the time. Like them, he was 'of a generation that had not participated in the war, had not experienced the triumphant idealism of bringing peace on earth. The atmosphere in the mid-fifties smacked of disillusion. Youth went sour on everything associated with the past'. Elvis worshipped James Dean; he had seen *Rebel Without a Cause* at least a dozen times and knew every one of Dean's lines in the film by heart. The way Elvis sang, each of his gestures and his facial contortions expressed the same defiance and scornful pity of the world as he had found it, the determination to break out of the smug, stultifying atmosphere which prevailed. Like all the later rock stars, it was the way he looked and what he stood for as much as his singing which made his fans adore him. His energy was incredible, and it promised liberation. He was so raw and dynamic that no prison of gentility could hold him. He had once been a truck driver and he brought the tough, cheeky arrogance of the truck driver into his act: 'On stage he bounced like a jeep driver crossing a ploughed field.' Sure he was vulgar, but you do not expect a hurricane to be decorous.

Elvis was born on 8th January, 1935, in Tupelo, Mississippi, son of Vernon and Gladys Presley. He was an adored only child who was cherished doubly by his parents because an identical twin brother had died at birth. The house where Elvis was born and spent his childhood could have comfortably fitted into the living room of the mansion he acquired in Memphis, Tennessee, when he became a superstar. The Presley family was extremely poor and Elvis was a child of the Great Depression. As a friend and neighbour recalls of their lives at this period: 'We never went real hungry, but we worked at it sometimes.' Like so many Southerners,

Elvis' parents were deeply religious. They would take their little boy to church services, camp meetings and revivals so that from the age of two he was steeped in the gospel music and the hymns the Southern whites had borrowed from the blacks. One of his grade school teachers remembers Elvis as no more than 'sweet and average', but even then he loved to sing. He won a singing prize when he was ten and got his first guitar at eleven because his parents could not afford to buy him the bicycle he really wanted.

The family moved to Memphis when Elvis was thirteen; they lived in grim slum conditions, but at least Memphis was a centre for country music and it was there that young Presley really got acquainted with the hillbilly style and the Blues. Thus gospel and hymns, both black and white, country music, which was predominantly white, and the Blues which was black music, all influenced Elvis and were later present in his musical style. The combination of these different strains was a very important element in his eventual success as a singer. As Jay Cocks put it, 'Presley gave rock and blues a gloss of country-and-western and a rockabilly beat, but he preserved the undertones of insinuating sexuality, accentuated rock's and blues' rough edges of danger from the sharp beat to streetwise lyrics.'

It was truly symbolic that the first record Elvis cut professionally in 1954 should have had, on one side, the white country-style ballad *Blue Moon of Kentucky* and on the other side a black blues song called *That's All Right, Mama*. What made it even more symbolic was that Elvis' version of the country song had a definite blues sound whereas the instrumentalization of the blues number had a distinct country twang. As one of his biographers pointed out, Elvis' voice was integrated before the US Supreme Court banned racial segregation. Sam Phillips, the first person to get Elvis under contract for his company, Sun Records, had always said, 'If I could find a white man who had the Negro sound and the Negro feel, I could make a billion dollars'. Phillips found Elvis, but was to 'sell' him again, to RCA in 1956, so that he only made $35,000 out of his discovery; Elvis would indeed go on to make nearly a billion, but for other people.

What was the young Elvis really like before fame crystallized his image as one of toughness, perfect self-confidence and defiance? By all accounts, he was a shy, obedient, polite and quiet-spoken boy. His paralyzing shyness was quite a handicap when he tried to get his singing career started. He could hardly bring himself to stand on a stage; perhaps some of the wildness he later displayed in his performances was an attempt to overcome the inhibitions of stage-fright. Whatever his private fantasies of rebellion, Elvis neither acted nor looked the part of a rebel during his high school years. 'Nobody knew I sang, I wasn't popular at school, I wasn't dating anybody,' he freely admitted. He grew

the sideburns which were to become so famous because he wanted to look like a truck driver, an understandable ideal of virility and success for a poor boy whose father was first a farm labourer, then a worker in a canning factory. After Elvis left school, there were a few years of ambition, often frustrated, playing on local radio stations, at bars and country fairs. He cut some songs for Sun Records during this period, but they were only moderately successful. He was no more than a local success until he was snapped up by RCA which was signing on a lot of rock singers after the phenomenal hit made by Bill Haley's *Rock Around the Clock*. Elvis cut his first record for RCA in January 1956; it was called *Heartbreak Hotel*, and from that moment he never looked back.

He went from hit to hit, sold millions of records (well over 500 million so far) and grossed a hundred million dollars within the first two years. He was soon being paid $25,000 a night for personal appearances which was twice the previous record. His name was soon used to sell everything: teenagers all over the world were making him rich by wearing Elvis Presley T-shirts, bobbysocks and bermuda shorts. They brushed their hair with Elvis Presley brushes and their teeth with Elvis Presley toothbrushes. They wrote with Elvis Presley ballpoint pens in Elvis Presley diaries. They chewed Elvis Presley bubblegum while they cuddled Elvis Presley plush hound-dogs. Elvis did not have to worry about pleasing parents or making concessions to the music critics who usually loathed him. The kids would always be on his side and the more adults attacked him, the better for his reputation and his wallet. Inevitably in 1956, Elvis the new superstar went to Hollywood and made a film, *Love Me Tender*. It was the first of the thirty-three films he would star in over the next eighteen years and which became an industry in themselves. Once Elvis' manager, Colonel Tom

Parker, had established the undeniable fact that there was no easier or quicker way for 'his' boy to make money, the obedient singer retired from the less well-paid and more exacting world of live performances or television shows to become a money-spinner who made everyone connected with his movies rich and who got paid a cool million each time for his pains (not counting the fat royalties he received on the albums made from the soundtrack of each film). Elvis has been adored by many and crucified by quite a few others for his film performances; some were dreadful, but not all. Some of the first, like *Love Me Tender, Jailhouse Rock* (1957) and *Loving You* (1957) were a lot better than most of what came later. By the sixties, with films like *Blue Hawaii* (1961), *Love in Las Vegas* (*Viva Las Vegas* in the U.S., 1964) and *Paradise Hawaiian Style* (1966), it was obvious that Elvis was fast becoming that 'bland, castrated monster' Charles Murray spoke of with a shudder. How had it happened?

All teenagers finally grow up, and not even Elvis could escape the process. Yesterday's symbol of youthful have-not rebellion turns into today's fat cat. It's hard to sound convincingly defiant when you're very rich. Elvis has often been called 'the father of rock and roll' which is meant as a great compliment; yet a father is a father and his descendants, blood or spiritual, must ultimately rebel against him. What had begun as pure anti-Establishment became, with time and success, an integral part of the Establishment. When religious leader Billy Graham had said back in 1957 that he would not want his daughter to meet Elvis, most American fathers would have agreed with him. But when the American president, Jimmy Carter, declared after Elvis had died that he had been an outstanding example to the

nation's youth, no-one raised an eyebrow. The idea of a president extolling the virtues of someone like Elvis would have seemed preposterous twenty years earlier. Was it a long climb up or a long way down from the singer's original image?

The change in Elvis had set in early in his career. By the sixties, Elvis no longer seemed what he had been to his original fans. A lot of the blame for the change was laid on the doorstep of 'the poor ol' Colonel', who was usually regarded as the singer's *eminence grise,* if anything can be considered grey about this colourful character. Parker had started off in the carnival world; show biz was in his blood and he remained a huckster all his life. He had graduated from the world of circus performer to that of manager for circus acts and had eventually drifted into the management of musicians, which is how he came into Elvis's life when the youngster was not yet a superstar.

As a kid, Parker had worked in an act called the Great Parker Pony Circus. When he became Elvis's manager in 1956, Elvis became his greatest Parker Pony and the whole world a circus in which to exhibit his latest prodigy. His influence on the malleable young singer must have been considerable for Parker was not only a manager but a Svengali and a Frankenstein at heart. As someone once said of Parker: 'When Tom's your manager, he's all you. He lives and breathes his

artist.' Undeniably, it was his influence which set Elvis on the rails of respectability, turning the young hellcat into a tame pussy. Parker had once caught some sparrows, painted them yellow and sold them as canaries. Elvis's fans were soon grumbling that the Colonel was doing the reverse to their idol: he was

turning the image of their gaudy, exotic singing-bird into that of a drab nice-guy. But it was not only Parker who accomplished the transformation of Elvis from a bad example to the nation's youth into a good one. Actually, the seeds of respectability had been sown long before. Under the hair grease and the rhinestone-spangled jackets, the good example had been there all along. Elvis had always been a nice, law-abiding, god-fearing American boy. The pro-Elvis faction preferred to overlook that side of him, just as the anti-Elvis faction would have refused to acknowledge it.

To begin with, Elvis was, and always had been, religious. 'God gave me a voice. If I turned against God, I'd be finished,' he had piously declared way back. A 1956 photograph of Elvis and his parents singing a hymn with unfeigned fervour so shocked some of his fans that they decided it was only a joke and that their rebel hero was putting them on. Later on, Elvis gambled, slept with girls, lived fast, drank and got divorced, but he never turned against God. During his career he often sang carols at Christmas pageants or introduced gospel groups at shows. 'I don't sing in this. Just listen to them . . . It's a beautiful song,' he would plead with the audience. Elvis was also modest, a virtue people enjoy in a celebrity. 'I don't aim to let this fame business get me,' he insisted, and it never completely did. He would attribute his success to just plain luck and his appealing common-sense approach to the whole madness of stardom was sincere. He had been ambitious and he loved success, but he always kept it in its true proportions. 'When I was a boy,' he once said, 'I was the hero in comic books and movies. I grew up believing in that dream. Now I've lived it out. That's all a man can ask for.' He saw what had happened to him as a comic-book fantasy come true: Elvis the Superman of Rock,

the Batman of the Blues. He was ready to settle for that.

Under the teenage rebel image, Elvis was also a devoted son. He adored his mother while she was alive and venerated her memory after she died in 1958. Long after her death, he said of her: 'If I never do anything really wrong, it's all because of her. She wouldn't let me do anything wrong.' He was also patriotic. When he was drafted into the Army, he cheerfully shaved off his sideburns and served a tour of duty in Germany. Elvis in uniform, Elvis not trying to get off the hook, refusing privilege and insisting on being treated like any recruit did more to inspire feelings of duty to their country in American youths than any sermons or lectures by the Draft Board. In his movies, Elvis was reluctant to play negative characters. He showed a bit of his original defiance when he played a sympathetic convict in *Jailhouse Rock* (1957) but soon he was the straight hero all the way, the great guy who helps to get others out of trouble and makes everyone happy with his music.

Pious, modest, mother-loving, patriotic – no wonder

Elvis was held up as a good rather than a bad example to the nation's youth by the time he died. Besides, Elvis' story could serve as an example in another and very real sense: twenty years on, his career had become the great American success story of the dirt poor boy who had climbed his way to fame and millions. The boy whose parents could not afford to buy him a bicycle now had a fleet of Cadillacs. He could acquire not just any old luxury yacht but the *Potomac,* no less, which was the presidential yacht on which Churchill and Roosevelt had drawn up the Atlantic Charter. The boy who had lived in a slum now lived in a colonial mansion. Streets were named after the kid who had once been a guitar-strumming truck driver with greased-back hair. A rags to riches story is always inspiring in a capitalist nation, and Elvis' career is probably the biggest and the quickest rags to riches saga in history.

But as everyone knows, celebrity is hard to live with. It takes a heavy toll on the psyche of even the most well-balanced star. Elvis did better than most; he survived superstardom for over twenty years, but in the end he was no exception to the maxim that 'Success Kills'. At nineteen, he had been unknown. He could prowl the streets, eat a hotdog in a snack-bar, go to a movie, chat up a girl, just like any other nineteen-year-old American male. By the time he was twenty-one, he could go nowhere and do nothing without attracting a crowd. He had to live surrounded by bodyguards, his house walled in by high fences to keep out hysterical fans. In fact, whenever a teenage girl was reported missing from her home, anywhere in America, one of the first places that the police would look for the runaway was outside the gates of Elvis' mansion. If he wanted to go to an amusement park or a bowling alley, he had to rent the place after closing-hours. For security reasons, he had to rent the entire floor of any hotel he stayed at. The guerrilla leader in the war of the generations had to live by night, guerrilla fashion, to plan his every move, to hide, to run away from his own troops of teenage admirers. A growing sense of isolation and alienation was inevitable. It was made worse by the fact that wealth and fame in such proportions could only act as a magnet for sycophants and spies. Elvis was a king, but as has been pointed out: 'In the court of the King, who can be trusted? Who is truly a friend and who a fawning opportunist? Who acts from love and who from hidden greed and hate?' Elvis was not the first king to become paranoid and distrustful after seeing many a courtier turn into a traitor.

Elvis was the prisoner of his fame and wealth, and there was no turning back. This was difficult enough but what was even more destructive was being the prisoner of his own image. If you have been a symbol and a god to millions, you have to live up to the model

towards him for what he had once represented. Like Dorian Gray stabbing the portrait of himself which had grown old in his place, so Elvis' fans stabbed at the ageing portrait of their youth which the singer had become. But in doing so, they were killing their own youth, and just like Dorian Gray's portrait the image of Elvis was miraculously restored by death to the pristine ideal it had once been. As soon as he died (of a heart-attack and, some rumoured, of an abuse of drugs), everyone was ready to forgive him for having lived so long, to see in him only that which he had represented. In obituaries of Elvis all over the world, people lamented their own vanished youth with his passing. Descriptions of Elvis' later decadence were washed away by nostalgia-drenched accounts of how he had been in his heyday, just as recent photographs of him were dwarfed by huge shots of him at twenty.

The news of Presley's death made headlines all over the world for a week. Even the stolid London *Times* gave him the longest obituary ever accorded to a popular singer. His records were selling out everywhere within hours of his death and his old films were hastily released. As for his lying-in and funeral, there had been nothing like it since the death of Valentino. 80,000 mourners surrounded his house, swooning by the dozen from heat and grief. The 30,000 who got into the house for a glimpse of the body behaved with predictable hysteria: they sobbed and screamed a final farewell to their idol. Two people were killed when a drunken driver ploughed into the crowd. The cortege of white Cadillacs led a procession down the Elvis Presley Boulevard to the cemetery which was piled high with floral tributes in the shape of guitars and hound dogs.

you have created, or else watch out. What could Elvis do when the mirror told him that he no longer looked like the lad who had once been an idol? No wonder he spent his fortieth birthday in bed because he felt too depressed to get up, that he would have violent temper tantrums whenever his weight shot up. Elvis was the chief victim of his youthful image. As one of his fans sadly said after Elvis died, 'It was all we could give him: an adulation and idolatry that dehumanized him, left him as flat and two dimensional as the Elvis poster on my wall. Just as – to a certain extent – everybody who plays or consumes rock and roll has become something of what Elvis made them, Elvis became what we made *him* . . . The human poster was gruesome by the end, and much of his pain must have come from the fact that he knew it.'

A few years ago a writer on rock wrote: 'Elvis oughta die real soon. He deserves it already both because he's no good no more (so he deserves to die like a dirty dog) and because he's still okay and at least used to be (so he deserves a better peace than all the cretins squalking at him saying he's no damn good). . . . Whatever way he dies, hopefully it'll be soon.' By the seventies, a lot of Elvis' early fans felt this way about him; it was a mixture of resentment and sardonic pity for their idol's fall from grace and an enduring gratitude

It was immediately obvious that Elvis' cult would know a second flowering as sensational in its way as the first. Young boys who were not born when the fifties rock scene came to an end had recently 'rediscovered' its songs and fashions; they were all ready to mourn the death of the king side by side with middle-aged rockers like the ones who gathered at the Nottingham Palais in England to recall their dead idol and their own vanished youth. Roy Hollingworth described these rockers in *Melody Maker*: 'Most of them were dusty and stale and full of dandruff. It seemed as though they had nowhere to go anymore. Elvis was dead. And loads of these miners and technicians and fitters and just honest fellows who'd built and modelled their whole existence on Presley, were dead too. But He wasn't. It was like seeing the remnants of Napoleon's all-conquering army coming home from Moscow, knowing that it had all gone wrong. These troops suddenly had nothing to do.' Teenage girls brought up on a pablum diet of old Elvis movies endlessly reshown on TV mourned not the 'elderly, bloated monster' of forty-two, older than many of their fathers, but the beautiful, sugary crooner

of their favourite sixties records and movies. The middle-aged mothers of these girls were probably the most affected: they had never forgotten the electrifying thrill of first seeing young Elvis on TV when he froze into place, legs askew, head lowered, hand poised above his guitar, waiting for the band to give him his cue before he launched in that inimitable way of his in the wild 'Wull it's one for the money, two for the show, three to get ready and go cats goooh'! of *Blue Suede Shoes*.

Have Elvis' more severe fans forgiven their idol for copping out some time around 1962? Just about everyone has come round to the idea that you cannot blame a fellow for wanting to live to forty-two and for not looking as slim and attractive by then as he did at nineteen. What Elvis can legitimately be blamed for is the artistic laziness which made him allow others to water down his image so as to make it ever more commercial; Elvis was no intellectual and he did not take his own 'art' as seriously as his more discriminating fans. Apparently, to him and to those who influenced him, his talent was not something to be prized and nutured for its own sake; it was merchandise to be sold to the highest

121

bidder. The Colonel had decreed that whatever brought in the most loot had to be best and who was Elvis to disagree with the Colonel? If he ever had his doubts, and there were signs that by the late sixties he did, Elvis did not trust his personal judgement sufficiently to make the necessary changes. So he added artistic dissatisfaction to his growing list of discontents: health, weight, age and love life.

What of Elvis's love life? It is a subject which has fascinated millions and has made millionaires of the writers of gossip sheets, yet it remains mysterious. Love and sex were always what Elvis was supposed to be about. His fans found him almost unbearably sexy. His detractors accused him of erotomania because of what he did with his voice and body, the way he dressed and played on young girls' emotions as well as on his guitar strings. Elvis was undeniably a sex symbol and he was hated for this as fervently as he was loved. After his death, George Gale wrote in *The Daily Express*: 'Presley seemed to brutalize sex, to deprive it of love and affection, and to glorify all that is ugly and violent in its representation. He is the first and foremost exponent of punk rock.' While it is quite true that Elvis cashed in on the hostility of the older generation to win over the younger one, as the punk rockers have been doing, anyone who listens to the words of a Presley song or who sees him in a film is struck by the extreme, almost mushy, romanticism of the singer. About 95 per cent of his songs are about love, with sex scarcely ever rearing its ugly head. Elvis sang about love in all its guises: puppy love, hopeful love, hopeless love, lost love, reproachful love, joyful love; whatever sort of love it was, the message which was always conveyed was that he was sincere, and that the emotion was for keeps. Many of Elvis's songs dripped with masochism. The man who had the largest pick of willing girls in the world always dwelled on the pangs of unrequited love, on the misery of the rejected suitor, on the despair of wanting and not being wanted back. All this is a long way from the arrogant sexual conqueror who was supposed to have deprived sex of love and affection.

How much of love's sorrow Elvis experienced and how much was only a convention of fifties' pop songs is another matter. The handsome young singer had little difficulty in getting girlfriends even when he was unknown, and once he became famous the sky was the limit as far as sexual conquest was concerned. The 'Memphis Mafia' – a group of young men who acted as the singer's bodyguards, servants and pals – always kept a large supply of more than willing girls handy for the King to choose from. Ellen Polton, a girl who had been invited to meet Elvis out in California, has described what she alleged was a typical scene. Elvis would be 'seated at the centre of a horseshoe shaped couch, feet up on the coffee table, captain's hat on his head, with half a dozen girls seated on the couch on

each side of him'. Like a pasha in his harem, Elvis would lazily look each girl over and finally smile at the lucky winner of his favours for that evening. The rest would have to make do with the members of his mafia if they ever wanted to get invited to have a second go at the first prize.

Elvis' name was linked romantically with those of dozens, if not hundreds of various starlets, beauty queens, models and most of the leading ladies in his films. Yet the only woman who can truly claim to have had a lasting romance with Elvis was Priscilla Beaulieu, the Air Force Captain's daughter he had met while he was doing his military service in Germany. Priscilla was only fourteen at the time, but their relationship lasted over the next few years and Elvis married her in 1967. Nine months later, Elvis' only child, Lisa Marie, was born and she became the third great love of his life after his mother and Priscilla. But his marriage to Priscilla came to an end when he found his wife in the arms of his judo instructor. He divorced her in 1973. Even a king wants to keep his queen forever and the end of the marriage was undoubtedly a contributory factor to the end of Elvis. He had declared on his wedding day: 'I decided it would be best if I waited till I really knew for sure. And now I'm really sure.' Perhaps because he came from a close-knit family, Elvis' concept of happiness had been, as it is for many, to settle down with the right person; during the early months of his marriage, he had been ridiculously pleased to be married, flaunting his wedding ring. While shooting a movie he would ostentatiously keep it on his finger right up to a take, quickly remove it, then put it on again immediately after the shot. Bill Bixby, who played with him in *Speedway* (1968), described the newly-wedded husband and father-to-be: 'Elvis was happier than I had ever seen him. He seemed totally content. I remember him whistling and humming . . . everything seemed to be falling into place.' But the king of rock and roll was not to be happy for long; he would become within a few short years unhappier than most ordinary mortals. May he rest in peace.

123

Left and right: The legendary rock and roll hero, Eddie Cochran, who was killed in a car crash in England in April 1960 at just 21. Bottom: Country and Western star Jim Reeves.

Of course, there are other figures from the ranks of fifties rock'n'roll who have also built up vast posthumous followings, especially now when, twenty years on, the whole era has taken on mythic proportions and has become the Valhalla for a whole generation who were not born when it was actually happening. Eddie Cochran and Gene Vincent are considered among the giants of 'pure' rock'n'roll, while country singer Jim Reeves, whose music came from the same roots and who was killed in an air crash on 31st July, 1964, has his own devoted following among country and western fans. On the soul side, before black music began to fuse with white, Sam Cooke had a huge following which has grown in stature since the death of his great disciple, Otis Redding. All these in their way personified the almost naive verve of early rock'n'roll and all have influenced and contributed to the subsequent course of popular music's development. Their deaths have been caused by a variety of tragic misfortunes – most, like Buddy Holly's, caused by transportation accidents while touring, although Sam Cooke's death in a shooting incident has unsavoury undertones and Gene Vincent's death from alcoholism was perhaps more pathetic than heroic.

Eddie Cochran is probably the greatest of these fifties figures. Cochran was twenty-one when he was killed in a car crash on the way to London Airport in 1960, and it is ironic that he was killed in Britain where at the time his following was much greater than in his native America. Eddie was an excellent guitarist and composer, and like Buddy Holly, had an impressive musical record which began at the age of sixteen. He was one of the most perfect representatives of the fifties youth spirit, managing to look both like the wholesome all-American boy who was held up as a model to teenagers of the time and like the superrocker that parents feared their sons would imitate. He bridged the gap between Buddy Holly's clean cut image and Elvis's raw animal magnetism. He could look

brooding and poetically melancholy in some of his photographs, not unlike James Dean, the archetypal symbol of fifties intellectualized romanticism, yet he was also buoyant enough at other times to delight the supersquares. The boy from Minnesota who started bashing his guitar at the age of twelve and who was a pro by his seventeenth birthday is one of the most enduring mythic figures of the vanished rock decade, though he is still better remembered and more admired in Europe than in his own country. Above all he is remembered for his electrifying appearance in the classic rock'n'roll film, *The Girl Can't Help It* (1957) and for a few great rock songs released both before and after his death: *Sittin' In the Balcony, Twenty Flight Rock, Summertime Blues* (the ultimate teenage anthem), *C'mon Everybody* and *Three Steps to Heaven*, which was climbing to the top of the charts at the time of his death.

One can only conjecture about Eddie Cochran's career in the sixties had he survived. His appearance in *The Girl Can't Help It* was due to be followed by further film work, and, like Buddy Holly with Maria, Eddie had found a steadying influence in his fiancée Sharron Sheely, who survived the fatal car crash. He had apparently been looking forward to taking life a little easier after the British tour, stepping out of the limelight for a while to concentrate on producing with his co-writer, Jerry Capehart. The partners had been looking forward to furthering the career of a recent discovery, Glen Campbell. Was the ballad style of this

125

Below: Gene Vincent and the Blue Caps in 1956.
Vincent survived the car crash that killed Cochran
but died aged 36 in 1971.

smooth country singer an example of the direction in which Eddie wanted to go? Early death froze Eddie Cochran within the fifties rock'n'roll mould; it is sadly fitting in a way that he did not survive 'his' decade.

Another survivor of that same car crash was the inimitable Gene Vincent (who was touring with Eddie Cochran), the enigmatic and unforgettable live performer who is best remembered for his song *Be-Bop-A-Lula*. Vincent, who came from Norfolk, Virginia, was an ordinary young man doing his Naval Service when he survived an earlier disastrous motorcycle accident which left him lame for life. This accident would prove vital to Gene's future destiny, since it was during his long sojourn in the hospital that he began to sing. After he took part in a local talent show, he was asked by a local disc jockey to make a professional recording. The limp became Vincent's trademark; along with his pasty-white complexion, his black leather clothes and his greased-back hair, it guaranteed that he would never go unnoticed. Paradoxically, he would eventually die not in an accident but of so-called natural causes in 1971, aged only thirty-six. After such a history of accidents it seems almost odd that he died of an internal haemorrhage which, like Elvis Presley's heart attack, was only the final result of several contributory factors, including in Gene's case a severe drinking problem. But Gene had been so long out of the mainstream of rock, and so much remembered for his rocker image in the fifties, that many devoted fans believe that he died

years earlier than he actually did. It was as if, with his 'bike boy' image, they attributed a more fitting death to someone who was only 'dead' in the commercial sense. Gene Vincent, another singer who died a bit too late for the good of his legend but has remained a mythical figure to many, is like a link between the rock musicians who died through accidents, and those whose life style meant they all but killed themselves.

While all these white rock'n'rollers were respectively impressing and shocking the youth and adulthood of middle America in the fifties, black music was developing its own more commercial, self-conscious image; an image to be copied avidly by the British R&B movement of the early sixties. The movement away from the music of hopeless despair embodied in the pure blues of men like Howlin' Wolf and Muddy Waters or of future happiness in the other world embodied in gospel music, reached its apotheosis in Sam Cooke, the father of today's soul music.

Most people recognize the Sam Cooke standards – even if they have not heard the originals they will have heard the myriad cover versions of songs like *Wonderful World*, *Cupid* and *Another Saturday Night*. But it is unlikely that they would have known or even guessed at the reaction of contemporary black fans when Sam Cooke died, shot by the wife of a motel manager in a Los Angeles suburb on 11th December, 1964. 'Thousands of screaming, crying, pushing people thronged the area surrounding A. R. Leak's Funeral Home . . . in a

Below left: Sam Cooke, the father of soul music.
Below right: Otis Redding, soul superstar of the
sixties, died in 1967 aged only 26.

frantic attempt to see the body of singer Sam Cooke,'
was the way the *Chicago Defender* described the funeral.
As at Valentino's lying-in-state, a plate glass door gave
way in the chapel, hundreds of people were jostled and
crushed and many of the huge crowd paying its last
respects were disappointed in their desire to take a last
look at the body. For whatever the circumstances of
his death (which involved accusations of attempted
rape and the final clubbing to death of the wounded
singer by the motel manager before the police arrived),
to black America Sam Cooke was a hero.

Sam Cooke was born in 1937 in Chicago, son of a
minister, and began his singing career with a gospel
group called the Soul Stirrers. It wasn't long before he
made the transition from gospel to commercial soul,
recording at first under an assumed name, and then
abandoning his religious singing in favour of pop. The
Keen label released his first single, *You Send Me*, in
1957, and it sold more than 1½ million copies to a predominantly black audience. According to *Rolling Stone*'s
Joe McEwen, Cooke's manager, J. W. Alexander, had
intended all along that Sam Cooke should become the
same sort of idol to black teenage girls that Elvis or
Buddy Holly were to whites. It was a new idea, and it
worked – and went even further when Cooke signed
with RCA. Now he bridged the gap between black and
white, and it became increasingly obvious that there was
a wider, mixed audience for soul music.

Sam Cooke was the idol of many later artists, black
and white, especially Otis Redding, who in turn was
idolized by Janis Joplin – a sad chain of admiration in
the circumstances. Otis was another victim of the pace
at which rock musicians have to live if they want to get
to the top and stay there. Redding was a near superstar
at the time of his death and has remained a legend to
many, although he always acknowledged his debt to
Sam Cooke and kept the latter's memory green by including Cooke songs in most of his albums and live
performances. Otis Redding, who was born in Macon,
Georgia, in 1941, had started his career by imitating the
frenetic style of Little Richard, but eventually developed,
via Sam Cooke's influence, his own soul style. As with
so many other R&B and soul performers of the early
sixties, Otis Redding was picked up by white rock stars
in Britain who 're-exported' the Stax Records top solo
singer to their white audiences in the States. (Black
audiences did not need to be told.) As *The NME Book of
Rock* wryly states, 'in England by 1965, no self-respect-
ing mod was complete without a copy of the album
Otis Blue tucked under his arm'.

Redding's appearance at the 1967 Monterey Pop
Festival set the seal on his superstar status. He was
about to take the throne of top black performer away
from Ray Charles when he was killed, along with most
members of his protégé band, the Bar Kays, as his plane
crashed into an icy lake in December, 1967. Many of
the other great soul singers, who could thank Otis's
success for bringing them to a wider audience, were
pallbearers at his funeral, including Joe Tex, Solomon
Burke and Percy Sledge, and his classic single *Dock of
the Bay*, which was released posthumously, sold a million copies within a month.

6. GENIUS FOR EXCESS

It was inevitable that three of the great rock stars of the sixties who could not stay the course – Brian Jones, Jimi Hendrix and Janis Joplin – should be lumped together after their deaths. How strangely linked their destinies seem now! They were born within a few months of each other in the early forties and they died within a few months of each other at the end of the decade which had brought them glory: the white boy, the black boy and the white girl with a black girl's blues. All three parading in fancy dress, plumes, velvets, beads and bangles. All three hopped to the eyeballs in drink and drugs. All three flaunting the sexual freedom of the sixties until sex became a substitute for satisfaction and the emphasis was on kicks and quantity. All three had struggled for success and adulation and yet were left strangely dissatisfied when they achieved it. All three were basically shy, sweet individuals under the brass and the greasepaint. All three lived it up as though tomorrow might never come, and eventually it did not: none of them lived beyond thirty.

Taken together, Jimi, Janis and Jones embody almost every facet of the Great Rock Boom of the sixties. Brian Jones was a perfect hybrid, embodying in his music the cross-cultural ties between England and America that were such a feature of the sixties rock scene.

Jimi Hendrix embodied other facets of the rock revolution and the pop culture of the sixties. He was black and American and unassailably authentic. Yet it was one of the paradoxes of the times he lived in that he had to go to England and sing with a white group before he became a superstar, making his name in Europe before American audiences would accept him. Perhaps he would have been *too* authentic if he had remained in the United States, playing with an all-black group. His music and his image would have lacked the synthetic element which is a vital ingredient of pop stardom. While Jimi remained in the States, playing and singing the blues, writing ballads about raical oppression, playing with other black musicians in Greenwich Village jazz clubs, he was only a virtuoso guitarist with a reputation among *aficionados*. When he moved to Swinging London in 1967, started dressing in the flamboyant gear of Carnaby Street and doing stunts like burning his guitar during his performances, he became one of the great rock stars. As a *Rolling Stone* writer put it, Jimi was 'the flower generation's electric nigger dandy – its king stud and golden calf, its maker of mighty dope music, its most outrageously visible force'. Jimi wove all the strands of the sixties musical currents into a revolutionary pattern of his own, combining black and white, psychedelic with folk, European with American, *avant-garde* with more than a dash of the old-style Elvis Presley beat. His performances had the wildness demanded by his times, the raw visual impact and excitement of a good circus act. He did not just play music that was nice to listen to but which was also fun to watch: he would play his guitar with his tongue, with his teeth, behind his back, lying on the floor, masturbating with it and often smashing it at the conclusion of a concert. In the age of the total act, Jimi was the total musician.

Janis Joplin, too, propelled herself to stardom by her stage performances as well as by her singing. Her audiences fondly remember how, 'her bottle of booze placed proudly atop her amplifier, she paraded the stage like a debauched Carnival Queen, or King Kong in drag.' During her songs she danced, screamed and broke off singing to call out to her fans. She would come on, 'stomping and posing like an imperious whore, stroking her mike and whipping her hair around', and it would drive the public wild before she had even sung a note. But she embodied other facets of the rock scene as well. To begin with, she represented the West Coast contribution to the pop world, with all its overtones of hippie freedom and its San Francisco flower-child mystique. She also understood the blues the way no white singer had ever done before. Until Janis, you either had to be black to sing the blues or else to do a convincing imitation of a black singer. Janis used the blues to create her own sound because she grasped in her innermost being that having the blues was not the prerogative of any one colour or class. Janis had started off her career by doing imitations of Bessie Smith and Odetta, but eventually she realized that it was enough to be Janis Joplin, a white middle-class girl from a comfortable background, to feel the blues deep down and to express them in her own way. When asked once how she had learned to sing the blues with such genuine feeling, she answered: 'I didn't learn shit, man, I just opened my mouth and that's what I sounded like, man. You can't make up something you don't feel.'

But Janis was not just a pure blues singer; like all the top rock stars of her time, a lot of different musical trends contributed to her colour scheme. The Joplin style was unique, yet it was also true to the sixties, combining rock, folk, blues and pop.

Brian Jones, Jimi Hendrix and Janis Joplin all became virtually dependent on drugs and alcohol, even or perhaps especially during their most successful periods. All three had fooled around with drugs before they grew famous, but it is an expensive habit when you are playing five dollars-a-night gigs. Once money stopped being a problem drugs started playing a key role in their lives: they were soon using drugs to get themselves into the right mood for a concert, drugs to get started the morning after, drugs to keep going through the day, drugs to give themselves the kicks they felt a superstar was entitled to, or drugs to keep loneliness, anxiety and self-doubt at bay. Drugs and booze because they are a musician's way of life, because they help an insecure youngster identify with illustrious predecessors like Bessie Smith, Billie Holiday and Charlie Parker. But also drugs because they were such a part of the sixties scene.

There they are, the three Js, all dead at the close of the sixties, all cult figures in the seventies; they make a winsome trio when you look at pictures of them in their heyday. But even as they grin and ham in front of the camera, you can find a lingering sadness around their eyes, a tremulous bravado in their smiles; caught unawares by the candid camera as they relax or walk down a street, they look lost and frightened. Is it with hindsight that we detect a doomed, tragic quality in those young, unlined faces? Or is it because, as many who knew them claim, Brian, Jimi and Janis were aware all along that their time would be brief? Their premonitions of early death are on record. When they died, most of their friends realized, or thought they did, that they had always known it would have to end that way.

But when we look at photographs of them now, another, more positive aspect of their personalities also emerges; we see how clearly they contributed to their times in other ways than through their music. Brian, Jimi and Janis embodied some of the most liberating elements of the sixties culture; the innovations implicit in their image and their style brought pleasure to millions of young people who imitated them in order to feel more free. A friend said of Brian: 'If he gave nothing else to the world, Brian Jones was the first heterosexual male to start wearing costume jewellery from Saks Fifth Avenue.' Brian did the lavender-suede-boots and day-glo sequin bit beautifully, elegantly, without the sexual ambivalence of Mick Jagger or David Bowie. The message got through to the general public, and by the close of the sixties, a man could enjoy the thrill of being a sex-object, discarding the shirt-and-tie uniform of the fifties male, without being hounded off the street or getting beaten up for being gay.

Jimi Hendrix had his message of liberation too, and because he was black it was subtly different from Brian's. Jimi wore no uniform, yet he managed to epitomize the Black-is-Beautiful slogan in a non-dogmatic or racist way. He wore his hair in the ultimate Afro, yet at the same time, 'he was the first *black* man to dress like an English fop and an eighteenth century dandy'. And why not, he seemed to be saying. Forget about the colour of your skin and wear whatever makes you feel good. Mix and match any old style until you feel like the real you; do not try to look like a white man, which you are not, but do not force yourself to look like an African, which you are not either. The Panthers had made young American blacks take pride in being black. Jimi's uninhibited style and its obvious success made them take pride in just being themselves.

Janis did for the girls what Brian had done for the boys and Jimi for the blacks. She was living proof of the feminist claim that you did not have to approximate a stereotyped ideal to be desirable. She demonstrated by her own example that it was possible to be overweight and pimply and yet still project a real kind of beauty. Her beauty was not always apparent, but that too was a part of the message: 'She taught America that beauty didn't *have* to be a constant, it could ebb and flow and surprise you by being there one minute and not the next.' There was also something far more liberating about the Janis image than some of the sterner dictums of the women's movement. The militant feminists wanted to free women from the synthetic styles they had once felt obliged to conform to, but their own decrees were almost as constricting: make-up was out, skirts and finery were chauvinist ways of turning women into sex objects for males. Janis cheerfully wore feathers, beads and long dresses because that was what she *liked* to wear. She went camping in silver, high-heeled boots. She wore floozy-style black net stockings with her mini-skirts, and plunging necklines to show off her tits; yet you did not feel for a moment that she did any of this because she was a slave to the convention that women must look feminine to try and please men. She did it because she wanted to make the best of her assets and to look as good as she possibly could; *that* was real freedom and girls everywhere heeded the call.

Though it may appear trivial to the serious-minded, it can be quite significant to create and promulgate a style, a look or a hairdo until it is so universally adopted that what once appeared outrageous becomes commonplace, even *passé*. Styles reflect their times and are only the outward symbols of forces at work, social changes in the making. Rebellions and aspirations make themselves visually manifest in the way people choose to dress. Sexual freedom, Black liberation, the Women's Movement were some of the most important currents to emerge out of the sixties and their impact is still making itself felt. Brian, Jimi and Janis expressed and furthered these trends in their clothes and in their styles of living. They will be remembered for this almost as much as for their music.

JONES

Brian Jones was born in Cheltenham on 28th February, 1942. The Rolling Stones would later make much of their working-class background, but Lewis Brian Hopkin-Jones was strictly middle-class: his father was an engineer and his mother taught piano. He learnt how to read music and studied musical theory as a child, and this would stand him in good stead when the Rolling Stones came into being, for he was the only member of the group who could read music and who was versatile enough to learn how to play a wide variety of instruments. After a normal, uneventful childhood came a difficult and restless adolescence. Brian was a true British child of his times: his youth exemplified the trend which had started back in the fifties and had found its verbal expression in John Osborne's play, *Look Back in Anger*. This trend was characterized by a shift away from the Establishment values and the class system which had dominated English society since Queen Victoria's reign. Brian Jones was a public school boy destined by his parents and by tradition to go to university. Like many others of his generation, he rebelled against the pre-ordained pattern by dropping out of school and adopting attitudes traditionally associated with the shiftless lower-classes: getting drunk regularly, bumming around and siring two illegitimate children while he was still in his teens. He drifted into the world of rock bands, a working-class phenomenon, where if your background was at all 'posh' you kept pretty quiet about it, adopting the manners, the accent and the clothes of your 'common' mates.

For a time Brian stayed on in Cheltenham after dropping out of school there. He had taught himself to play the guitar and other instruments, the clarinet and the

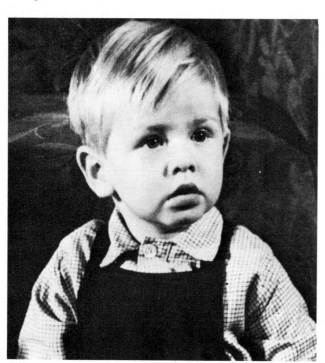

alto sax. He 'gigged' for local traditional jazz bands around the West Country and got to know Alexis Korner while the latter was on tour with his band, Blues Incorporated. At the beginning of the sixties, Brian drifted away from his worried parents and, inevitably, turned up in London. He learned about working-class poverty in a Hammersmith slum, surviving on a diet of cold tinned spaghetti and working at odd jobs now and again, such as bus conductor and cashier. But music, and especially Rhythm and Blues – 'the city Negro's pop' as he called it – continued to be his first love. He frequented the Ealing Blues Club in West London, which was one of the foremost venues for Rhythm and Blues bands in the capital. It was there he first ran into Mick Jagger and Keith Richard. The three youngsters discovered a common ambition: to form their own Rhythm and Blues band – and pretty soon they moved into a Chelsea flat together.

Jones, Jagger and Richard brought together a motley group of musicians from blues and jazz backgrounds who called themselves the Rolling Stones. By the end of 1963 the Rolling Stones line up consisted of Mick Jagger, Keith Richard, Brian Jones, Bill Wyman, Charlie Watts and Ian Stewart on piano. It was when they managed to land the coveted Saturday afternoon spot at the Crawdaddy Club in Richmond that Andrew Loog Oldham saw them. At nineteen, Oldham had already passed through singing into management and he immediately realized the raw potential of this new group. It was he too who eased out Ian Stewart, one of the founder members with Brian Jones, because he did not look right. With the inspired slogan, 'The Rolling Stones aren't another group – they're a way of life' Andrew Oldham set out to package the Stones with a true salesman's flair.

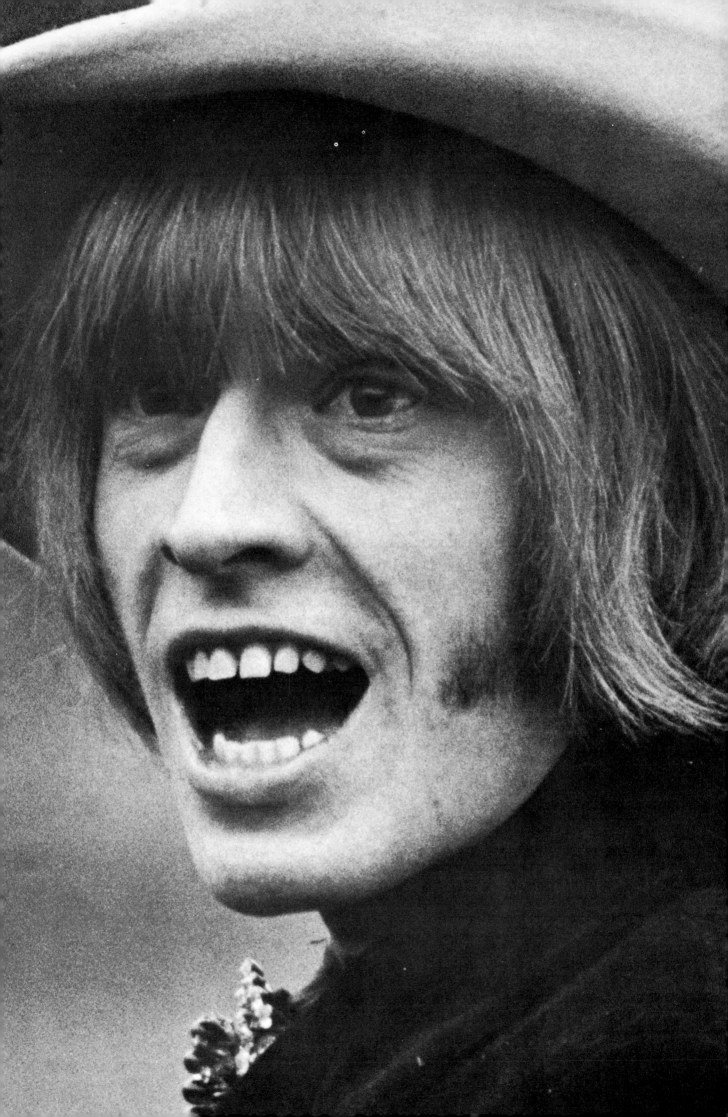

Success comes quickly in the world of popular music – when it comes at all. The world was ready for the Rolling Stones. By the end of 1963 they were famous; by 1964 they were rich. Brian's role during this early phase was crucial. As the other members of the group readily admitted in later years, it was Brian's enthusiasm and determination which buoyed up the group during its hesitant beginnings. It was his chemistry which made the group jell, his musical knowledge which enabled the other members to develop their range. His professional experience was slender but it exceeded theirs and his determination was an important factor in holding out and not falling apart after a few months like so many other new groups. In the days when Mick Jagger still believed he would become a professional economist and would just sing a little on the side, Brian already knew exactly what he wanted: he was once mistaken for one of the famous Beatles and the experience thrilled him.

By 1964, the Rolling Stones were being subjected to exactly the same adulation. Newspaper headlines like: ROLLING STONES FLEE RIOTS, WOMEN P.C.S. FAINT AT STONES SHOW, GUARDS TRAMPLED AS STONES' FANS GO WILD, were soon common. At first Brian seemed to enjoy it. He relished turning on with exaggeratedly camp and provocative movements, 'mincing away' as Roy Carr wrote, 'with narcissistic flicks of his flaxen hair . . . playing out his new-found role of jean-creaming demi-god for all it was worth'. The group went from one smash hit song and wild concert to another throughout 1964, 1965, 1966 and 1967. They toured Europe, Australia and America, recorded, among others, the albums: *The Rolling Stones 1 and 2, Out of Our Heads, Aftermath* and *Their Satanic Majesties' Request.* In the way that their image was rougher and wilder than that of the Beatles, so audience reaction to them and fan behaviour could be unpredictable, hysterical and downright dangerous. On one occasion they were besieged by a horde of girls armed with scissors to try to cut off locks of their hair. During a concert they were sometimes sent flying into the orchestra pit by over-enthusiastic fans. They were also highly unpopular with large sections of the adult population and were forever being torn to shreds by the press. They were singled out for special treament by policemen and customs officials; hotels turned down their bookings, and they lived in a strange, delirious climate of mixed love and hatred. It took a thick skin to cope with these extreme reactions and perhaps Brian's skin was not thick enough. Some of the strain began to tell on him; as Keith Richard later recalled in an interview, 'When I first met Brian, he was like a little Welsh bull . . . As he went along he got more and more fragile and delicate. His personality, and physically. I think that touring did a lot to break him. We worked our asses off from '63 to '66, right through those three years,

non-stop. I believe we had two weeks off.' It sounds pretty rough, but as Richard added: 'That's nothing, I mean I tell that to B. B. King and he'll say "I been doing it for years". But for cats like Brian . . . ' Keith Richard's voice trails away at this point; he doesn't know either why Brian could not stand the pace. After all, the other Stones thrived on it.

Quite a lot of the trouble was rooted in Brian's gradual loss of the limelight to Mick Jagger. After the Rolling Stones became world famous, it became more and more evident that Brian was no longer 'the undisputed leader' of the group as he had once prided himself on being. Girls might still go for Brian, but it was Mick Jagger the journalists wanted to interview and to whom they always referred as the leader of the Stones. This was partly due to Jagger's strong personality and to his more unusual features, but it was chiefly that, in Jagger's own words, 'It was accepted by the public that the singer with the band was the leader and, as I just happened to be the singer, most people singled me out as the leader . . . that was the thing that fucked Brian up – because he was so desperate for attention. He wanted to be admired and loved and all that . . . which he was by a lot of people, but it wasn't enough for him.' In fact the story of Mick and Brian's love-hate relationship is more complex than Jagger suggests here. There existed a long rivalry between them which, logically, had to end in the elimination of one or the other from the group, and since Jagger was much the stronger of the two it had to be Brian. Jagger used his closer ties with Keith Richard and Charlie Watts to make Brian feel the odd man out, finally rejecting the songs Brian wrote to use only his own compositions or Keith's. He took advantage of

Brian's growing drug problem to persuade the group that it could not rely on its guitarist and to do without him at recording sessions. All this tended to confirm Brian in his already existing paranoia and made him withdraw further into himself. When he lost his steady girlfriend, Anita Pallenberg to Keith Richard, his sense of isolation from the group must have been complete. On a visit home to see his parents, he wistfully regretted ever having left the town of Cheltenham he had once so longed to escape from. Those who saw him in London nightclubs were struck by his melancholy remoteness: 'Despite his flamboyance and his decadent affectations, he was strangely naïve and withdrawn, a changeling in London's brittle clubs.' A Chelsea restaurant owner recalls that Brian used to come alone to watch early evening television in the bar with the chef, before the restaurant opened. He did not seem to require conversation, just companionship.

His relationship with Mick Jagger deteriorated further. According to one of Jagger's biographers, Anthony Scaduto, he attacked Mick with a knife not long before his death, and after a fruitless attempt at stabbing him, Brian proceeded to throw himself into the water-filled moat of the house at which they were staying, shouting to Jagger, 'I don't want to live on the same earth with you. I can't kill you, so I'll die instead.' As Jagger's star grew brighter, so Brian's grew dimmer; whether his everincreasing consumption of drugs was a cause or an effect of this, it certainly did not help matters. The drugs he took in large quantity destroyed his creativity as well as his self-confidence. They wrecked him physically and also brought him endless difficulties at the hands of the law, confirming him in his paranoia that everybody was out to get him. By 1967, police raids, busts, court sessions and heavy fines had become a regular, if inconvenient feature of the Stones' lives. According to Mick Jagger, their frequency interfered with the business of producing records: 'We never knew who was going to be in jail when, and when to book a session, *for almost a year!*

Harassment of the various members of the Rolling Stones over the drug issue reached such proportions in England that, in 1967, even the conservative *Times*

finally took their side, declaring that they were being needlessly persecuted and were being used as scapegoats because they were public figures. *The Times* editorial was aptly entitled 'Who breaks a butterfly on a wheel?', after Oscar Wilde whose notoriety had also brought him persecution. Jagger and Richard at that time presented a show of bravado; but Brian Jones did not have their resilience and by the time of the newspaper article he was indeed a broken butterfly. A prison sentence of nine months for possession of Indian hemp was commuted to three years' probation and a fine of £1,000 in December 1967, after three psychiatrists declared that he was 'an extremely frightened young man', one of them adding 'with suicidal tendencies'. Brian had collapsed from nervous strain both immediately after the preliminary hearing in July 1967 and in December after the sentence was finally set aside by the Appeal Court.

In May 1968 he was busted yet again. There was more than suspicion now that as William Rees-Mogg had written in *The Times* about Mick Jagger, this was yet another case where 'a single figure becomes the focus for public concern about some aspect of public morality.' Certainly the reported remarks of Judge Leslie Block

(the chairman of the Sussex quarter sessions who sentenced Mick Jagger and Keith Richard in June 1967), while Brian's first case was still *sub judice*, seemed to imply that the establishment was out to make an example of the Stones. Judge Block observed jocularly at a Sussex society dinner that 'We did our best, your fellow countrymen, I and my fellow magistrates, to cut those Stones down to size, but alas, it was not to be because the Court of Criminal Appeal let them roll free.' But Brian was in no fit state to be a crusader, to face the establishment defiantly in the way the other Stones did. His personal problems with the group, his sense of isolation and paranoia were fuelled by this public assault on him just because he was a member of the Rolling Stones. Perhaps it was this which undid him: even in terms of public disapproval it seemed it was not Brian Jones as a private individual, or even Brian Jones as an individual superstar who was being busted, but just Brian Jones as a member of the collective phenomenon called the Rolling Stones.

Whatever was the truth, the final arrest was an important factor in the breaking of Brian. Although the case itself began with a roar (he was let out on £2,000 bail) and ended in a whimper (he was fined £50 and

drew further into himself, He drowned on 3rd July, 1969 aged 25 in his swimming pool. Below: Brian's parents, sister and girlfriend Suki Poitier at his funeral. Below right: The last portrait.

£105 costs), the damage had been done. During the last year of his life, Brian gradually withdrew, becoming increasingly vague. He only spoke in whispers, so that you had 'to put an ear against his mouth to hear what he was saying'. Even at a distance, it was obvious that Brian was fading out. At Monterey, in his Chinese robes and lace, he looked barely present, an iridescent ghost on the threshold of the drugs that sustained him. Inevitably, he had become a liability to the Stones. As Jagger has said about the final months: 'Brian wasn't in any condition to play. He couldn't play. He was far too fucked up in his mind to play . . . we felt like we had a wooden leg.' Brian hardly contributed anything to the last Stones album he worked on, *Beggars Banquet*. This album, full of ambiguous and provocative tracks, signalled the change of atmosphere at the end of the sixties from flower power to panic in the streets. Brian perhaps could not face the future: even his new home in Sussex seemed to point to a desire to return to the ease of childhood, since it was Cotchford Farm, where A. A. Milne wrote about Winnie-the-Pooh.

In June 1969, the group dropped Brian and took on Mick Taylor in his place. Officially, Brian left over disagreements about songs. 'I no longer see eye to eye with the discs we are cutting' he was reported as saying. Mick Taylor, previously guitarist with the John Mayall group, was to make his public debut with the Stones in a free concert in London's Hyde Park on 5th July, 1969. Perhaps this was too much for Brian to bear. The teenagers' idol who had craved attention was being replaced by a virtual unknown barely out of his teens. Only two days before the concert, on the night of 2nd-3rd July, Brian was pulled unconscious from the bottom of the pool at Cotchford Farm. His girlfriend, Anna Wohlin, herself a nurse, tried to revive him with artificial respiration, while an ambulance was called. But it was too late; Brian was dead by the time a doctor arrived.

His former Stones colleagues were shattered. They went ahead with the Hyde Park concert on 5th July, dedicating it to Brian's memory. Two hundred and fifty thousand people saw the Rolling Stones give one of their most memorable live performances in front of a huge blown-up photograph of Brian and accompanied by a cloud of white butterflies released into the summer air. Mick spoke for everyone when he said that day: 'I am so shocked and wordless and sad, I have really lost something. I hope he is finding peace.'

But who knows whether it was peace that Brian was seeking, or whether indeed he meant to drown himself at all? Was it an unfortunate asthma attack? Coincidence? Was he under the influence of drink or drugs? Al Aronowitz called him 'the little princeling who had run out of toys to play with'. It seems fairer to remember Brian Jones' own epitaph, as it was read out at his funeral in Cheltenham: 'Please don't judge me too harshly.' Whatever clues his final months of life may have provided as to the real state of his mind, he took the secret of his final moments with him to the grave.

HENDRIX

Jimi Hendrix, the 'electric nigger dandy' of the psychedelic decade, may well be the most representative figure of his era. His music, his personality and his style are quintessentially sixties. There is a crazy poetry not only in Jimi Hendrix's music but about his whole image, and his death at the end of the sixties, though sad, also seems a form of poetic justice. Of the great mythic figures whose posters adorn the walls of today's and yesterday's teenagers, the juxtaposition of Che Guevara and Jimi Hendrix is a common one. The two could not have been more different in real life; perhaps the only thing they really had in common was that both were supremely photogenic. Yet they perfectly represent the two opposite and often conflicting poles of the sixties spirit. On the one hand, we have Che who evokes memories of the youth revolution, the anti-war demonstrations and the student barricades of May 1968, the spirit of protest which rocked the streets and campuses of the world during that decade. On the other, we have Hendrix the standard-bearer of individualism, the champion of the 'do-your-own-thing' life-style, seeking inner liberation rather than political freedom.

Like all great legends, Jimi Hendrix is at once transparent and mysterious. A hero's image is so stimulating that the facts of his life can seem prosaic by comparison, his biographical data almost dull because it resembles everyone else's until the events occur which lead to the flowering of his myth. Hendrix is no exception to this rule; until he turned into *the* Jimi Hendrix we know today, his life story was not unlike that of many talented black musicians. Even his appearance – which would become striking to the point of being bizarre – seems hardly unusual in early photographs of him when, short-

haired and wearing a suit and tie, he poses with a group that called itself the Squires.

James Mitchell Hendrix was born on 27th November, 1942, in Seattle, Washington. Like every North American with Negro blood, he is always referred to as 'black', but in fact his racial antecedents also included white, Cherokee Indian and Mexican blood. The mixture of races would show up clearly in Jimi's features, in his temperament and even in his music which was never as black as that played by Southern musicians of pure African descent. Jimi's father was a sober, quiet, hard-working man, a gardener by profession. His mother, who died when he was ten, loved dressing up, having a good time and drinking more than was good for her. Again the mixture of paternal and maternal personality-types would show up in Jimi's nature, which was both quiet and wild, reticent and excessive, divided between a taste for work well-done and loose living. The dichotomy of his nature was apparent from an early age. One of his aunts remembered him as being 'very shy and humble' as a child. But he was also turned out of a Baptist church when he was only eight for being dressed too extravagantly.

He discovered the two ruling passions of his life – music and sex – before he was in his teens. His musical education had begun early, though it was of an unsophisticated sort: it consisted of watching, listening to and trying to imitate his father skilfully playing the spoons and blowing on the comb. Before he was ten, he was given a guitar by his uncle and he never again put

Jimi Hendrix epitomized sixties' flamboyance.
Left: With his girlfriend Cathy Etchingham. Below
centre: Performing at the Golden Gate Park, San
Francisco, 1969. The Monterey Pop Festival (1967)

down his 'axe' for very long after that. He immediately
showed an unusual flair for playing the instrument
though he was left-handed, and he could pick up any
tune he heard on the radio. At the age of twelve he had
sex with a girl for the first time. As he later recalled it: 'I
could hardly get it in – but when I did it was sooooooo
nice!' Sex got him thrown out of school three years
later: scolded by a woman teacher for holding a girl's
hand in class, Jimi coolly replied: 'What's the matter?
Are you jealous?'

Like many another black teenager out of school and
out of work, Jimi could easily have drifted straight into
the world of juvenile delinquency. Already he liked
flashy clothes so much that he sometimes stole them
from clothing stores. But instead, with his father's eager
consent, he enlisted in the U.S. Airborne Paratroopers
when he was seventeen. As he himself described it, his
time in the Paratroopers was divided between 'screaming *aghhhhhhh*! and *I'm faallliiiiiing*', as he jumped out
of airplanes, and going to 'sleazy bars with their neon
signs blinking a welcome to all of us lonely suckers, and
the urine-perfumed benches where you could sit with a
whore straight from Satan . . . ' After his discharge he
got a job playing the guitar with a group called the
Flames, then worked for a time touring the States with
Little Richard, afterwards playing with the Isley
Brothers, picking up experience on the road and improving his guitar style all the while.

All black American musicians end up in New York
sooner or later and in 1964 Jimi followed the road leading to the Big Apple – 'rotten to the core but irresistible'
as Curtis Knight described it. With so many talented
rhythm and blues and jazz musicians concentrated in
one place, competition was stiff and jobs not always
easy to get or well-paid, even for someone as obviously
gifted as Jimi. Miles Davis, who heard him play at a
club in Greenwich Village in 1965, later claimed, 'Even
then I could see genius and scope in Jimi's playing – he

went in all directions making his musical statement'.
But Jimi's musical style was too unusual and *avant-
garde* for many clubs or discotheques and his life was not
easy even though true *aficionados* recognized his worth
and were eager to spread the word about the new young
virtuoso. The Animals, a very popular British rock group
which was touring the States, heard on the grapevine
about Jimi, and went to hear him play at a fashionable
club called Ondines. Chas Chandler, the bassist of the
Animals, was extremely impressed; he grasped the
potential impact that Hendrix could make in London,
whereas Jimi was somewhat lost in the talented crowd
of New York's musical world. Chandler persuaded Hendrix to go to England with him and became his manager.
(In fact Hendrix had already signed with an American
manager, Ed Chalpin, which was later to prove prob-
lematic.) Hendrix and Chandler left in 1966 to try out
the London scene, which was in full swing at the time.

Chandler was right. In England, Jimi stood out in
a way he could not do back in New York, despite his
talent. Here, Jimi was startling, amazing, unique, and
his sheer skill as a musician had all of London's
guitarists throwing up their hands in despair. Chandler's

*had made a star of Jimi in the USA. His per-
formance there became legendary. Below right: At
the Albert Hall, February 1969.*

next stroke of genius was to team up Hendrix with two
white English musicians, Noel Redding on bass and
Mitch Mitchell on drums. This prevented the new group,
baptized the Jimi Hendrix Experience, from being
labelled either black or American at a time when white
English rock groups were all the rage on both sides of
the Atlantic. Success did not come overnight, but it did
not take long. Hendrix's talent soon surfaced; when he
got a chance to play, he was always impressive and the
word got around fast. To begin with, Jimi had the added
advantage of being a 'musician's musician'. Even Mick
Jagger and John Lennon were impressed. He also made
excellent copy, and the papers were always happy to
run an interview with the soft-spoken, sharp-thinking,
super-cool young performer.

When the Experience played in concert halls rather
than nightclubs, audience response was so enthusiastic
and the stage act so wild that Jimi Hendrix became
impossible to ignore. He became news. All his singles,
including *Hey Joe*, *Purple Haze* and *The Wind Cries
Mary* went high up the British charts. His reputation
soon spread to the rest of Europe, and he caused a sensation wherever he toured: Scandinavia, Germany,

France, Holland, Belgium and Italy. When he had left
the States only a few months earlier, he was nothing
more than a respected musician. When he returned in
1967, he was a superstar. His performance at the Monterey Pop Festival that June consecrated his position
in his own country, as did a subsequent tour of the
States in 1968. His albums, *Are You Experienced?*
(1967), *Alexis: Bold as Love* (1968) and *Electric Ladyland* (1968) took the message to whatever parts of the
world Jimi had not yet covered. But *Electric Ladyland*,
a double album, showed the beginnings of change in the
Experience's successful 'electric hippy' formula, and it
was Jimi who was most anxious to begin to progress
musically. Besides this there were serious personality
problems between Jimi and Noel Redding so no one in
the music business was surprised when the Experience
broke up in November 1968, although their millions of
fans were shocked and disappointed.

From the Experience's farewell concerts in January
1969 it seemed that time was running out for Jimi.
Within eighteen months he was dead, choked by his
own vomit after an overdose of sleeping tablets on 18th
September, 1970. He was twenty-seven years old and
had been a star for three years. As with Brian Jones, and
later, Janis Joplin, his death shocked rather than sur-

prised his friends and admirers. Chas Chandler summed up this feeling of inevitability. 'Somehow I wasn't surprised' he is quoted as saying in Chris Welch's biography of Hendrix. 'I don't believe for one minute that he killed himself. But something had to happen and there was no way of stoppin' it. You just get a feeling sometimes. It was as if the last couple of years had prepared us for it. It was like a message I had been waiting for.' Jimi was a heavy drug user, and could also drink his way through a quart and a half of whisky at a sitting. Many refused to admit his death was suicide, but all could acknowledge that his life style had long been a form of self-murder and that behind his craving for drink and drugs lay a craving not for pleasure but for oblivion. What had gone wrong?

Jimi had certainly contemplated killing himself at least once before. The scars on his wrists were evidence that he had attempted to commit suicide with a razor. But that had been back in the old, penniless days in New York when lack of funds and success had driven the down-and-out musician to near despair. At first superstardom had not seemed to have the disastrous effect on Jimi's psyche that it had on Brian Jones'. In his quiet way, Jimi had adjusted to fame and to its fruits: the money, the girls and the freedom, at first, to play when and what he liked. A modest, rather shy person, the publicity and adulation probably didn't mean all that much to his ego; but he obviously appreciated the creature comforts he could now afford, along with musical recognition.

Yet Jimi had always been a moody man; long before his great success his moody spells had disconcerted those around him. 'Often Jimi would lie in bed for a couple of days on end, not interested in anything', Cathy Etchingham, an early girlfriend, remembered. 'Even when he wasn't getting high on drugs, there would be times when he would lock himself up in his room and refuse to speak to anybody. Or else, in company, he would withdraw into hermetic silences and reject all attempts at communication.' At such moments he exuded a sense of loneliness so total that even those closest to him felt they could not get through. Once he had become a star, his very fame created a sense of isolation: 'No-one felt the strength to take him out of that web,' one girl singer said of Jimi after seeing him in that mood at the Isle of Wight Pop Festival a few weeks before his death. 'It was almost as if we had to stand by and watch . . . it came out of him being the superstar and us just being the person on the side.' His German girlfriend, Monika Danneman, described the long walks she took with Jimi in Hyde Park during the last few days of his life in the early Autumn of 1970: 'Often Jimi would not speak for long periods of time, as if he were storing up and digesting his last communication with earth . . . and I walked with him silently, knowing and understanding his spiritual loneliness during these times.'

There has been some controversy about how Jimi felt concerning the colour of his skin, how much it affected his attitude towards life or was a factor in his self-destructive streak. Some of those who knew him thought it was important both to his music and to his state of mind. Others did not. Eric Burdon of the Animals was so convinced it mattered enormously that he advised people to attend Jimi's performances: 'If you want to see what an American black is going through today, where his mind is at, go and see Jimi Hendrix and you'll realize why there are race riots in America and why the country is close to civil war . . . He is exorcising generations of anger.' Jimi's road manager, Gerry Stickells, was equally convinced this was *not* so: 'To me, Jimi wasn't black man – he was a white man. He didn't think like a coloured guy and he certainly didn't appeal to a coloured audience at all. Not that he wasn't sympathetic to their cause. He just didn't really think about it.'

If Hendrix was deeply disturbed by the race issue, he certainly played it very cool. Brought up outside the deep South or the ghettoes of America's north-eastern cities, he had not experienced the same degree of racial discrimination as many American blacks. He felt somewhat guilty about not relating strongly to the Black Power movement that was a growing social and political force, but he was too much of an individualist to allow any organization to take him over. He once pushed his proclaimed indifference to the issue of racism to the extent of declaring to an interviewer: 'Man, I'd even play South Africa as long as there wasn't any physical violence, and if they tried to get me in other ways I just wouldn't take much of it. Anyway, they can only call you names.' However, this did not prevent him joining an admittedly ill-fated all-black group, the Band of Gypsies, with Bill Cox and Buddy Miles. Like the Experience this group was dogged by internal disagreement and only played two concerts on New Year's Eve, 1969 and the end of January, 1970. The second was stopped in the middle by Hendrix who walked off, after telling the audience, 'I'm sorry but we just can't get it together.'

Jimi did not only have puzzling spells of moodiness but also wild outbursts of destructive rage that were as inexplicable as they were uncontrollable. His violence would sometimes be directed at people, often at inanimate objects. In 1967, on a tour of Sweden with the Experience, he had landed in jail for smashing everything in his hotel room to smithereens one night. The following day, when asked why he had done it, he replied: 'I can't remember. Are you sure it wasn't me dreaming?' Was it drink and drugs that were setting off these bouts of anger or was it Jimi working out pent-up frustration, giving vent to an inner turmoil so deep that he could not or did not wish to explain it? The anger was often impersonal, unrelated to any specific cause or occasion: 'One moment he would be quiet and gentle and the next moment he would smash up a room, no matter whose house he was in, and hit anyone who interfered, man or woman', Cathy Etchingham recalled. Jimi's much-publicized attacks on his guitar, which made people call him 'the wild man of pop' and which many thought were only a stage gimmick, were often prompted by real fury against his audience and himself. His last American concert, in his home town of Seattle ended in this way with Jimi shouting 'Fuck you! Fuck you!' at the audience. Jimi once described how he had felt the first time he set fire to his guitar on stage: 'Me and this guitar had been in spiritual conflict all evening anyway. I told it do one thing and it did another and I was really fed up with it. I wanted to kill it . . . I was ready to tear it apart with my bare hands.' Someone standing backstage in the wings recalled the chilling impression Jimi had made on her on another of these occasions: 'It was quite fantastic – he was livid with fury. I saw his face as he turned his back on the audience: he really hated that guitar . . . I couldn't bear to look at his face again when he was smashing the guitar. When he came back into the dressing-room he just sat down in silence.'

Fits of rage alternating with moody spells of withdrawal are not symptoms of contentment or adjustment. Jimi was not very articulate; he often complained about different aspects of his life, ranting against what he called 'pop slavery', the exhausting pace of his pop-star existence, his artistic frustrations or his problems with backers and his financial difficulties. From the break-up of the Experience in November 1968, Hendrix's professional life had been dogged by a series of failures and disagreements, some of his own making, some not. It has been suggested that some of the difficulties arose from Hendrix's relationship with his manager, a perennial problem for entertainers, but other events, like the concert in Denver broken up by police with tear gas, and the arrest for possession of heroin at Toronto (for which he was later acquitted)

cannot have done much for Jimi's peace of mind. Some have even claimed that Jimi *wasn't* depressed at the time of his death because he was beginning to see the light at the end of the tunnel in his struggle for artistic integrity, by a planned change to more 'sympathetic' management. Joe Boyd, who made a film about Hendrix, wasn't so sure. He felt that Hendrix would never have made the final break, even if he had lived: 'From what I know of Jimi's pattern throughout the rest of his life I don't think he was capable of doing this – he hated confrontations so much.' It may well be that Jimi's management difficulties were brought on by his own personality. He never satisfactorily explained why he was subject to those spells of deep gloom and uncontrollable rage. Others have suffered from the same sort of pressures from the music business but have managed not to go under. Hendrix's unpredictability would have made the handling of his affairs confusing and difficult for the most sensitive and patient manager, since Jimi himself seems to have been fundamentally unclear about what he wanted.

The Coroner declared an open verdict at the Inquest on his death, stating that 'the question why Hendrix took so many sleeping pills cannot be safely answered'. Jimi did not leave any concrete indication that he planned to kill himself, but the evidence does point to it being a deliberate act. On that last evening Monika Danneman caught Jimi pouring all her sleeping pills into his hand. When she tried to snatch the bottle away from him, he cunningly reassured her by explaining that he had only been counting the pills, but then he proceeded to swallow them once her back was turned. There is also no doubt that Jimi knew what he was doing at the time; he did not appear to be drugged or drunk. Jimi took nine Vesperax pills (the normal dose is one half, and it seems he apparently commonly took two), but had only drunk a little white wine very much earlier in the evening. The mystery lies in the time he took the pills – after apparently spending the evening quietly with Monika he inexplicably went out to see someone in the early hours of the morning. There was an alleged call for help on Chas Chandler's answering service timed at 1:30 a.m. Chandler returned the call at 10 a.m. that same morning to be answered by Jimi himself, who asked Chas to call back later. Within an hour he was dead. So what happened in the early hours of 18th Sepember which made Hendrix seek some sort of oblivion when he got home and take well over his normal dose of Vesperax? Was he really seeking to take his own life, or did he just want to escape temporarily? Some say it was drugs, others girl trouble, others management problems, others, simple despair. Whichever it was the result was death and it seemed an unsurprising end for someone who once said, 'Sadness is for when a baby is born into this heavy world – and joy should be exhibited at someone's death.'

JOPLIN

Janis was the greatest thing that ever happened to her hometown, Port Arthur, Texas, but Port Arthur did not know it at the time. Though some of its members would welcome her when she visited in early 1970, most thought Port Arthur could have managed well without its most famous daughter.

Janis was born in Port Arthur, on 19th January, 1943. Her father worked as supervisor in a Texaco oil refinery (Janis once referred to him as a secret intellectual), and she grew up in a neat, tree-shaded frame house just like millions of others in Middle America. As she remembers from her early years: 'I was a sensitive child. I had a lot of hurts and confusions. You know, it's hard when you're a kid to be different, you're full of things and you don't know what it's about . . .'

As often happens, it took other people a few years to realize that Janis was as different as she herself felt she was. It was not until her teens that the inhabitants of Port Arthur and her own family started noticing how special Janis was. Intelligent, articulate and endowed with a forceful personality, Janis's defence was to show scorn and dislike for the conventions and values of her extremely conservative environment. By the time she entered high school, her behaviour had become aggressively provocative. In an age when girls were still expected to be ladylike, she hung out with a group of disreputable boys, drank hard liquor and swore like a trooper, a habit she kept throughout her life and which later amused and pleased her fans as much as it had disgusted and horrified the inhabitants in Port Arthur.

By the time she was sixteen she had the reputation for being promiscuous, but this is doubtful. One of her closest friends at Port Arthur declared, 'She was probably more innocent than nine out of ten of the girls who graduated from high school with her.' Pretending to be loose was just another way of refusing to conform to the fifties' feminine image of chastity and daintiness. Another attack on the image was wearing jeans and shirts and keeping her hair long and stringy in the days of spit-curls and crinolines. In the America of the Eisenhower years, refusing to wear lipstick or to perm your hair would have made a girl ugly even if she had been truly beautiful, which Janis was not. As a schoolmate remembers Janis at high school: 'She dressed sloppy, she was overweight, didn't wear make-up, just refused to compromise.'

Janis' classmates were quick to retaliate against her nonconformism and her attack on their standards. They berated her, shunned her, nicknamed her 'pig' at school and tortured her with their taunts. Janis' best friend Karleen told Janis' biographer, Myra Friedman, that Janis would laugh, 'playing along to get along. But she'd go home and cry'. At the University of Texas in Austin which she attended for a year after graduating from high school, she was nominated 'Ugliest Man on Campus'. This was the last straw; she had to leave. Janis had pretended not to care, taking refuge in behaving and dressing even more obnoxiously, but those long years as an outcast and a pariah left her deeply scarred, for underneath her loud, aggressive attitude lay a sensitivity and a thirst for love and acceptance so deep that for a short period she even tried to remodel her image into one that would please Port Arthur. But it did not last and it was then that she began to drink. The permanent rejection she suffered throughout her teens created a sense of alienation and self-doubt within her which no amount of acceptance in later years would cure. It would make her success seem forever unreal to her. As she once said: 'When people would clap and tell me I was good, I used to wonder "Is that real, or is that something I've learned to do with my voice?" . . . I used to ask guys I was balling "Do I ball like I sing?" Is it really me? . . . that's what I wonder sometimes when I'm talking. Is this person that's talking me?'

What saved Janis from total isolation and despair during her teens was the discovery that she could sing. She always loved listening to Bessie Smith and Billie Holiday records, and one evening as a joke, she started doing an impersonation of Bessie Smith for the few friends she had; they were impressed. After that, she started singing in local bars and coffee houses, thus getting to meet people who were more congenial to her and who were also prepared to appreciate her the way she was. She continued singing in Austin, learned to accompany herself on an autoharp, and hung out at a converted filling station called Threadgill's where a

group of people who loved country and blues music congregated every week. Vocally, Janis could switch with ease from sweet, high-pitched bluegrass to the grainy, whisky-voiced blues style of Ma Rainey and Bessie Smith. But she was still shy about singing in public and did not yet contemplate becoming a professional singer. After she dropped out of college, she ended up in San Francisco in 1962. She managed to get on the dole after one short-lived job and fell in with the North Beach remnant of the great beatnik community celebrated by Jack Kerouac in the fifties. It was there, inevitably, that she discovered the drug scene. As she described herself later to David Dalton, she was at this period of her life 'wide-eyed, bright-eyed and bushy-tailed. Just a plain, overweight chick. I wanted something more than bowling alleys and drive-ins. I'd've fucked anything, taken anything . . . I did. I'd take it, suck it, lick it, smoke it, shoot it, drop it, fall in love with it . . . "Hey man, what is it? I'll try it. How do you do it? Do you suck it? No? You swallow it? I'll swallow it".'

At that pace, Janis could not last long either physically or mentally. She took to speed, taking Methedrine intravenously, and by 1965 when she limped back to Port Arthur, her weight had dropped to 88 pounds. Yet during her stay in San Francisco she had acquired enough of a reputation as a casual singer of brilliance and emotional power for a group of musicians called Big Brother and the Holding Company to decide when they were looking for a singer that they wanted her. Despite Janis' fear of the drug scene which had almost killed her the previous year, she was back on the West Coast playing with Big Brother in 1966. After hesitant beginnings, the group took off. The following year, in June 1967, they played at the Monterey pop festival, and Janis caused a sensation. After Monterey, she was a hit, she was a star. The recordings she made for Columbia with Big Brother, then with her own Kozmic Blues Band and with Full Tilt Boogie made her world-

famous. Janis' music was soul blues to begin with – she idolized Otis Redding and was shattered when he was killed. But she synthesized soul and rock in a unique way. It is generally agreed that her best recorded work is on the second Big Brother album *Cheap Thrills*, and on the posthumous album *Pearl* that she was working on when she died. Her reputation while she was alive was largely based on her electrifying live performances, seen by thousands on her widely acclaimed concert tours in America, Canada and Europe.

So why did Janis die of an overdose of heroin all alone one night on 4th October, 1970, in the Los Angeles motel where she was living during her last recording session? She was twenty-seven and she had known only three and a half years of stardom. Kris Kristofferson, the film actor and singer, wrote an epitaph for her:

'Just say she was someone
So far from home
Whose life was so lonesome
She died all alone

*synthesized soul and rock in a unique way. Right:
'I mean you may not end up happy but I'm fucked
if I'm not going to try.'*

Who dreamed pretty dreams
That never came true
Lord, why was she born
So black and blue?'

Kristofferson had been one of Janis' more regular boyfriends and had known her over a number of years, but even he could not discover why had Janis been born 'so black and blue'. In his epitaph, he takes it for granted that she was lonesome, though in her position she could have had anyone she wanted for company; he says that her dreams never came true, though her career was the ultimate dream-come-true of any rock musician. Perhaps, as Kristofferson rightly suggests, either you are born black and blue or you are not, and no amount of friends, money or fame will stop you feeling lonely and depressed.

Janis died only three weeks after Jimi Hendrix. When she heard of Jimi's death, she said 'Goddam it, he beat me to it!' She made several more references to Jimi which seem to indicate that she was thinking of killing herself in the near future, wondering if her own death would get much publicity and if she could afford to die in the same year as another famous pop star. Yet, as with Hendrix, many of her friends refused to believe Janis' death was anything but a tragic accident. Sure, a lot of them had thought Janis might also die young; all of them had witnessed her blind urges towards self-destruction and had warned her that she would have to pay her dues if she carried on boozing and taking dope they way she did. Yet there was so much life in Janis, so much vitality! It was obvious to everyone that there was a part of her which wanted to live and to be happy. Her life-loving impulse seemed to counterbalance her darker sides. She herself had once declared: 'I mean, you may not end up happy but I'm fucked if I'm not going to try.'

Janis was full of paradoxes: miserable and joyous, weak but strong, self-pitying yet gutsy. She sang songs that were full of despair, yet the sadness in them was not a whining sort of misery. It was tough, an almost aggressive kind of unhappiness which made you feel the singer was going through a bad patch but was planning to pull out of it soon. She was a fighter. She fought for the right to be herself back in Port Arthur, even when the pressures to conform were well-nigh intolerable. She fought for artistic recognition and the right to sing the way she felt she ought to sing, and she won. She fought against the ugly-girl label and turned herself into a fashion-setter. She fought down the horrified stares of the squares who couldn't believe what they saw when she turned up in airports and hotel lobbies decked in her outrageous clothes. She fought the police

to keep this up had to reinforce it with external stimuli. Nothing and nobody could slake her thirst for love and approval. She refused to believe the evidence, public and private, of the affection and admiration she was able to arouse. 'Tell me I'm good! Tell me you love me!' she would scream at her concerts. But even when the audience roared back its approval as it always did, Janis never quite believed in it. 'Nobody wants an old chick like me', she would moan about her fans, 'they want young girls. They'll *forget* me. They don't love me, man, *nobody* loves me!'

Janis' difficulty in finding love even where love existed was not confined to her relationship with her audiences. In her private life her insecurity was even worse. She was never satisfied by the emotional responses of her lovers. She was bisexual, but though her friendships with women meant a lot to her, she really craved a lasting heterosexual relationship. If she never settled down with any one person, it wasn't because there was a shortage of good men to fall in love with. Several of her lovers were fine people who were prepared to care for her in a genuine and permanent way. Some of them, like Kristofferson and Country Joe McDonald, were well-known and successful in their own right and could not be accused of wanting to latch on to Janis just because she was famous. When asked what he had liked about Janis, Country Joe gave an answer which could have satisfied any woman: 'I thought she had a nice sense of humour, and she was smart, and I thought she was pretty. She was just very interesting and we seemed to get along very well.'

During the closing years of her life, Janis had two serious affairs, the first with a young man called David Niehaus, whom she met on a vacation in Brazil, the second with a wealthy New Yorker called Seth Morgan. Neither of these men were connected with the world of rock music. Both wanted to save Janis from that world since it was obviously destroying her. They tried to take her out of the limelight, at least temporarily. But Janis would have none of it. Though she complained that men wanted to bed her because she was Janis Joplin, her fragile ego also needed to feel that they were interested in her because she was a famous singer. In love with the idea of love being total acceptance and total reassurance, Janis sought being wanted in many arms. But love as *she* conceived of it still eluded her and this added to her despair. As she once said: 'Blues are easy to write. Just a lonely woman's song. Looking for one good man. And I've been looking. It's an eternal blues. About me trying to act tough and nobody noticed I wasn't . . . I'm so lonely oh-oh-ooh, and some guy'll come along and say, "Well, it gives you more soul". Fuuuuck you, man! I DON'T WANT ANY MORE!'

In one way fame harmed Janis, but not in the way it had harmed Brian Jones. Janis could stand the pressures of celebrity, she was resilient and bouncy enough

in Florida, getting herself two indictments for vulgar and indecent language at a concert at Tampa, in November 1968. She fought her addiction to drugs when it got too heavy and managed to kick the habit several times. When she was 'clean' she would speak of her spells as a junkie with disgust: 'I looked grey, I looked defeated.'

Janis did not like defeat. When her hang-ups got too bad, she finally gave in to her manager Albert Grossman's demand that she get help from a doctor, Doctor Rothschild. Even he found her 'unsettling'. 'Just intellectually bordering on brilliant' was his assessment: 'She really could think circles around most people. One of her problems was that intellectually she was so advanced and her emotions were childlike and uncontrollable.' She bought a house outside San Francisco so that she could feel she had a home to go to after the long rootless spells on the road. She got a dog to have something to love. She looked for the right man and never stopped hoping that she would find him in the end. She even toyed with the idea of giving up her career if the pace grew too killing. But Janis was ambitious – there was never really any question of her giving up. She wanted to be a star but could not cope with what being a star really meant. She revelled in the wild girl image that fans and media jointly demanded of her, but

for that, but what she could not bear was the personal disappointment: success had come and it had not cured her feelings of unhappiness or her gnawing self-doubts. As her biographer and friend, Myra Friedman, said: 'Janis had sought too many answers in fame, had looked to its glories for something so unattainable and mighty that adulation by contrast was a meagre gift.' What was it that Janis had been looking for and why did it destroy her not to find it? As with all depressives, she could always supply reasons. But as Myra Friedman underlines, 'her infinitely genuine suffering was often attached to people, events, worries, fears that had little or nothing to do with the real source of her hell'. Janis would be plunged into gloom by a fancied slight, a minor problem, a detail of organization. Depression is illogical and so we cast about for reasons which will make it seem more rational and better-founded than it really is. Janis was prone to bouts of hysterical self-pity during which she blamed any and everything for her unhappiness, yet when she had her head together and was being reflective, she knew her troubles lay within herself rather than in her external circumstances. Often she would say: 'I'm the victim of my insides', or 'I think too much'. The closest she ever got to conveying how she really felt about life and why it hurt too much was when she explained a song she had written called Kozmic Blues (it had to be spelt like that, she insisted: 'It's too down and lonely a trip to be taken seriously, it has to be a Crumb cartoon'): 'I remember when I was a kid they always told me "Oh, you're unhappy now because you're going through adolescence, as soon as you get to be a grown up everything's going to be cool". I really believed that, you know. Or, as soon as you grow up and meet the right man, or – if I could get laid, if only I could get a little bread together, everything will be all right. And then, one day, I finally realized that it ain't all right and it ain't never gonna be all right, there's always something wrong . . . I'm a middle-class white chick from a family that would love to send me to college and I didn't wanna. I had a job – I didn't dig it. I had a car, I didn't dig it, I had it easy . . . and then one day I realized in a flash, that it wasn't an up-hill incline that one day was going to be all right, it was your whole life. You'd never touch that fucking carrot, man, and that's what the Kozmic Blues are, 'cause you ain't never going to get it.' The cosmic despair of feeling that she would never find things all right, the realization that privilege and fortune would never fill the void of her depression, would never cure her hopelessness, explain why Janis grew unhappier as time passed, when, logically, she should have grown happier: each of her public triumphs must have seemed like a bitter private defeat since it could only confirm her suspicion that even glory did not bring the satisfaction and fulfilment she was looking for.

So Janis was black and blue, but did she want to die? There was a permanent tug of war between the life and the death force going on inside her. On the one hand, she had scoffed: 'I've had interviewers come up to me and say, "Tell me, Janis, do you think you'll die a young and unhappy death?" Well, I say, "I hope, not man!"' On the other hand, shortly before her death, she tried to reassure her publicist that she was not on drugs by saying 'You don't have to worry about the junk. I'll never touch it again – not unless I do it deliberately to go out.' Yet all the evidence points to an upturn in Janis' fortunes just before her death. The latest recording session was going well and she was planning to marry Seth Morgan – she had put through a call to City Hall on the afternoon of the day she died, but because it was a Saturday there had been nobody in the offices to take it. At the same time, she *was* back on heroin after a break of nearly six months. The reasons for this are hazy. In her strange, obtuse way perhaps Janis could not allow herself the luxury of straightening out. She met up with her old addict friends during her period of abstinence, in particular Peggy Caserta helped Janis return to the drug. But Janis was alone in her room at the Landmark Hotel when she took the fatal fix. It could not really be called an overdose – the actual quantity of heroin was no greater than she had normally been used to, but the dose was pure and concentrated. Her tolerance was low after the 'clean' period during the previous summer and her body finally gave in. The coroner also reported signs of alcohol in the blood, and her liver was affected by long-term heavy drinking.

Janis Joplin's remains were cremated according to the terms of her will. The ashes were scattered from an aeroplane along the California coast which had been the scene of so many of her triumphs and despairs.

MORRISON

Jim Morrison was probably one of the most truly intellectual of the sixties rock casualties, and in his way as much of a quintessential victim as Hendrix, Joplin and Jones. Jim was lead singer of the Doors, known for the profundity of the songs they sang, songs composed mostly by Morrison himself. For Morrison not only had an exciting stage presence and a voice so strong it could make itself heard without a mike during a riot; he was also a gifted poet, 'a man of words', as he described himself and one of the most creative talents of the great rock decade.

James Douglas Morrison was born in Florida on 8th December, 1943. His father, a high-ranking naval officer, brought his children up strictly and Jim's later revolt would often express extreme hostility to his family and the traditional values it stood for. The Morrisons moved to Virginia in the late fifties and Jim was sent to high school in Washington, D.C. Not as much of an exhibitionist as Janis Joplin, whom he resembled in many other respects, Jim demonstrated his rebelliousness in quiet ways at first, refusing to join in the activities that were expected of 'good' American teenagers of that period: sports, clubs, etc. He went to college in Florida for a time, then moved to California in 1964 to study film-making at U.C.L.A. His fascination with films would never leave him for it was tied up with another of his enduring preoccupations – death; as he once said, 'The attraction of the cinema lies in the fear of death. Movies create a kind of false eternity.' During his subsequent career as a rock star, Jim made several short films of a surrealist sort which resembled the poetic imagery of his poems and songs. One was called *Hiway*; another, *The Unknown Soldier*, illustrated one of his anti-war songs, while yet another, *Feast of Friends,* was a free-form documentary of the life of a pop group on the road.

While he was still at U.C.L.A., Jim became friendly with Ray Manzarek, a fellow student who was paying his way through college by singing in a jazz group at weekends. Though Morrison had already started writing song-poems, he had never thought of singing them himself, let alone of becoming a professional rock singer. But the idea took shape under the influence of Manzarek. Morrison and Manzarek had both drifted inevitably into the mid-sixties beach culture of the Californian coast where acid (LSD) was the favoured stimulant. Manzarek remembered the first time Jim recited *Moonlight Drive* to him, and how in the euphoria of the moment it seemed there was no reason why they should not get a group together and 'make a million dollars'. By 1965, Jim and Ray had formed their group, calling themselves the Doors with Jim as lead singer-composer, Ray Manzarek as organist, Robbie Krieger as guitarist and John Densmore as drummer. The intellectual, sometimes mystical

nature of Morrison's songs was reflected in his choice of the group's name: it was drawn from a line by William Blake: 'There are things that are known and things that are unknown; in between are doors.'

The new group was quickly recognized as being one of the most original and dynamic in the States, largely because of the quality of Morrison's songs and his impact as a performer. They were snapped up by Jac Holzman of Elektra after he saw them at the Whisky-A-Go-Go in L.A. and their first album *The Doors* was one of the best-selling of the era. The single that came from it, *Light My Fire,* became, as Lester Bangs has said, 'the anthem of a generation'. After it reached number one in the summer of 1967 (that special 'summer of love', high spot of the decadent decade), the Doors' concert fee shot up from $750 a night to $7000 for two. At first Jim Morrison was rather withdrawn on stage, but as his audiences grew larger and he allowed his pent-up emotions to surface, his manner grew wild and uninhibited. His performances eventually became a form of rock theatre, his singing punctuated by screams and harangues to the public. One of his early tricks was to throw flaming lighters into the audience during *Light My Fire*; for three years audiences would light thousands of matches during subsequent performances. Another trick was the use of pauses during

performances – sometimes between songs, sometimes between lines, sometimes between syllables. Morrison claimed that these silences could draw out the hostility and bring the group (or himself) and the audience closer together.

The contents and the delivery of Jim Morrison songs were perfectly representative of the spirit of their times – they were anti-social, despairing, charged with sex and violence, full of hatred for restrictions and hope for a new order of things where the young at least would run their lives in the way they chose. The anti-militaristic spirit of many Morrison songs reflected the feeling of the Vietnam war years as well as the singer's private score against his career officer father. When he sang 'They got the guns but we got the numbers' (in *Five to One*), Morrison was in many ways ahead of his time, for this has been the theme of many songs of the latter seventies. Perhaps this accounts in part for his lasting cult following.

In another of his songs, *When the Music's Over*, Jim would end with the words, 'We want the world, and we want it NOW!', unleashing storms of approval on the part of his young audiences that often ended in near riots. The shock value of his songs was nowhere more apparent than in his song *The End*, where the nihilism, the conflict of generations and obsession with sex and death, the ambivalence of his relationship with his parents, all found total expression in the final stanza, where the character in the songs tells his father that he wants to kill him, and ends 'Mother, I want to . . . ' At this point Morrison would let out an ear-splitting shriek which shattered whatever composure his listeners still

had. Such violence, coupled with the fact that he was extraordinarily handsome in a grim yet angelic way, made Morrison seem like an irresistible force, an anti-prophet for the young and a lethal enemy for all previously established values.

Inevitably, Morrison and the Doors became a focus for attack and victimization by the conventional forces of society. Nothing illustrates better how wide was the gap between them in the mid-sixties than a television company's attempt to censor one line of *Light My Fire* which the Doors were due to perform live on the Ed Sullivan Show. The line objected to was inoffensive: 'Baby, we can't get much higher.' Morrison agreed to sing an alternative – and did so in rehearsal – but characteristically he reverted to the original when the show went out later. Doors' performances were frequently cancelled at the last minute through the efforts of local do-gooders (parallels can be drawn with the concerts given by so-called Punk bands in Britain in the mid-seventies) and audiences were regularly clubbed by policemen during concerts. Jim Morrison was himself arrested while actually giving a performance, once in New Haven, Connecticut in 1967, for verbally attacking the police and 'incitement to riot', and a second time in Miami in 1969 for supposedly exposing himself on

at the Isle of Wight Festival, August 1970. He
died the following year. Below centre: Morrison's
grave in the Pere Lachaise Cemetery, France.

stage. This was too much for Morrison, within whom the forces of destruction had already been long at work. A heavy user of LSD and an alcoholic who could get drunk at any time of the day or night on whatever happened to be handy, Morrison seemed hell bent on killing himself young. He once described his drinking as 'not suicide but slow capitulation'. What he was capitulating to was his own need to block out the sense of frustration, despair and growing paranoia. Like Brian Jones, whose withdrawal in his last year made him a liability to the Rolling Stones, Jim Morrison's drinking made him a drag on the rest of the Doors. His performances became debauched parodies of his former sensual act, and he grew fat and pathetic. Audiences became sceptical, the Doors' credibility declined (although the album *L.A. Woman*, 1971, was a *tour de force* which showed much of the old spark), and the 'indecent exposure' event put the lid on it. Morrison decided to end

his rock star existence and to retire to France for good. Perhaps it was his last bid for life, though his official reason was that he felt too old (at twenty-seven) to go on being a rock star, and that anyway he was too alienated from the other members of his group to continue with them.

Jim went to Paris with his wife Pamela, whom he had married in 1970. His relationship with Pamela was enigmatic – in spite of the inevitable groupies and the fact that he sometimes treated her in a humiliating, domineering way, she had managed to stay with him for some years, and he had dedicated the song *Queen of the Highway* (from *Morrison Hotel*, 1970) to her. But Paris was not the answer. After several months of heavy drinking and bouts of depression, he died suddenly in the summer of 1971, while taking a hot bath in the middle of the night. His death was attributed to heart failure and he was buried at the Père Lachaise cemetery, but as there was no autopsy, the exact cause of his death can never be established. There are some who even claim that he did not die at all, as always happens in the aftermath of shock when someone young and famous dies. The mystery has been heightened since the only reliable witness, Pamela, herself died of a heroin overdose in 1974. Jim Morrison, the high priest of open, all-out war between the generations, died before he could become a member of the older generation he hated. Although all his family were alive, he had once filled in the section under 'Family' in a biographical questionnaire with the laconic word 'Deceased'. No member of his family attended his funeral.

153

By the early seventies four of the greatest rock stars of the sixties had dropped out for good; their deaths were like the closing statement of what had been an exciting but excessive decade. Yet Brian Jones, Jimi Hendrix, Janis Joplin and Jim Morrison were not the last to go, as they had not been the first. Other martyrs of the drug scene, of the negative aspects of fame and the devastating life-style of the successful rock musician, would succeed them, proving that they were not so much children of their times as children of their circumstances. They were followed by an apparently never-ending list of casualties. As Keith Richard recalls, 'Rock'n'roll has a very high fatality rate. It used to be plane crashes. Then it was wicked management. More recently it has been drug overdoses. A lotta my best friends, like Gram Parsons, went that way and Gram was supposed to have cleaned up when he died . . . I don't particularly blame junk for some of their deaths – simply because they would have done it on something else. Like Brian [Jones] always used to say "I'll not make it much beyond 30", and Gram Parsons also had that kind of thing about it.' Keith Richards' friend Gram Parsons had been the foremost exponent of the fusion of country music and rock, especially through his contribution to the Byrds' seminal album, *Sweetheart of the Rodeo* (1968). Born in 1946, at Winterhaven, Florida, Gram was brought up in New Orleans after the early death of his father. He ran away from home in his early teens and was already singing semi-professionally at age 16. After his time with the Byrds he formed the Flying Burrito Brothers, but left in 1970, went to Europe with Keith and finally made two solo albums, which incidentally set Emmylou Harris on her way to stardom. But, as Richards has indicated, Parsons also had a self-destructive streak and died of an overdose on 19th September, 1973. A

bizarre story surrounds his funeral: in response to the alleged wish of Parsons himself, his friend and road manager, Phil Kaufman, hijacked the body and burnt it at the Joshua Tree National Monument.

Two years earlier Duane Allman was killed in a motor-cycle accident on 29th October, 1971 in Macon, Georgia, aged 24. As lead guitarist of the Allman Brothers Band, Duane had gained a world reputation as a player of bottle-neck slide guitar, reaching its apotheosis in the electrifying duet with Eric Clapton in *Layla,* title track of Clapton's famous 'Derek and The Dominoes' album. Then there was Cass Elliott, Mama Cass, the big, plump bitch goddess who sang sweetly and raucously along with the Mamas and the Papas, one of the top folk-rock groups of the sixties. Everyone

154

loved Mama Cass, and her success was as huge as her build, until the group split up and its four members went their separate way. Afterwards, Mama Cass tried to make it on her own. Whether she would have got by or not will never be known, for she died while on tour, in much the same circumstances as Hendrix, alone in her hotel room in London on 29th July, 1974. She was only thirty-one. Two years later, another talented and successful rock musician died in his sleep: Paul Kossoff, the lead guitarist of the British group, Free. Kossoff was one of the more promising post-sixties musicians. But although his career did not take off until the seventies, he had inherited the sixties' rock world tradition of hard, self-destructive living and indiscriminate drug-taking. In the autumn of 1975, Paul suffered a near fatal heart attack as a result of his addiction. On doctor's orders, he reduced his work load and was given the all clear for a U.K. tour in April, 1976. But his system still could not cope. He died, from a second heart attack, on 19th March, 1976, on a transatlantic flight.

The following year, the English rock star Marc Bolan was killed in a car crash, while being driven home by his girl friend, Gloria Jones. Bolan had been the blue-eyed, baby-faced East Londoner and teen idol known to millions as lead singer to T.Rex, the archetypal glitter rock group of the early seventies. But as the teenybopper audience switched its loyalties to newcomers like David Cassidy and Donny Osmond, Bolan, like Jim Morrison, deteriorated into inactivity and drink. He was in the process of making a low key come-back when the accident happened a few days before his thirtieth birthday, in 1977. His legend was consolidated by the accident – many rock contemporaries, including David Bowie, attended the funeral and the cemetery overflowed with floral tributes, including a swan constructed entirely from white flowers in remembrance of his most famous

hit song, *Ride a White Swan*.

More recently there was Keith Moon, who died of an overdose of the drug Heminevrin on September 7th, 1978. Keith had been drummer with The Who since the group's foundation in 1962. The Who – whose famous hits included one of the best ever songs about rebellious youth, *My Generation* – were famous for their aggressive and destructive live performances.

Keith Moon was known as the wild man of rock – he once drove a car into a swimming pool – but he was also a dedicated musician with an aggressive drumming style admired by fellow-professionals in the music business. He was also liked personally. His bizarre and

erratic behaviour was considered by close friends to be a cover for his basic uncertainty in the frantic world of rock. Yet it was he who was acknowledged as the one group member who kept in closest touch with the fans, and it seems likely that he will be remembererd where others will not.

Like many other sixties groups, The Who had a period of quiet in the middle seventies, although they still had a large and loyal body of fans, especially since the huge success of the rock opera, *Tommy*. In the year preceding Moon's death, The Who were effecting not so much a come-back as a renewed period of activity, including a hit album and a film, *The Kids Are Alright*. Their popularity was never greater. The Who's music seemed to be as immediate in 1978 as it had been in 1964.

Yet it did not come as a particular surprise to those who were close to Keith Moon that he should take more than thirty sedative tablets, even though he had seemed his usual cheerful self at a party given by Paul McCartney the previous evening, prior to a screening of the film *The Buddy Holly Story*. Pete Townshend said 'It's something we have been expecting for twenty years, but when it happens you just can't take it in. Keith has always appeared so close to blowing himself up in the past that we've become used to living with the feeling'. The sedatives he took were apparently prescribed by his doctor because of tension and sleeplessness but they can also be used as an aid to withdrawal from alcoholism. It was well known that Moon had had a serious drinking problem and was trying to overcome it.

The future of The Who now seems in doubt. Pete Townshend said 'Keith was an irreplaceable member of what was really a family group'. Yet in spite of the security of that family, like so many others, Keith seems to have followed the famous line in The Who's own song, *My Generation*: 'Hope I die before I get old.'

These dead rock stars are representatives of a law which has applied to many artists and performers. Danny Fields, a publicist for Elektra and Atlantic records, had something interesting to say about the connection between the use and abuse of drugs and the 'star' personality. He said it about Janis Joplin, but it applies equally well to all the entertainers who have destroyed themselves via drink, hard drugs or barbiturates: 'I just don't know where the person ends and the drugs begin. Drugs become part of your chemistry. You see, this thing about stars is that they sail out and they don't think of danger, because if they did they wouldn't be where they are, they wouldn't have done what they did. They've got this quality that you and I don't have, like, let it all fly, whammo, full sail, full tilt, like Janis. They're always dancing on the edge, and that's why they're so great. At that point where everyone else would stop or hesitate and couldn't make it, they just go right out on the tight wire.'

It is all too likely that the traits which go into the personality of a star performer (and without which even great talent would not suffice), must include a love of risk which, in its constructive phase, enables the individual to project himself dazzlingly, where a more timorous type could not. But in a destructive phase, the mechanism of caution and self-preservation will not function properly. The individual literally does not know when to stop. Or even if he knows and wishes to stop, he does not have the means of acting on his knowledge. It is a genius for excess which made his star shine so vividly in the first place, but it can all too easily kill him in the end.

7. ORIENTAL SUPERMAN

In the sixties almost no one outside South-East Asia or the Chinese colonies dotted around the world had ever seen a Chinese movie. But by the early seventies, kung fu films had become an established part of international mass culture, as ubiquitous as Mickey Mouse or Batman. In many capitals of the world there is now a special heading for kung fu movies in lists of films currently showing in the city's cinemas. Much of this transformation can be credited to the influence of one Chinese film actor and martial artist, Bruce Lee. As Raymond Chow, one of Hong Kong's top film producers, was to say: 'You have no idea of the trouble we ran into when we first started to push our films overseas. The reaction was: "What? A Chinese film?" Then Bruce Lee changed all that.'

In the world of movie entertainment, the star system is still all-important: statistics show that most people choose to see a film because of its star. What Chinese **LEE** movies had lacked before Bruce Lee was a superstar who would give international audiences the impetus to go and discover what Chinese action films were like. Even though Lee's career was so brief, his successors and imitators have cashed in on the vogue for Oriental films which Lee set off, and which is still far from over. Yet as Raymond Chow points out, the Hong Kong film boom was due not only to Lee but also to the economic crisis from which the other film centres around the world were suffering. There was a potential market ready to be tapped which had grown weary of the traditional action film: thrillers, cowboy and gangster movies had been around for half a century and it was getting harder all the time to do anything which had not been done before. As a result, new offerings either tended to seem stale or self-conscious, as directors desperately looked for new angles, unexplored psychological or socio-political dimensions.

Interest in Oriental philosophies and disciplines of every sort was a feature of the sixties scenes and an offshoot of the hippie culture. Growing numbers of people in the West were intrigued by, and often eager to imitate, Oriental ways of thinking, eating and dressing. By the late sixties, this curiosity about the 'mysterious East' had much to do with the West's awareness of the war in Vietnam and the emergence of Red China from behind its bamboo curtain. Interest reached its peak with the admission of Red China into the United Nations and Nixon's visit to Peking. All these events,

widely covered in the mass media, helped to prepare the world scene for Chinese action films in general and for Bruce Lee in particular.

Who was Bruce Lee? To begin with, he was an American citizen by birth. He was born on 27th November, 1940 in San Francisco, in the year of the Dragon, at the hour of the Dragon, hence his nickname, 'the little Dragon'. His mother was Eurasian and his father was a well-known actor in the Cantonese opera which happened to be touring the United States at the time of Bruce's birth. The family returned to Hong Kong when Lee was an infant and he grew up in a crowded Hong Kong apartment which housed sixteen people, plus nine dogs and a variety of other pets. The little boy spent much of his time playing in the streets and, by his own admission, became something of a hoodlum by the time he was in his teens. Bruce was a difficult, lively child who liked nothing more than getting into fights and nothing less than going to school. Despite his laziness, he was capable of prodigious concentration when he read about subjects which interested him and he would be an avid book collector all his life. He had inherited his father's talent for acting and made his film debut at age six in a movie called *The Beginning of a Boy*. By the time he was eighteen, he had acted in eighteen films.

Quick-tempered and never one to back down in an argument, living in a rowdy world of urban schoolboy gangs, young Lee soon discovered the need for an effective method of self-defence. He began to study the martial arts at thirteen and it rapidly became his ruling passion in life. His small size and slight physique were handicaps that his stubborn nature gave him the determination to overcome. Even when he was fully grown, Lee never weighed over 130 lbs and he was only 5 ft 4 in tall. Studying the martial arts taught him self-discipline and control while it increased his chances of coming out the victor in his street encounters. The fact that Lee had come to take an interest in self defence for the purely practical purpose of winning fights influenced his whole approach to the subject; he would never lose sight of the chief goal, which was to win, long after kung fu had ceased to be just a means to get out of a scrape and had become his art form, his way of earning a livelihood and his whole philosophy of life. The personal theories and techniques he developed were conditioned by the consideration of what actually worked, what would give a fighter the edge over his opponent,

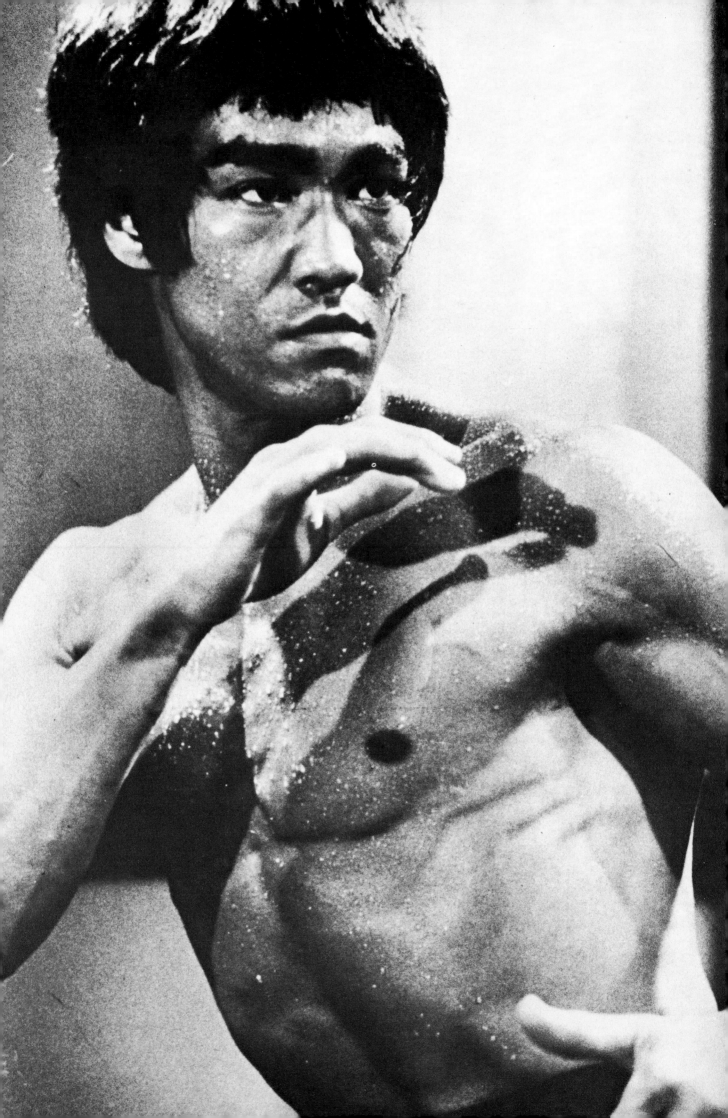

and he discarded whatever was merely traditional or looked good. Bruce Lee was a winner and an innovator by temperament. He had no patience for the elaborate ritual and the poses adopted in many fighting styles which had little to do with the primary aim of achieving victory and which in his view could actually get in the way of doing so. 'Ninety per cent of Oriental self-defence is baloney,' he declared in his outspoken way to a Seattle interviewer when Americans began to take an interest in his ideas on the topic. After he had opened a martial arts school in the United States, he was asked which of the highly prized coloured belts he possessed to indicate his degree of skill in karate; he replied irreverently: 'I don't have any belt whatsoever. . . . Unless you can really do it, that belt doesn't mean anything. I think it might be useful to hold up your pants but that's about it.' Such non-conformist views were to make him highly unpopular with the purists, especially since he amply proved the superiority of his technique in contests with traditional fighters; but Lee's whole attitude appealed to the younger, more dynamic elements in the world of the martial arts and especially to Occidentals interested in the subject.

Lee went to live in the United States when he was eighteen and attended college in Seattle, Washington; there he opened his first martial arts school to earn a living while he finished his studies. His whole outlook and his ideas on kung fu became increasingly Westernized with an ever growing emphasis on effectiveness and a typically American wariness of tradition and convention. 'Efficiency is what works,' he was fond of repeating to his pupils. He also said: 'To express your-

self freely, you must eliminate everything old in yourself. If you follow classical methods, you understand routines and traditions but you no longer understand yourself.' As he perfected his own special method, known as *jeet kune do,* he did not hesitate to incorporate American boxing and wrestling tricks into its various moves, as well as any elements in the hundreds of different Oriental fighting styles which proved to be really effective. *Jeet kune do* means 'the way of the intercepting fist' and concentrates on upsetting the opponent's centre of gravity; it is more aggressive than many other self-defence methods where the primary purpose is to block an assailant's blows rather than to deal them. For one thing, *jeet kune do* relies on the element of surprise, which often means attacking first. It requires considerable muscular strength and previous training; Lee was the first to advise women not to count too heavily on their skill when faced with a powerful would-be aggressor. His laconic advice to them was: 'Hit 'em in the groin . . . and run like hell!' *Jeet kune do* also demands tremendous agility, speed of movement and a lightning swift perception of what moves the other fellow is planning to make, which means remaining calm enough to observe him closely however violent the encounter. This combination of physical and mental quickness, which requires perfect body control and highly developed reflexes, was exactly what Bruce Lee possessed. His leg kicks were so quick that

he was sometimes called 'the man with three legs'; many
of his fighting scenes had to be shot in slow motion for
television, his gestures would have been all but invisible
on the screen otherwise.

Always an ardent proselytizer and a wholehearted
believer in the value of what he was doing, Lee tried to
infuse his new American friends with his own enthusiasm for *jeet kune do*. Before long he married one of
the pupils at his first school, a young American co-ed
named Linda Emery. Linda has described how it was
right after tossing her effortlessly onto a mat several
feet away during a lesson, that Bruce asked her to go
out with him for the first time! In 1964, the newly
weds moved to Los Angeles and Lee immediately opened
another school which quickly attracted Hollywood personalities such as Steve McQueen and James Coburn.
It was inevitable that Lee should begin to dream of
demonstrating his fighting and acting skills on the
screen, given his high degree of ambition, his contact
with stars, his past career as a child actor and his presence in the world's leading movie capital. His extro-
verted, lively nature, his by now amazing abilities as a
fighter and his photogenic appearance gave him high
hopes. His goal soon was to become no less than the
first Chinese international superstar. After seeing Lee
in action at a karate tournament, the producer of the
Batman television series signed him up for the part of
Kato, the sauve black-masked chauffeur in a new detec-
tive series called *The Green Hornet*. Over the next few
years, Lee appeared in other successful television productions like *Longstreet* and *Marlowe*. By the late sixties, he was well-known and the Hollywood wealthies
who flocked to his school were ready to pay him up to
$250 an hour for his private tuition in *jeet kune do*.
Yet Lee was unhappy about his career: he was still not
a major film star and there weren't enough roles available in the United States for a would-be Oriental superman. He therefore decided to try his luck in Hong
Kong, where the *Green Hornet* series had turned him
into a hero.

When Lee returned to Hong Kong in 1970, having
signed a $10,000 contract with a major studio called
Golden Harvest Productions, the Asian film market
was ripe for him. Hong Kong and Taiwan were producing about two hundred films annually and a sizeable
proportion of these were action films, or kung fu movies
as they came to be known. The fact that 3 to 5 per
cent of these films' budgets went into buying gallons
of brightly coloured artificial blood gives some idea
of their general content. The majority of Chinese films
were hastily shot and slipshod by Hollywood standards:
directors thought nothing of using different props and
extras from one day to the next for scenes which were
supposed to remain the same. The level of acting was
not often high and even more often stilted and melo-
dramatic. Continuity and motivation were sacrificed

to the public's insatiable demand for endless fighting
scenes. Yet these movies, sometimes called 'chop
sockies' or 'Won ton westerns' in the film trade, were
well suited to Lee's special abilities; they catered to an
audience of connoisseurs in the martial arts who would
recognize his natural superiority as a fighter; the in-
ordinately long fight sequences were usually lovingly
shot and visually beautiful. In these films, Bruce Lee
would be given ample opportunity to display all he was
capable of without running the risk that a producer
would cut his fighting scenes on the grounds that he
was not well-known enough, that audiences would get
bored, or that the rest of the plot would suffer if the
fights went on for too long.

The first thing Lee did after signing his contract
was to go and see as many Chinese action films as he
could. He was unimpressed; his characteristically outspoken view was that they were all 'terrible. . . . Everybody always fighting the same way, and fighting all the
time. They were unrealistic, always a lot of overacting'.
His equally characteristic reaction was to believe that
he would change all that. By contract he had the right
to say how his films should be made and especially how
the fights were to be orchestrated. The result was immediately apparent in his first film, *The Big Boss* (1971).
Throughout the first half of this film, there was no
fighting at all, which served to build up the tension and
to whet the audience's appetite for the climactic fight
sequences in the second half. In this film, Lee displayed
to the full his inventiveness and stylishness as a fighter

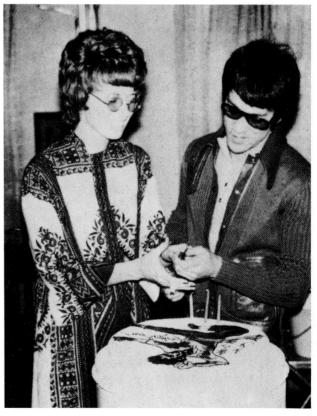

as well as his box-office potential as an actor.

But Lee's avowed ambition was to be a world star. Each of his subsequent films was a bid for the international market. The theme of his next film, *Fist of Fury* (1972), was still specifically Asiatic with its tale of rivalry between martial schools and its chauvinistic story of virtuous Chinese defeating wicked Japanese. The film turned Lee into a hero and a champion of his race, but it also confirmed his vibrant screen presence and revealed him to be even more charismatic and powerful than in his earlier endeavour. It was obvious by now that the key to Lee's success lay in his 'wholeness' as a performer. Lee himself summed it up admirably to an interviewer: 'I never depend solely on my fighting skill to fulfil any of my fighting roles . . . I believe it is more my personality and the expression of my body and myself. I am not acting. I am just doing my thing. . . . See, I have this intensity in me so that the audience believes in what I do because I believe in what I do.' *The Big Boss* and *Fist of Fury* were released in many parts of the globe, and slowly but surely, began to win over non-Asian audiences who had never seen a Chinese action film before.

Lee was at last becoming an international star. He decided to write, produce and direct his third picture himself, as well as starring in it and staging all the fight sequences. Though many have been critical of *Way of The Dragon* (1972) and though Lee himself later claimed it had been aimed at the Asian market, the film was full of innovations which seemed designed to have the broadest appeal: it was the first Hong Kong production ever shot on location in Europe. Each fight was rigorously different from all the others and many of the actors, including the fighters, were European or American. The film contained a lot of comedy and the character Lee played was often intentionally funny and endearing rather than loftily heroic and humourless like most action film heroes. Lee's last completed film,

Enter the Dragon (1973) went even further to widen the appeal of kung fu films. *Enter the Dragon* was a co-production between Warner Brothers and Lee's own company. It brought together no less than two hundred martial artists from around the world and had a typically James Bond-style plot in which Lee played a government agent sent out to crack a vice and drug ring run from an island fortress by an all powerful and sinister Doctor No figure. The film's combination of slick fantasy, beautiful girls and trick photography was far closer to Western-type escapist adventure films than to traditional Chinese action movies. As Lee had hoped, the film was a smash hit in the United States, which was the little dragon's revenge against Hollywood's relative neglect of his talents during his years there. But, ironically, Lee did not live long enough to see his dream come true. He died suddenly in July 1973 just before the film was released.

This abrupt end astounded his fans. In fact, there had been a warning signal but it had been hushed up. Two and a half months earlier, Lee had fainted during the dubbing of *Enter The Dragon*; he had been rushed to hospital suffering from a high fever and strange convulsions. The doctors diagnosed a swelling of the brain and possible malfunction of the kidneys though they could find no specific disease to account for it. This first attack had been alarming, but it was over rapidly and a few weeks later Lee flew to Los Angeles to consult

believes in what I do, because I believe in what I do.' Right: Bruce Lee's death left several of his projects incomplete; on location for The Game of Death.

with a team of medical experts; the physicians reassured him and declared that he had the body of an eighteen-year-old boy. Lee turned to Hong Kong in high spirits, telling people he planned to live to be a hundred. Less than two months later he was dead, aged only thirty-two.

On the fatal day, Lee had gone with his producer, Raymond Chow, to the home of an actress called Betty Ting-Pei who was to have a role in his next film, *The Game of Death*. Lee complained of a headache and took a tablet of Equagesic to cure it. Chow had to leave and Lee retired to Betty's room to rest before the three of them went out to dinner as they had planned. When Chow returned, Lee was sleeping soundly, far too soundly. Chow was unable to wake him up, even by slapping his face, and a doctor was summoned. But Lee was in a coma and all attempts to revive him failed, both there and at the hospital to which he was taken.

When any superstar dies there is always a public reaction of shock and disbelief; wild rumours are fanned by the lurid press, the testimonials of purported friends and the wishful thinking of incredulous fans. It is hard for many, impossible for some, to accept the idea that a young and apparently healthy person can die of natural causes or can be killed in a truly 'accidental' accident. It was persistently claimed that Valentino had been shot by a rival or by the Mafia, that Carole Lombard's plane had been sabotaged, that James Dean had not really

died in his car accident, that Marilyn Monroe had not committed suicide but had been liquidated for mysterious political reasons because of her acquaintance with the Kennedy brothers. In the case of Bruce Lee, death by natural causes seemed even more improbable and there were not one but any number of theories concerning the 'real' way he had died. After all, Lee had been the ultimate exponent of physical fitness, a symbol of perfect health and vitality. His whole life had been dedicated to the principle of keeping his body in superb shape. He ran up to eight miles every day, spent at least two hours doing his daily exercises and often continued exercising even while he read, watched television or ate a meal! He neither smoked nor drank alcohol and even refused to touch coffee for health reasons. A health food fanatic, he lived off fresh fruit and vegetable juices, vitamins and high-protein, body-building drinks. Apart from the occasional puff at a cannabis 'joint', he shunned any practice which might impair his magnificent state of fitness. So when the pathologists who did a post-mortem on Lee testified that his death had probably been caused by an acute allergic reaction to the tablet of Equagesic (a variety of aspirin) he had taken to cure his headache, this verdict was generally deemed preposterous, though it was confirmed by an eminent professor who was flown over from England specially and who had performed no less than ninety thousand autopsies during his career. The fittest, healthiest and toughest of Oriental supermen killed by an aspirin? How could those who looked upon Bruce Lee as a sort

163

師傅千古

菩創載

苦練

of demi-god or at least as someone endowed with extra-human powers accept such a conclusion?

The 'real' story behind Lee's disappearance had to be more mysterious, exotic, frightening and even a bit magical, as befits a mythical hero's end. The inscrutable East lends itself perfectly to strange theories, and the world of martial sects even better: these societies have the reputation of possessing jealousy-guarded secret practices and are known for their implacable determination to wreak revenge on traitors and enemies of their cause.

The theory that it was a hostile martial sect which killed Lee by some fiendish method is based on the assumption that Lee had offended them by criticizing the most revered martial theories on many occasions. Worse, he had given away some of their cherished secrets; he had taught Westerners tricks and techniques of unarmed self-defence which Orientals had originally devised to get the better of taller, more muscular Caucasian enemies in hand to hand combat. But there were other, more mundane theories about who Lee's murderers were. Had Lee been killed by one of the powerful Hong Kong Triad gangs because he refused to pay it protection money?

For those who could not buy the theory of the undetectable murder there remained the theory that Bruce Lee was not dead at all. Despite the fact that Bruce Lee had two funerals, one in Hong Kong and one in Seattle, that there are a number of photographs of him lying in his coffin, that his doctors, his wife and his mother did not doubt the identity of his corpse for a moment, a book called *Bruce Lee Lives?* was published recently claiming that Lee is alive and well, and helping the Hong Kong anti-drug squad to defeat the opium trade under a new name and identity.

Even setting aside any of the wilder theories mentioned above, the circumstances of Bruce Lee's sudden death *are* mysterious insofar as the autopsy revealed no traces of disease and all his vital organs were found to be healthy. Perhaps this mystery will never be cleared up to everyone's satisfaction, but we can at least try to analyze the seeming mystery of his fantastic success both during his lifetime and since his death. Lee's name has been linked to those of many great men. Some have claimed that he was almost as big a figure for most Chinese as Mao Tse Tung. Others have declared that watching Lee in action was comparable to seeing Nijinsky dancing or Beethoven playing the piano. Others still have said in all seriousness that Lee was 'the Edison, Einstein and Leonardo da Vinci of the martial arts'. After such comparisons, what one author wrote about the dead Bruce Lee sounds modest: 'He's a cult. He's a legend not only with movie fans but among karate and experts in the martial arts from Timbuctoo to Vladivostock: a James Dean, Marilyn Monroe, Rudolph Valentino, Muhammad Ali figures all rolled into one.' Undoubtedly, Lee must have been a prodigy in the field of martial arts to earn such respect from people, many of whom were experts in the subject, such as Chuck Morris who played opposite Lee in *The Way of the Dragon* and who is the seven times US and world karate champion.

Yet Lee's undisputed mastery as a fighter would not have been sufficient (not outside South-East Asia, at any rate) to turn him into the box-office star he became. It required something more than that and Lee possessed it. By all accounts his off-stage personality was exceptionally charismatic, though quite a few of those who met him were put off by his arrogance and his tendency to show off. Lee had the star's quality of being able to project his personality in a convincing and exciting way. In films, his tremendous vitality and animal magnetism came across not only in his superb fighting scenes but in his straight scenes as well. Though not handsome in the conventional manner of a screen 'heart-throb', he had considerable charm; his fey expression and blunt, urchin-like features appealed to non-Asiatic audiences as well as to Asian ones. Lee was a natural actor with an inborn gift for appearing genuinely spontaneous. The American director of *Enter the Dragon* had been startled to discover the ease with which Lee could create a believable well-rounded character. He could probably have made a name for himself as a film actor even if he had not been a martial

artist, but it was the combination of these two talents which made him true mythic material.

Bruce Lee was, first and foremost, a superman to whom a lot of ordinary mortals could relate. He was 'the man beyond us yet ourselves' that countless young have-nots round the world still identify with: they too are often country boys adrift in a big, dangerous and cruel megalopolis. Lee's simple message of legitimate revenge and taking the law into one's own hands cannot fail to please those who have a grudge against society or against their bosses for keeping them down, and who feel that the law is not interested in their problems because they lack socio-economic power. In his films, Lee starts out as nothing: poor, uneducated, despised, discriminated against. Through sheer determination, the power of his self-trained muscles and of his self-taught fighting skill, he comes out the victor against those in a better position: the stronger, taller, wealthier, more privileged than he. If the bulk of Lee's fans round the world tends to be uneducated and economically deprived it is not necessarily because the cultural level of the kung fu genre is low but more because it represents, in the most primal and obvious way possible, the ultimate physical and moral triumph of the unsung urban underdog.

8. IDOLS OF FLESH & BLOOD

'I will be dead in five years' time, but while I am here I will travel many highways and I will, of necessity, die at a time when my message of love, peace and freedom can be shared with people all over the world.' These words could be taken for a quotation from the New Testament but, in fact, they are supposed to have been spoken by Jimi Hendrix to his friend and apostle, Curtis Knight. All the people in this book have at some stage and by some people been virtually deified, and treated with the deference accorded to martyrs. The terms 'idol', 'demi-god', 'god' and 'goddess' have often been used in connection with stars during this century. We say that we 'worship' and 'adore' them without giving a thought to the religious connotation of these terms. We do not even stop to consider the paradox which Edgar Morin underlined when he wrote: 'The camera appeared destined to reproduce reality; instead it began to manufacture dreams. It seemed that the screen would reflect human beings as if in a mirror; instead it gave the twentieth century its demi-gods, the stars.'

If living human beings can be deified, it is even easier to attribute extrahuman qualities and powers to dead ones; the dead are not there to refute their own sanctity by actions and words bearing the obvious stamp of humanity. Some of the world's major religions have evolved from the worship of dead ancestors, as have the great majority of primitive faiths. In one of the tribes studied by the anthropologist Margaret Mead, all individuals automatically became household gods when they died, no matter how commonplace they had been in their lifetime; each had the power to communicate with the living and to interfere with the activities of those he had left behind. It is therefore perfectly natural that, in an age when belief in traditional religions is declining, so many people look for new forms of spiritual consolation such as the cult of dead stars, a belief in their messianic qualities and in the possibility of communicating with their spirits.

Traditionally, human beings believed to possess divine or extra-human attributes had special powers. While they lived, they exerted a particular fascination on all those who came near them. They had a message for humanity or had a mission to accomplish during their brief sojourn on earth. It was often their destiny to die as martyrs to the harshness or lack of understanding of their fellow men. After they died, they were usually able to enter into spiritual communication with the living or even sometimes be reincarnated in another

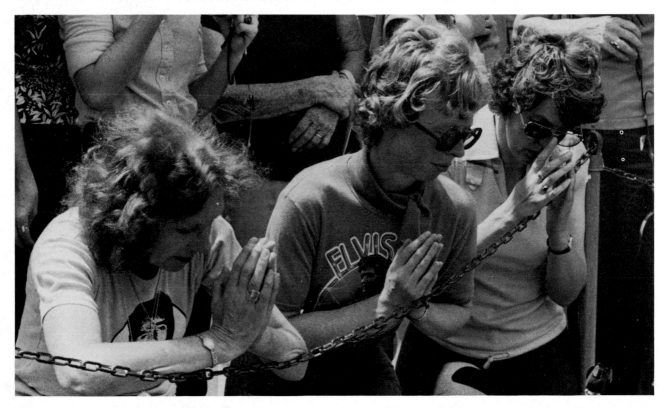

shape. Many of the people in this book have been endowed with some or all of these traits. Of nearly all of them it was said that they had a premonition of their own deaths. At thirty-one, Valentino would lament the fact to Pola Negri that he had not met her sooner, since it was already 'too late'; when she saw him off as he left for New York, where he was to die shortly after, she recalls: 'I don't know how I knew, but I knew . . . I would never see him again.' Pola Negri has often rather unfairly been depicted as hysterical and histrionic, but the more sober friends of Carole Lombard, Gérard Philipe, James Dean, Buddy Holly, Jimi Hendrix

or Janis Joplin were to insist that each of these stars in turn had predicted his own death, sometimes with uncanny accuracy as to the actual date. The extremely sensible Linda Lee was to write after her husband Bruce's death that he '. . . realized unconsciously . . . that it was urgent to do great things in the shortest possible time' and that Bruce was convinced during the last months of his life that little time remained to him, though he had never been healthier.

The prescience of oncoming death is often coupled with a sense of mission, at least so it is claimed by the friends and admirers of the dead. According to Curtis Knight, Jimi Hendrix spoke on many occasions 'about his being sent here from another world as a messenger and about how we must suffer and reach a certain spiritual height before we would be allowed a permanent place in the spiritual world'. A similar sense of mission to be accomplished on earth has been attributed to Brian Jones by his friend, Al Aronowitz, who reported a vision Brian had once at dawn as he was leaving a night-club: 'It was as if the heavens had called upon him to look up and see the face of a goddess angel telling him to work for human good. It was a vision that guided him for as long as I knew him and yet he always kept cursing himself as one who used his power for evil.'

A charismatic quality of the sort attributed to Jesus has frequently been reported of stars who died young. There is much of the apostle Peter in the way a Japanese friend of Bruce Lee described his first encounter with the dead star: 'It was like an electric force which attracted you to him. He was half my age yet I found myself ready to follow him like some superhuman being.' James Coburn, who was also a friend of Lee's, reasonably pointed out that, if in a group, 'Bruce only had to say three words for everybody to make a circle around him', then surely it was 'the same magnetism, the same appeal which his film audiences feel'. As the Catholic mystics knew, it is difficult to dissociate animal magnetism from spiritual attraction: we do not know what Jesus really looked like but he and all the most popular saints have been depicted throughout the ages as handsome human beings.

In the same way that the conquistadores built their churches on the site of Aztec and Inca temples, using the very stones of the buildings they were replacing, so we encounter Christian symbols in the mythology of those who died young which lend them an aura of sanctity and spiritual authenticity. The most famous example is that of James Dean in *Giant* standing as though crucified to the gun slung over his shoulders. The image of the real Gérard Philipe has merged with those of him playing an angel or the Christ-like Prince Myshkin. Hendrix up on the stage with his musicians has been likened to 'Christ between his two thieves', while Janis Joplin's wild hair and grief-filled face have earned her comparisons to Mary Magdalene at the foot of the cross.

The belief that it is possible to enter into spiritual contact with the dead turned Natacha Rambova's posthumous memoirs of Valentino into a best-seller. Rudy's spirit dictated reassuring descriptions of his new existence 'Up There' to his ex-wife, telling her how 'my friends have taken me to see the theatres. They are enormous and very, very beautiful. They are built of thought substance which comes from true poets' ideals'. Up there, there was 'so much love I have never seen before. Everyone seems to beam with it'. Caruso, the singer Rudy had admired, had become his special friend Up There: 'He does not look just as he used to either. He looks more like his music sounded.' But some men thought that Rudy's spirit would be better off on earth, for a number actually wrote to Pola Negri informing her she had to marry them, since her dead lover's soul had entered their bodies and expected to be reunited with her. In later years, others would fancy that they were the spiritual reincarnation of James Dean, just as a posthumous account supposedly dictated by Jimmy to someone he had never met would sell half a million copies. Another tract 'dictated' to a medium by the dead Dean from 'Somewhere Beyond Eden', began with the words: 'Dear Friends on Earth: From somewhere beyond the eons of eternity from the hours of time, I am writing to my living friends on earth.'

There has to be a natural scepticism to most of these claims. The people who have made them on behalf of dead stars range from heartbroken wives to hard-bitten opportunists, from staunch, lifelong friends of the deceased to people who had never met them, from in-

dividual admirers who genuinely believed the claims they were making, to charlatans who asked for nothing less than to get rich on the proceeds, like medieval sellers of indulgences or phoney holy relics. What is intriguing is the readiness of millions to believe or at least to try and believe in the continued spiritual existence of their demi-gods, to build and then worship at altars consecrated to the dead stars and to acquire at exorbitant prices relics of their passage on earth. We have already seen how the shrines built to the memories of the dead, the pilgrimages to their places of birth or to their graves all contribute to the perpetuation of their memories. What the cults have revealed is the underlying yearning for faith in something or someone which has not been satisfied by twentieth century ideology. Reverence for the memory of dead stars, the passionate tenderness people feel for them, betrays the gap left in the lives of so many now that they no longer cherish household saints or pray before domestic icons. The New Age of Enlightenment is still a long way off: erode religious faith and people will create new religions to fill the vacuum. Like pilgrimages of old, fans still trek south to view Buddy Holly's grave at Lubbock, conveniently situated close to the highway. Some of the fan club reunions around a dead star's memories have been church masses in all but name only. In the cult headquarters of the James Dean Death Club, there were 'forty or fifty candles on a shelf that were lighted each week when the cultists gathered to play wild Wagnerian music and talk in low, exalted tones about James Dean, the non-conformist'. To some degree all these dead heroes can be looked upon as the saints and martyrs of a new religion.

Many people who readily concede that a dead cult figure holds a very special place in their hearts will nevertheless deny that they harbour religious feelings for their chosen idol. They feel that his superhuman qualities reside only in his exceptional talent or looks. Those who refute the claim that the stars who died young possessed quasi-divine qualities, may wonder if they possessed any other traits which might provide clues to their success both as stars during their lifetime and as cult figures after their death. Of course they were all photogenic, all famous, all rich and all outstanding in their individual fields, but if we look more closely we can discover further, less obvious similarities. Though it is impossible to generalize about so many very different individuals, belonging to different sexes, cultures, generations, and art forms, we find certain qualities recurring that can roughly be classified as sexuality, immaturity and innovation.

To begin with, most dead cult figures in the world of popular entertainment were intensely sexual beings, many of whom gave out sufficient erotic vibrations to attract both sexes. A fair proportion of the dead stars appealed emotionally to the non-homosexual members of their own sex because they had a way of combining seductive masculine and feminine traits: a good example of this diffused sexual appeal was the comment one girl fan made about Janis Joplin: that unlike many other women singers, when Janis sang a love song she made all the girls in the audience feel included and never seemed to be addressing herself solely to the males who were present. Rudolph Valentino, Gérard Philipe, James Dean, Montgomery Clift, Brian Jones, Janis Joplin, Jim Morrison and Elvis Presley possessed sufficient sexual ambivalence to arouse strong emotional reactions in both sexes, while stars like Carole Lombard and Bruce Lee were at least as popular with members of their own sex as with members of the opposite one.

The strong sexual appeal projected on screen and stage by the dead star was often the projection of a powerful sex-drive or an irresistible need to attract in real life. The force of this drive was tangible in their screen or stage persona, and they themselves acknowledged that they saw in their audiences symbolic sexual partners on whom to practice their arts of seduction. As Janis Joplin once said after a concert: 'I've just made love to five thousand people . . . the only love I have is with the audience.' Jimi Hendrix was even more explicit: 'Man, when I stepped on that stage in my black military jacket with the gold braids, with all those foxes in the audiences, I decided I would make love to all of them with my guitar, and I know that they had to feel it, because I felt it.' It was chiefly the public's response to their vibrant sexual appeal which made many of them stars, whatever their other talents. Going to a Joplin concert has been described as 'Like getting laid lovingly and well', while someone else has said that what Hendrix 'does to a guitar could get him arrested for assault'; Jimi's performances, like those of Presley or Brian Jones, 'made the girls practically come out of their dresses'. Jim Morrison captured the underlying sexual hysteria of pop music when he defined rock musicians in the following terms: 'Erotic politicians, that's what we are. We're interested in everything about revolt, disorder and *all* activity that appears to have no meaning.'

It may be argued that all the stars of popular entertainment are sex-symbols and that most of them probably lead intense sex lives, but the sexuality of those who died young is often bound up in their continuing success after death. The early death of a star leaves a sense of sexual loss and frustration: his fans must now remain irremediably unfulfilled in their desire for physical possession. Yet the death of a star can also console them for non-possession: alive, the star seemed even further from reach than dead, since he or she had their own love affairs. Dead, the star becomes common property and no longer belongs to a real-life sweetheart, husband or wife. He becomes a sort of demon lover, an incubus who visits the dream life of all who care to con-

Many stars project an image of eternal
adolescence. The vulnerable little-girl-lost look of
Marilyn Monroe in The Seven-Year Itch (below);
the misunderstood, helpless look of James Dean
in East of Eden (below left); the dreamy schoolboy

jure his spirit. The nostalgia we feel for those dead stars is tinged with the regret felt for the deprivation of imagined erotic satisfaction which might have been experienced with them had we been fortunate enough to meet them while they were still alive.

The people in this book were young when they died, but they were not children. Yet in our memories their image is often one of eternal adolescence. Nearly all of them projected a kind of immaturity associated with the teenage years and even with childhood: the whispery, little-girl-lost sound of Marilyn Monroe's voice as she sang 'My heart belongs to daddy'; the babyish hiccup in a Buddy Holly song; the misunderstood little-boy look in James Dean's eyes; the dreamy schoolboy manner of Gérard Philipe (who was still being offered adolescent roles in his mid-thirties); the juvenile, 'I'm gonna show the world' defiance of Elvis Presley or Eddie Cochran. Even the less obvious candidates for an image of eternal adolescence had a childish streak in their make-up which played on adult sympathies. Bruce Lee's tousled hair and cute facial expressions often gave him an urchin-like appeal, and as Verina Glaessner put it, 'His image swings constantly between that of the little boy who upset the apple-cart and the bone-hard body fanatic.' There is something of the ragamuffin in John Garfield's film portrayals which goes right back to the hoodlum youth he never really outgrew. Even Valentino's suave façade did not conceal something childish which brought out the incestuous mother in older women; as Pola Negri said of him 'He appealed more to the maternal than to the amorous. He was rather like a vulnerable child all decked out in fancy clothes'. The same was often said of Janis Joplin's whorish finery which many thought made her look like a funny little girl who had put on her mother's lipstick and was now wobbling crazily in oversized high-heeled

shoes. The otherwise adult Carole Lombard was notorious for her tomboy practical jokes. Even the sophisticated Jean Harlow was called 'the Baby' by everyone who knew her, so childish was her manner, so infantlike her dimples and her light-blue eyes despite the sexiness and the knowing smile.

Children and young adolescents are vulnerable, a quality we cherish because it touches on our sensibilities, brings out our better instincts of protectiveness and indulgence. When a star dies young, people focus on the childish, immature aspects of his personality which make his death seem even more touching; this immaturity plucks the heartstrings to breaking point and can also help to explain the often irrational circumstances of the star's death. For it is well-known that children are irresponsible and foolhardy, that they are not sufficiently well-equipped to face the pressures and obligations of adult living. When a child died in the nineteenth century, it was commonly said that he or she 'was too good for this world'. Perhaps we wish to believe that when a star dies young he was too good

manner of Gérard Philipe (below right). Right:
Hysterical fans in the 70s mobbing Marc Bolan
on stage.

for this world because, in many respects, he was too
innocent and spiritually pure to survive. Brian Jones,
who died in the house at Pooh Corner, is only one
example of the many who have remained Christopher
Robins and Peter Pans forever in the collective memory
of the fans who mourn them.

Stars who died young represented something new
in their field of entertainment. Originality can do a lot
to guarantee the survival of an image; innovators themselves, or perfect representatives of a new trend, many
of the people discussed in this book liberated their audiences from previous, constricting stereotypes. It was
through them that the fans discovered personal needs
for freedom or fantasy which had not yet been catered
to by anyone else. We have seen how Valentino taught
women that they were entitled to expect sexual finesse
and polish on the part of their heroes or real-life partners, that these attributes were not to be confined to
cads. We have seen how Jean Harlow, Carole Lombard
and Marilyn Monroe gave men the hope that a good
woman could also be a sexy one, that they would not
be forced to opt either for the practised but unprincipled seductress or the virtuous but asexual heroine.
John Garfield, Montgomery Clift, James Dean and

Cybulski (and in certain respects Gérard Philipe) all
proved in their individual ways that neurosis could be
fascinating to women, that weakness, non-aggression
or faltering were not necessarily unmanly; this discovery must have reassured many a growing boy who
recognized himself far better in these new-style heroes
than in the super-virile men who usually paraded on the
screen. The way the new rock musicians threw themselves about on the stage and off it, the way they
screamed out their pain or their *joie de vivre*, urged
young people to indulge in their need to let it all hang
out, to give bodily expression to their innermost
emotions. Many people recall with enthusiasm the
sense of liberation they experienced when they first discovered their favourite cult hero, the very real influence
he or she had on their lives. They feel he helped them to
find out what they were really like; he kicked the way
out of old ruts and opened up new trails for them to
follow. Thus many a dead star is remembered with
gratitude as well as with reverence or affection by his
admirers, who feel they owe something of their true
identity to his influence.

Millions of words have been written about the people
discussed in this book but little has ever been said about
those who put them there in the first place: the devotees,
the fans of both living and dead stars. In the same way
that we can wonder what dead cult heroes had in common, so we can also ask ourselves what their fans have
in common. The cinema has existed for over seven
decades and the star system for at least five, but one
fact has remained constant and it holds as true for the
pop music scene as for the movies: you don't have to

173

be very young to be a *bona fide* fan, but it helps. The worshippers of dead stars do not escape this rule. This does not mean that there aren't a lot of older fans around, but they are in a minority. What older fans there are tend to have started 'cultivating' a particular star in their early youth and have remained hooked out of loyalty to their idol and to the memory of their own youth which he or she symbolized: a lot of middle-aged male fans of James Dean and Elvis Presley fall into this category. Traditionally a large proportion of older female fans are supposed to be housewives with too much time on their hands and too few satisfactions in their personal relationships to fulfil their real need for excitement and romance. These are the truly 'fanatical' fans, not those who merely profess to admire this or that star, but the ones who spend much or all their free time reading about them and joining fan clubs dedicated to their idols.

There is a good reason why the majority of fans are young people on the brink of adult life. A survey made by UNESCO a few years ago underlined that the cinema and its stars exert a particularly powerful pull on adolescents everywhere and have been, since the media has existed, important means of discovering adult pleasures like love, sex and adventure at an age when many grown-up activities are denied them. This was just as true for the parents and grandparents of today's adolescents: back in 1935, twenty-eight million American kids under twenty-one went to the cinema at least once a week. In a relatively small country like England, five million people under eighteen saw more than one film a week in 1939. Because of television teenagers may actually be going to cinemas less frequently now than they did then, but they are seeing four or five full-length feature films a week on their TV set. Most of the psychiatrists quoted in the UNESCO survey spoke at great length about the need children have at puberty to discover new 'role models' as they outgrow the notion that their own parents are ideal personality types; at this stage the effect of movies is probably not so much to provide the young with entertainment as to supply them with a variety of new models with whom to identify. This was confirmed by a survey which revealed that 60 per cent of boys between twelve and fourteen often play at pretending to be their favourite film hero, while a majority of girls admit that they enjoy reconstituting the love scenes they see on the screen. The survey went on to demonstrate that the most avid adolescent film-goers are children who are unhappy at home and who feel misunderstood by their elders or by their peers, which accounts for the perennial popularity of the brooding or delinquent adolescent theme in the cinema. For obvious reasons youngsters at 'the awkward age' prefer to dream at the pictures and to turn favourite stars into fantasy companions than to face the more difficult task of coping with real

situations and people. The need to escape from real-life challenges at an age when one is particularly prone to feelings of inadequacy is just as much part of the attraction of the pop music world as that of the movies. For every pretty, self-assured little groupie who is bold enough to try and batter down the bedroom door of her favourite rock musician, there are fifty lonely girls with complexes about their looks who feel too unsure of themselves even to try and charm the boy next door.

None of this means that, to be a true fan, one has to be maladjusted, unattractive or unhappy. Almost everyone in this century, at least in the West or in Western-influenced societies, is, has been or will be a fan at some stage of life. Young people become fans not only for negative reasons like insecurity or escapism, but for very positive reasons as well such as enthusiasm, idealism, a dislike of mediocrity and the wish to identify with what seems most worthy of esteem. It is not easy

to disassociate the fans of living stars from the cultists of dead ones; the two forms of worship overlap. One can easily worship the living Marlon Brando along with the dead James Dean, or the living Brigitte Bardot side by side with the dead Marilyn Monroe. Or else one can have been a fanatic admirer of Jimi Hendrix while he was alive and an equally dedicated admirer of his memory after he died. The cult of a dead star takes on morbid overtones if the worship is exclusive and quasi-obsessional, where the very fact that the star is dead and the actual circumstances of his demise become the all-important element in the cult. Older women like the ones who grieved for Valentino become cultists in this sense. The tragic fact of their idol's early death fed their propensity for melancholia and depression, for it reflected their own sense of wasted life and missed opportunities.

But the great majority of fans are healthy and happy

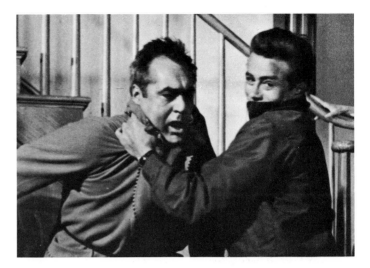

enough. Their devotion to the famous, alive or dead, does not get in the way of their private lives; it can often enhance their everyday existence by bringing them pleasure, providing them with a hobby and catering to their love of beauty. It can help them give expression to their tastes and their individuality, depending on which stars they choose to 'cultivate', 'collect' and 'desire ardently'.

The specific cult of dead stars can be beneficial to young people in one important way. In an age where the subject of death is suppressed as far as possible, venerating the memory of someone who died young is almost the only outlet for thinking about the whole idea of dying and for trying to come to terms with grief, mourning and the sense of injustice most people feel about death's inevitability. In the old days, religious and social conventions as well as the higher rate of mortality made people all too familiar with death. Relatives died at home, there were wakes, special days to remember the dead, feasts, ceremonies and prayers, visits to cemeteries and other observancies which forced individuals to acknowledge from childhood the fact that they were mortal, that they had to learn to control their fear of death as best they could and indulge in their sense of loss when someone they loved died, so that the healing process could begin. Today, it is often exclusively through descriptions of the deaths of celebrities that young people are able to satisfy what can really be called a healthy curiosity in death. While it is often taboo now to discuss and recall the memory of dead friends or relatives in too much detail, it is permissible and satisfying to cultivate the memory of dead stars, to evoke their merits, to cherish the recollection of who they were and what they did. This too is healthy and reassuring: to deny despite all the evidence that one's hero is really dead may be immature and escapist, but to write 'Che Lives' on a windowpane is an act of faith and hope. It is a way of proclaiming that the admired individual may be physically dead but that what he stood for, his unique personality and his achievements live on in the human spirit and in the memories of all those who loved him.

175

'Che Lives'? Guevara wasn't a film or rock star, so why should he have his fans, his cult, his face paraded on the T-shirts of young people, his poster hanging up side by side with that of Elvis Presley or Jimi Hendrix? Like all well-known political figures, Che had many admirers as well as many detractors during his lifetime. His books on political and military strategy, his high-ranking position in the Cuban government, his many official visits to foreign lands and his fiery speeches at the United Nations had all served to make him an international figure during the late fifties and early sixties, though his image was austere rather than romantic during those years. Who then could have predicted that Che would become, after his death, a cult hero on a par with James Dean, his image shorn of most of its political and ideological significance?

The revolution in mass media communication and entertainment has blurred the distinction between real life and the image of 'life' as depicted on the screem. Thus James Dean's image has become inextricably confused with that of the fictional characters he portrayed; conversely, Che Guevara's adventurous existence and heroic death have become a kind of fictional movie drama in which he plays the starring role in the story of his own life.

In this respect, the more attractive and appealing political figures of this century have become media heroes in their own right, subjected to the laws of the media, and as likely as popular entertainers to become cult heroes and saints if they happen to die prematurely and in tragic circumstances, not an unusual occurrence in the restless world of politics. The spread of world-wide mass communication systems has meant that individual political heroes can exist both within national boundaries and beyond them in a way that would have been unthinkable only a few generations ago. Whereas previously political ideas have been disseminated widely through the printed word, it used to take decades before their real influence could be felt by the ordinary citizen. Now, television and radio have changed all that – when

Mao Tse Tung spoke to foreign newsmen in Peking, the whole world knew what he said within hours; when John F. Kennedy was running for the presidency he used television in an unprecedented way as part of his campaign strategy; and when Che Guevara was killed in Bolivia his death was instrumental in sparking off a wave of student insurrection in most capitals of Europe, whose repercussions are still being felt. Personality has come to be as important in politics today as policy, and many politicians have become popular heroes as a result of media exposure.

Che Guevara is probably the best example of this recent phenomenon. He is also the prime example of the deification and worship of a dead political figure by those who know little about his true political or ideological affiliations. The Argentinian revolutionary was Fidel Castro's right hand man during the struggle to oust Batista from Cuba between 1956 and 1958. During the following years, Che dedicated himself to the creation of a true economic and social revolution in Cuba. In 1965 he disappeared, surfacing in 1967 as leader of the unsuccessful attempt to trigger a revolution in Bolivia, part of Guevara's visionary plan to unite Latin America. In his dispatch from the mountains of Bolivia he wrote 'The armed struggle is going on in Guatemala, Colombia, Venezuela and Bolivia; the first uprisings are cropping up in Brazil. Almost all the countries of this continent are ready for a type of struggle that, in order to achieve victory, cannot be content with anything less than establishing a government of socialist tendencies'. He wrote inspiringly of a future in which wars of liberation would flourish throughout the world. Within months Che had been captured and after an unsuccessful attempt by Bolivian officers to interrogate him, he was shot in October 1967, aged only thirty-nine.

Che Guevara is one of the most ardently admired and celebrated myth figures of the twentieth century. The young in particular have adopted his name, face and legend as symbols of courage, self-abnegation and faith in the possibility of change. Though Che certainly pos-

*John F. Kennedy and his brother
Robert possessed a natural glamour, an uncontrived panache. Below centre: John F. Kennedy
campaigning for the presidency in 1960. He was
assassinated in Dallas, Texas, 1963. Bottom*

sessed these qualities to a high degree, how many of his
youthful admirers know today what he really believed,
wrote and achieved in his lifetime? How much is his
deification due to his handsome face and romantic
death rather than to his highly original Marxist thinking
or his key involvement in the building of the new Cuban
state? Those who sport Che's face on their T-shirts or
name boutiques after him are unlikely to have read his
books about applied guerilla warfare and the international strategy of wars of liberation. All they have
retained of Che's image is a hazy notion of a young
man who rebelled against the establishment, who went
off on his own to save the world and who was willing
to get killed in the process. It is a pity because Che
Guevara himself was particularly interested in the ideological formation of young people; his most original
work, *Man and Socialism in Cuba*, was about the challenge of educating and shaping 'Twenty-First Century
Man'. Although, as Andrew Sinclair writes, Che's death
'provided the Marxists with their first saint', even the
urban middle-class student 'revolutionaries' of 1968,
who used Che as their personal symbol, had miscon-
ceived Che's ideal of a *rural* revolt that would sweep
away corruption in the urban environment. Now, ten
years and more from his death, his image has been pro-
cessed further still. He would have been bitterly disappointed by the sort of cult to his memory which has
existed since his death for that cult is mostly empty of
significance and is unlikely to convert anyone to Marxist
ideals or a heroic lifestyle.

John Fitzgerald Kennedy, the youngest man ever to
be elected president of the United States, also belongs
to the ranks of those political figures who have achieved
superstar status more by virtue of their good looks and
their tragic early deaths than for what they actually did
or who they really were. Not only was Jack Kennedy
handsome; as anyone can attest who has ever seen him
on film, television or in the flesh, Kennedy had charisma.
The way he moved, expressed himself, smiled and
gesticulated, instantly attracted attention, interest and
usually sympathy in quite a few people who were
opposed to his beliefs. He and his brother Robert possessed a natural glamour, an uncontrived panache which
many a film or musical star would have envied. Part of
this glamour came from the special position the
Kennedy family as a whole had held in American society
for a generation. If the United States were a monarchy,
the Kennedy family would be among the highest
echelons of the aristocratic hierarchy, and in John F.
Kennedy would have almost achieved royal status. Even
today the Kennedy name makes headlines, either
directly through the actions of Senator Edward Kennedy
and his family, or the sons and daughters of his dead
brothers, or indirectly, as the press follow those who
married into the family, especially John Kennedy's
widow Jackie who went on to marry the equally legen-

centre: His younger brother Robert, who was assassinated in similar circumstances to President Kennedy in Los Angeles, 1968, is besieged by fans on leaving the Acropolis, Washington.

dary Greek oil magnate Aristotle Onassis.

It can be said of John Kennedy as it can of Che Guevara that he had a number of solid achievements to his credit which should have entitled him to youth-hero status irrespective of his good looks or his early death from an assassin's bullet. Yet, like Che, JFK's actions performed during his lifetime have all but been obscured by the image of his photogenic face and his martyr's death. Who now recalls that JFK, aged only twenty-nine when he was elected to Congress, tirelessly fought for advanced welfare policies and progressive social and economic legislation? Who remembers that he was a Second World War hero or that he wrote a book which won the Pulitzer prize? The brilliance and beauty of his later destiny, the horror of his murder, the pathos of his funeral, the grief of his lovely wife and young children, as viewed on TV by millions the world over, almost made us forget that it was Kennedy who first openly criticized French colonial policy during the Algerian war, and that it was he who took the tremendous political gamble of expressing his sympathy publicly for the imprisoned Martin Luther King at the height of his presidential campaign.

Recently, less savoury aspects of his career have come to light and the progressive image has been tempered with knowledge that it was he who agreed to keep US troops in Vietnam in the early sixties, condoned the abortive 'Bay of Pigs' counter-revolutionary invasion of Cuba and, less seriously, was involved in various extra-marital affairs. None of these has managed to tarnish completely the Kennedy cult, which still revolves around those fine movie-star features of his and around the drama of his last moments in that fatal Dallas motorcade where a bullet cut him down in 1963.

What has been said about Jack Kennedy also holds true of the legend that has built up around the memory of his younger brother Robert, who was assassinated in similar circumstances in 1968, aged only forty-three. Less famous, but no less handsome than his brother, the cult of Robert Kennedy is less widespread or sentimental than that of John Kennedy, Che Guevara or Eva Peron but it is better founded and more realistic. Robert Kennedy's image was younger and more radical than his brother's, and this is why he is better remembered in the Third World than in the west. Bobby Kennedy was closely identified with a new, progressive current in American domestic and foreign policy during his years as Senator, Governor and Attorney-General. He was one of the most committed partisans of desegregation in the United States and fought to put an end to all forms of racial discrimination. He outraged most Americans by suggesting as early as in 1967 that the Vietcong should be offered a share in the Saigon government and that the United States should stop bombing North Vietnam. When he visited Africa in 1967 he received a delirious welcome for his eloquent speeches expressed genuine concern for all the 'people in the huts and villages of half the globe' which his brother had pledged to help in his 1960 inaugural address. None of this has been forgotten by his legions of admirers and Bobby Kennedy is a cult figure, a myth and a legend in his own right.

Of course, political heroes often achieve mythic status in their own lands, especially if they have embodied nationalist aspirations, but their fame may not travel in any significant way beyond their national borders. Eva Peron is one of the most extraordinary twentieth century examples of this phenomenon. Eva Peron was the first woman in Latin American politics to achieve mythic status, and she reached a position of real power almost by virtue of her good looks alone.

The film actress wife of Argentina's dictator president, Juan Peron, 'Evita' as all her admirers called her, became more popular than her husband during the years she reigned as first lady chiefly because she was so photogenic. Her 'rags to riches' story – the illegitimate peasant girl who rose to become first a well-known Argentinian film star and then wife of the most powerful man in the land – was irresistible copy for the newsreels, radio and TV programmes and magazine articles that were churned out week after week. Not that Peron was unaware of this: he used her public relations potential quite deliberately to secure his own political base in the country, especially during his rise to power. (The British Ambassador at the time, Sir John Balfour, has described the regime as 'political vaudeville' with Peron as impresario and Eva as leading actress.)

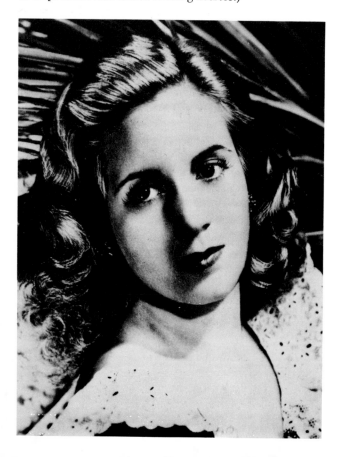

Evita's approach to politics was purely intuitive. What endeared her to 'the little people' whom she made her own was that she was herself of humble origin (she may even have been a call girl at one time) and from the start her name became linked with the cause of the poor and the needy who make up a sizeable proportion of Argentina's population. Yet the cult of Evita had a lot more to do with her bright blonde tresses and the madonna-like regularity of her features than with her concern for the sufferings of the proletariat. It was the photographs of Evita wearing sumptuous evening gowns which stunned and charmed her lower-class admirers just as much as the pictures of her visiting an orphanage or inaugurating a hospital. It is true, however, that having discovered her appeal to the poor, she set about working for them, changing her image, and abandoning the diamonds and furs for a more severe, 'purer' look. She formed the Eva Peron Foundation for the relief of the poor (although there are doubts about where some of the money went), she brought votes for women for the first time to Argentina and she was apparently passionately interested in the workings of the C.G.T., Argentina's central trade union organization. In 1951, when Peron was elected to a second term as president Eva was urged by popular pressure to accept the position of vice-president. She refused: she already knew she was dying.

Eva Peron died of cancer in 1952, aged only thirty-three. She became an instant cult figure and a modern saint, whose funeral rivalled that of royalty in grandeur,

years she reigned as first lady. When she died of cancer in 1952 aged only 33, she became an instant cult figure and a modern saint.

floral tributes and spontaneous national manifestations of passionate grief. There were sixteen days of public mourning for the so-called 'spiritual leader of the nation', a state funeral, and her body was embalmed for posterity. The dead, however, can often be more troublesome than the living since their bodies or even fragments of their bodies can become potent relics, especially in Catholic countries. It is better if they disappear altogether from the face of the earth. Thus Che Guevara's body was spirited away right after he was killed, and incinerated in the greatest secrecy by those who feared his memory. And thus also the military junta which ousted Peron soon after Evita's death was keen to dispose of the remains of 'Santa Evita', still adored by the poor, the *descamisados* of Argentina. The junta therefore arranged a macabre and elaborate subterfuge. Evita's coffin was whisked away by the Secret Police from the C.G.T. headquarters where it lay and was shipped abroad to be buried under a false name. Other coffins were also dispatched to different destinations under different names to make the right one even more difficult to identify. Evita's burial place may never have been found except for the fact that the Argentine President of the time (perhaps from pangs of conscience or even superstition) arranged for the whereabouts to be revealed in the event of his death. He was assassinated in 1970, and the coffin was subsequently found in a Milan cemetery, whereupon it was returned to Peron who was exiled in Madrid.

Evita's corpse eventually followed Peron back to Argentina in 1971 when he was invited back as President, an invitation he owed as much to the memory of his dead wife as to his own enduring popularity. Every effort was made to cast Isabel Peron, Evita's successor, in the role of a new Evita, but charisma is elusive; if it is there it can be exploited as artfully as Evita had done. But if it is lacking, as it was in Isabel, no amount of publicity, media exposure and gimmicky myth-making can really make a legend bloom. Isabel's failure to capture the imagination of the Argentine people, despite her game attempts to imitate her predecessor and the unlimited means at her disposal, point to the fact that there must have been something undeniably special, if not unique, in Evita's personality. In the years following her death the tendency among the sophisticated has been to scoff at her image (dismissed as vulgar), her achievements (deemed phoney), and her simplistic political views. But if we re-examine her in terms of her natural ability to conquer crowds and to make a lasting impression, she becomes a fascinating figure once again. This explains why there has been a revival of interest in Eva Peron's story in recent years, with many books published about her and culminating in a hit musical about her life, to be followed no doubt by a film. Though the subject of Evita has become fashionable again and one can almost speak of a second Evita cult, it cannot be compared in intensity and adoration to her first cult in her own country when her yellowing photograph was tacked up on the wall of every Argentine shanty town shack, to be quite literally venerated side by side with portraits of the saints and of the Pope.

Enduring cults have sprung up round the memories of other recent political figures, in particular with those connected with the rise of black consciousness in both America and the developing countries. Patrice Lumumba, Malcolm X and Martin Luther King were all charismatic personalities cut down in their prime, but it would be unfair to compare their legends to the quasi-deification of Eva Peron, Che Guevara and John Kennedy. There is something artificial, romanticized and overly glamorous about the myths of Che and John Kennedy, however justified their adulation was in fact. The admiration aroused by figures like Lumumba, Malcolm X and King was more firmly anchored in their actual deeds than in the beauty of their faces or the pathos of their deaths. Yet they have their place in a book about media-created mythology. It was the press and television which turned them into international celebrities, making people in all parts of the globe familiar not only with their words or actions but with the very essence of their personalities, which is where cults originate.

Patrice Lumumba, the independent Congo's first prime minister and a symbol of young African radicalism, became a household face and name during the few troubled months that he ruled his country in 1960.

The eyes of the whole world were upon him as he struggled vainly to keep his new nation together, against the secessionists, rival tribes and neo-colonialist business interests that were tearing it apart. He failed, was ousted and murdered by his enemies in 1961, aged only thirty-six. Lumumba has remained a legendary figure in many Third World countries and among young radicals because he was a martyr to the cause of national liberation and independence, because he struggled so valiantly to maintain his country's integrity and because, as has often been said, he was really 'murdered for his virtues'. Though he failed, his image is one of youthful idealism and sincerity taking a stand against a corrupt order, whether that order was the Belgian colonialists, Moise Tshombe or Mobutu.

The image of youthful openness and integrity taking a stand against older and more rigid structures was perfectly exemplified by the case of Malcolm X, one of the leading ministers of the Nation of Islam, a black Muslim sect founded by Elijah Muhammad in the United States. Malcolm X came into open conflict with this elderly authoritarian father figure. Malcolm X used his position, his orator's talent and his personal prestige to further the cause of Black Power and to establish links between black Americans and coloured people in other parts of the globe. But because he was growing even more popular than Elijah Muhammad, Malcolm X was eventually ousted from the Nation of Islam and assassinated by Elijah's followers shortly afterwards in 1965. To many Malcolm X still seems the classic symbol of progress versus conservation, or integrity versus the sell-out, and his assassination the necessary sacrifice of he who follows his conscience and refuses to compromise.

Martin Luther King, the black American clergyman who won a Nobel Peace Prize in the year Malcolm X was assassinated, was another of those legendary political figures whose face and personality became familiar to millions through the mass media, and who achieved mythical status not only for what he accomplished but for the emotional reactions the man himself could arouse. He had neither Guevara's Byronic physique nor the Kennedy brothers' glamour, but the millions of people who have seen him on film or television making his famous 'I have a dream' speech during the 1963 march on Washington can testify that King was star material and that his charisma transcended politics. King was the most famous representative since Ghandi of active non-violent tactics. It was he who led the boycotts, sit-ins, campaigns and marches which finally resulted in racial desegregation in the United States and set the pattern of protest for a decade to come. He became an international figure and was acclaimed on visits to India, West Africa, Latin America and Europe, where his personal struggle for racial equality made him almost as famous and often more popular than back in the States. His natural eloquence and his capacity for creating a sense of involvement in what he was doing, his tremendous sincerity and earnestness did as much to convert or to reconcile his fellow Americans to the principle of racial equality as his writings. It was often King's personal prestige alone which got nationwide press and TV coverage for the causes he defended. When he was assassinated in 1968, aged thirty-nine, he became a martyr to his cause. King's name will always be remembered for his personal contribution to the fight for minority rights everywhere, and he well deserves myth status, but it is doubtful whether he would have had the same dramatic impact in the pre-television era, when slower communications made it more difficult to break down deep seated prejudices.

9. LARGER THAN LIFE

Ever since there have been stars in the world of entertainment, they have been subjected to grinding pressures, both physical and moral and to temptations wellnigh irresistible. The rewards of fame are fantastic, but the artificiality of the position often leads to a sense of unreality, to a loss of identity which brings out psychological disorders such as schizophrenia, paranoia, alienation and megalomania. The star system has been in existence for much longer than we customarily assume: as long as popular entertainment has existed, the crowd has picked out its darlings, has adulated and rewarded its favourite balladeers, performers and players. Actresses like Lily Langtry and Sarah Bernhardt experienced delirious acclaim and assaults on their privacy long before Rudolph Valentino or the Rolling Stones.

But old-style stars usually had to work harder and longer to achieve stardom and were thus better prepared for it when it came. With the advent of cinema, radio, the record-player and television, a performer can quite literally go from bum to star overnight and most people's psyches find it hard to adjust. The first hazard lies in the temptation to self-indulgence when success comes, to gratify all of one's whims and pleasures. As Arthur Knight wrote in *The Liveliest Art* about the Hollywood of the twenties and thirties: 'Too many people had become too rich too quickly. Ill-prepared for sudden wealth, unaccustomed to such direct opulence, many among them began by reacting like children in a room full of beautiful brand-new toys. Only their toys included high-powered cars, bootlegged whisky, costly women and drugs. They began to believe in their own

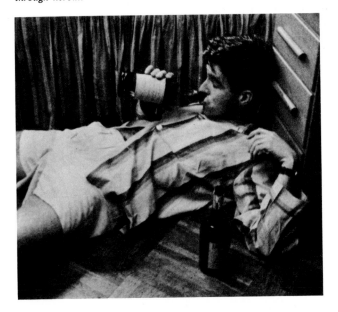

publicity. They were infallible kings and queens. But this fascination which the publicity men had taken so much trouble to create would finally lead to their doom.'

This comment has remained valid all along in the world of movies, and has been if anything even truer of the pop music scene. Most of the individuals jet-propelled into film and music stardom are young in years and rarely mature in other respects. They find themselves rich and raved about, lusted after by large numbers of desirable partners, egged on and manipulated by sycophants, urged to live up to their public image of gilded, highly-sexed, fast-living youth and often applauded for their excesses. 'What was I trying to prove? What in God's name was I trying to prove?' John Garfield would despairingly wonder at the end of his life when he recalled the infinite number of women he had lovelessly laid during his heyday of stardom; his promiscuity had only led to acute feelings of guilt, had wrecked his marriage to the wife he loved, had played havoc with the family life and the acting vocation he cared so deeply about. In fact all that Garfield had proved by his conduct was that, like Oscar Wilde and most of us, he could resist everything but temptation. Just as Montgomery Clift demonstrated with his booze, James Dean with his fast cars, and Janis Joplin with her drugs. The well-known result of having so many dangerous temptations thrust upon them is that a high proportion of twentieth century's stars have marriage problems, drink problems and drug problems, and a sizeable number get involved in serious accidents, have nervous breakdowns or fall foul of the law. Statistics have not been established comparing the accident-drink-divorce rate of film and pop stars with that of the population at large, but it is most unlikely that, as some might claim, it only appears to be higher because the peccadillos of the great are so well-chronicled. A glance at the lives of film and pop stars shows that the sober, clean-leaving, monogamous and well-balanced star is the exception rather than the rule.

Even those stars who might have started out self-disciplined, who could resist temptation better than most either because they had more will-power or because they were temperamentally less prone to self-indulgence, often end up taking refuge in the risky delights of drugs or drink just to escape from the many pressures of stardom. No one today is so naive as to believe that life at the top is a bed of roses, the notion originally propagated by the publicity men. The stars themselves were the first to complain about the psychic tribulations they underwent because of their fame. By the early thirties, the theme of unhappiness and heartbreak lying just below the surface of glamour and seeming happiness had become a common subject in the Hollywood fan magazines. It reflected the truth as the stars saw it, but it perhaps also reflected and catered to the magazine reader's wish to believe that screen fame was hellish as well as heavenly. Heavenly because we all want to believe there *is* a Heaven even if we do not have access to it. Hellish because otherwise it would be too unfair if only a happy few were allowed through the gates of Paradise on Earth and the rest were excluded. The latent sense of injustice the public feels about the real or imagined good fortune of its idols explains to some extent why the premature death of a star is so often made to sound in the popular press like a necessary retribution, the just price paid for unjust luck.

The fight for status and the terror of slipping in the world of popular entertainment have often been described. In the *Memoirs of a Star*, which Pola Negri wrote when she was an old lady, she spoke of the 'Hollywood of Dreams' she had known in the following terms: 'There lay behind the illusions the bitter truth of despairing frenzy. Superficially, this place was

dazzlingly beautiful; within, it was a mixture of fear and personal tragedy. Exquisite smiles charmed the whole world, but often hid an insecurity which led this small elite to excesses of depravity. Would the option be kept? Would tonight's star disappear by next morning? Would the next film make money? Would the box-office, the barometer of economic and emotional storms, suddenly collapse? The stakes in all this were almost inconceivably high. And the ransom was equally high, although paid for in another currency.' Even a star whose position was assured and who, temporarily at least, did not have to worry too much about options being kept or the next film making money was in a situation of extreme and permanent psychological stress. The pressure always to be at the top of your form, to look your best in all circumstances, to watch your every word and action so that it matched your public image was gruelling and could be pushed to incredible lengths, such as Buster Keaton's contract never to smile in public. The unreality of living up to a two-dimensional stereotype of oneself cannot fail to be dehumanizing, while unwanted publicity, false reports and endless invasions of privacy have always been a permanent irritant for the stars of the entertainment world. In a movie magazine article of the thirties, Myrna Loy groaned: 'If I could be the plain Myrna Williams I am at heart, instead of forever figuring out what Myrna Loy dare and dare not say . . . I have to be self-conscious most of the time. The most normal, insignificant move I make may be magnified in the public prints tomorrow. I've got to be, on all public occasions, the personality they sell at the box-office.' Yet she admitted in the same interview that there could be no question of turning back; success was the ultimate drug, whatever its drawbacks. Her long denunciation of stardom ended with the words: 'It's nine parts drudgery and fear and heartache to one part thrill and glamour. It's all the things I've said it is and more. And I love it – I love it.'

Several decades later, rock music stars were to discover the same principle – success and stardom were hellish in many respects and could even be lethal. Even so the lure of success is irresistible. Janis Joplin might moan to all who cared to listen that success was killing her, yet she rejected any suggestion that she ought to retire, even only temporarily, right up until success really did kill her. She could quite sincerely say of being a star: 'It's surreal. It's got nothing to do with me, really . . . I don't believe it, you know – I mean, you can't.' Yet she did and, as happens with other stars, her ego had become so bound up with her public image that she flew into a rage with a telephone operator who did not recognize her name, shrieking, 'Don't you know who I am! I'm Janis Joplin, the world's greatest singer!'

The pressures of stardom are not only psychological but physical as well. When an early film magazine article declared that 'Far too often the paths of glory lead but to the grave', it was not just histrionic. The life of a film actor or a pop singer can wear out the body along with the soul. Many top film stars have been ready to risk their health and sometimes their lives to prove they were the greatest. Lon Chaney, who died at forty-seven, tortured his body and permanently damaged his spine to achieve grotesque effects when creating the variety of mis-shapen characters for which he was famous. Tyrone Power died at fifty-five in a duelling accident on the location of a film. Clark Gable died in his late fifties from the heart attack he suffered after the strenuous roping tricks he insisted on performing in a temperature of 110°F for *The Misfits*, probably because he wanted to prove to the world and to himself that he was still the King of Hollywood and did not yet need a stunt man to stand in for him. Renee Adoree and Mabel Normand had to spend years in sanatoriums as a direct result of their exertions on the film set and Mabel Normand died at only thirty-two. Early Hollywood epics and serials often involved falling into icy rivers, marching in rags through real snow or crawling across the burning sands of Death Valley. It is startling to see how many film stars died well before their statistically allotted lifespan of seventy or seventy-five years. Douglas Fairbanks died at fifty-five, Judy Holliday at forty-two, Judy Garland at forty-eight, Errol Flynn at fifty, John Gilbert at thirty-nine, Leslie Howard at fifty, Paul Douglas at fifty-two, Mario Lanza at thirty-eight, Humphrey Bogart at

fifty-seven. The list is much longer and would seem to indicate that, though some of these stars died of other causes, longevity is not a feature of the acting profession. The downfall of the great cult figures discussed in this book was often attributed to actions they took to preserve their images. Thus the stomach disorder which killed Valentino was partially brought on by the drugs he took to avoid growing bald; it had been claimed repeatedly that Bruce Lee may have died from an abuse of body-building drugs; Elvis Presley definitely wrecked his health by consuming vast quantities of amphetamine-based pills to keep down his weight. When Valentino confessed his shameful secret of his hair loss to Pola Negri after collapsing with ulcer pains in her presence, she urged him to stop taking hair-restoring drugs and tried to persuade him that a lot of actors wore toupees or were attractive even though bald. According to her, Valentino replied with Italian dignity and perfect logic: 'Yes, but they are not Valentino.' No man wants to grow bold, weak or fat, but for Valentino to lose his hair, for Bruce Lee to lose his muscles and for Elvis Presley to get overweight was a major personal and professional catastrophe to be avoided at the risk of pain, ill-health and even death.

Rock musicians are not subjected to the hazards of plunging into icy rivers or being mauled by lions in film epics about the early Christians, yet their life is probably more exhausting than that of film actors, with the strain of late nights and of endless travelling, coupled with the exertions of performances. Singer James Brown is said to lose five pounds during the course of a two-hour concert. Many found it literally painful to watch Judy Garland or Edith Piaf giving a concert towards the

end of their lives, so much did both women seem to be pouring out their remaining vitality which each note they sang. Anyone who has ever had a drink to overcome an excruciating sense of fatigue can understand the temptation for the live entertainer to resort to a stimulant before going on stage. The need to boost one's flagging energy may not just be dictated by the physical strain of perfomance either but also by the artistic quality which will be required. Much of rock music depends on a 'spontaneous' creativity which the artist cannot always summon on request. If Janis Joplin has often been compared to Bessie Smith and Billie Holiday, or Jimi Hendrix to Charlie Parker, it is not only in terms of their talent or their voices but because the great stars of jazz were faced with similar problems. As Craig McGregor explained it: 'Whiskey, heroin, speed: they're familiar Mother's Helpers in both jazz and rock. In a way rock is a victim of some of the best things it has borrowed from jazz, including the concept of improvisation . . . Everything depends on the inspiration of the moment. Hence drugs: they kick you on, give you time to think, and help ease the lurking fear of many musicians that they might suddenly dry up, that the magical connection between mind, heart and horn might snap and never rejoin . . . you have to create everything anew every time you stand up at the mike.' Inevitably, it is the better and more conscientious musicians who are most afraid of drying up. The less gifted and the cynical won't care so much. They are happy to go on repeating themselves mechanically as long as they can earn a living that way; they have too little respect for their art form or for their audiences to feel greatly concerned about non-renewal. But authentic artists always care, even if their audience is not discriminating enough to tell the difference between a sub-standard performance and a great one.

Many fine performers do, of course, survive the physical and emotional strains of being stars, of work-

ing hard and growing old gracefully in a profession where age counts for so much. Some even seem to thrive on their difficult routines, to enjoy the demands made on them by their public. People like Maurice Chevalier, Louis Armstrong, Marlene Dietrich, Bing Crosby or Frank Sinatra appeared to be rejuvenated by concert tours which would have worn out people half or even a third of their age. Whatever treasures of energy they expended during their perfomances, they always gave the impression that they had more in reserve to give. It wasn't that their professional consciences were weaker than those of other, less fortunate artists who had to resort to drugs and other panaceas to keep going, but that they happened to be tough in limb and mind, which was lucky for them and for their fans. Keith Richard of the Rolling Stones has recently said, 'Hollywood is the end of the line for so many people. It's a killer and if you're weak you can be sure it'll get you.' The profession of star-actor-entertainer is an exacting one; in that risky garden of delight it is hard to survive unscathed and, in quite a few cases, to survive at all.

Whether it is better to die young or to live and grow old is a matter of opinion. It is certainly harder to grow old in the world of popular entertainment than in most others, especially today. Back in the thirties, an article in a fan magazine was already saying of film actors and actresses who had died young: 'Yet perhaps those that remain behind should not sorrow too much for the great ones who have gone. They had escaped the hand of unscrupulous Time, more cruel than Death. Death has cut in lasting marble what would have become dust. Many players have climbed to the heights and have lived to see their fame dwindle to nothing – forgotten even by the very people who once acclaimed them. To them that must be worse than death.' Forty years later, Lester Bangs echoed much the same feelings about the world of pop stardom: 'The problem of creating mythology with living people is that you have to watch them fall old and decay, or fall down and make fools of them-

selves. They can't live up to their own mythology. Mick Jagger is a perfect example. His face is turning all flabby and his big lips are hanging down. After all, he's getting old.' Whether Mick Jagger's fans agree with this verdict or not, the interesting fact is that it was made when Jagger was only thirty-three. The old stage actor who sang a popular Victorian ballad called 'I'm Only a Fallen Star' in which he bewailed the fact of inglorious ageing was presumably already in his sixties. Today it all happens much faster and Janis Joplin at twenty-seven was moaning that her fans 'don't want an old chick like me'. Yet it is not altogether true either that people love only those who die young. Many stars remain tremendously popular into middle and old age, and nothing proves that Marlon Brando, Bette Davis, Sophia Loren or Charlie Chaplin, to name only a few, would have become even greater cult figures or legendary 'sacred monsters' if they had not lived beyond the age of forty. Even more so, outside the field of entertainment, where the individual's physical appearance is less important than their achievements, the living and the dead, the young and the old, co-exist as cult-figures of mythical stature.

But in the field of popular entertainment disseminated by the mass media, dying young can definitely help to create a legend. The death of a young star brings reactions of sympathy and empathy which few feel as keenly when an old star dies. As Dave Laing said in his biography of Buddy Holly: 'The death in mid-career of a singer, a sportsman or a film-actor always has a more dramatic effect than that of a writer, painter or director because they are performers, people with an immediate physical presence for their audiences.' Given the role that television now plays in political life and in news coverage, statesmen and politicians should perhaps also be included in the category of people 'with an im-

mediate physical presence for their audiences'. But the image of political figure is regulated by other laws than those of an entertainer. It is hard to be mature or objective about something as purely childish as pleasure: when the pleasure given by a star is cut short by his death, fans tend to react as children do when they are deprived of their source of gratification: with astonishment, disbelief, anger and longing. The miracle of film, photography and radio waves keeps these emotions alive, for they allow the personalities and achievements of the dead to be reconstituted at will. We can go on regretting the loss of James Dean when watching *Rebel Without a Cause,* of Marilyn in *Bus Stop* and of Bruce Lee in *Enter the Dragon* for as long as these films are shown. A sense of loss can be revived each time we listen to Elvis singing *Hound Dog* or Jimi Hendrix playing *Foxy Lady.* We can suspend belief and almost forget that they are dead at all; after all, the sense of sound and sight knows differently. When seen in a film or heard on a record, they are with us in exactly the same fashion as they were while they were alive. It is only the intellect which knows that they have been dead ten or fifteen or twenty years. The frustration of having to admit the objective fact of their deaths while still responding to them emotionally as if they were alive is one of the chief reasons why enduring cults to their memory survive.

Twentieth century dead heroes, unlike those of other eras, will not lie still and allow themselves to be forgotten. They solicit remembrance endlessly with their faces, their names, their voices, as though they were begging to be thought about, to be loved, and admired as much as they were while they were alive. They are unreal and real at the same time, in ways that tantalize and irritate.

Their deaths as well as their lives appeal to fantasies of how things ought to be. While they were alive they lived for their fans the idealized existence of the beautiful, the rich, the talented; they were cherished by all, rewarded, indulged and were apparently effortlessly successful. And when they died, it was the rapid, beautiful, photogenic death of childhood fantasy when, feeling unloved and misunderstood, a child imagines himself dying painlessly and lying in his coffin, surrounded by horrified, grief-struck mourners all wailing: 'If only we had known' and 'He was so wonderful!'

Those who survive must inexorably grow older, yet dreams of eternal youth seem to have come true in the lasting image left behind by those who died young: their appearance is, of necessity, as young as on the day they died. Yet people all over the world, who are in their forties, fifties, sixties and over, see contemporaries in them. The ageing survivors can detect in those youthful images aspects of their inner selves which they feel can never age, whatever the external evidence of the passing years. They can point out a dead star to their growing children or grandchildren and say with pride: 'He or she belongs to my generation; just as he is a part of me, so I am a part of him.' The dead star's enduring youthfulness is the testimony and proof that each of us too was once young and, though successive generations invariably react with scepticism, no one who has been young once has ever outgrown the feeling, whatever age he may have lived to.

ACKNOWLEDGEMENTS

A book which covers such a wide-ranging topic necessarily involves the help and co-operation of many different individuals and organisations. I particularly wish to thank the excellent Bibliothèque de l'Institut des Hautes Etudes Cinématographiques in Paris, where I did so much of the research for this book.

I would like to express my thanks to John Howlett, John Tobler, Virginia Boston, Douglas Gibbons, Gay Haines and Ann Geaney who all in various ways helped with the original research and preparation of this book, and special thanks to Hubert Niogret for his advice and his informative article on Jimi Hendrix and Janis Joplin.

I would like to thank the following for the use of photographs from their archives and for their help in researching visual materials: Simon Crocker and the John Kobal Collection, John Beecher, Rob Burt, Roy Burchell and *Melody Maker*, Alan Lewis and *Sounds*, Fred Zentner of the Cinema Bookshop, the National Film Archive; also the following photographers for the use of their material: Sir Cecil Beaton, David Bonnar, Dezo Hoffman and Chris Walters; and the record and film companies responsible for many of the artists in this book: Elektra, Warner Brothers Records, M.C.A., R.C.A., and E.M.I.; Paramount Films, Columbia Pictures, Warner Brothers, Universal Pictures, Gala Films, Camera Eye Pictures Inc., United Artists Films, 20th Century Fox and M.G.M. Films; and I would also like to thank the following companies and agencies: Faber and Faber, The Bodley Head, Rolling Stones Archives, The Bettmann Archive, Camera Press, Keystone Press Agency, London Features International, Popperfoto and Rex Features. It has not been possible in all cases to trace the copyright sources, and my publishers would be glad to hear from any such unacknowledged copyright holders.

I would also like to express my gratitude to three people: Nicky Hayden for her collaboration and editing, and all the help and assistance she provided throughout with research and writing, especially for Chapters 5 and 6, and Sandra Wake and Terence Porter who, above and beyond the call of their duty as my publishers, have always been so helpful in supplying research material, ideas and suggestions for this book; also to Chris Lower who designed the book. The cover of a book is more often than not team work. For *Those Who Died Young* our thanks to Charlie Baird for the painting, Chris Lower and Bob Ughetti for the design and graphics.

And last but not least, Denise Alexandre and Derek Lindsay for their encouragement and forbearance during the writing of this book.

BIBLIOGRAPHY

Writing a book of this kind involves researching widely in books, periodicals and newspapers, as well as talking to individuals with specialist knowledge. This selected bibliography is designed to help those who want to find out more about some of the people in this book.

General
The Stars by Edgar Morin; *The Rebel Hero* by Joe Morella; *Celluloid Rock* by Philip Jenkinson and Alan Warner; *All You Need is Love* by Tony Palmer.

Biographies
Valentino by Alexander Walker; *Marilyn* by Norman Mailer; *Marilyn Monroe* by Norman Rosten; *Norma Jean: The Story of Marilyn Monroe* by Fred Lawrence Guiles; *Body and Soul: A Biography of John Garfield* by Larry Swindell; *Montgomery Clift* by Robert LeGuardia; *James Dean* by John Howlett; *Gable and Lombard* by Joe Morella and Edward Z. Epstein; *Buddy Holly* by John Goldrosen; *Elvis* by Jerry Hopkins; *The Rolling Stones: An Illustrated Record* by Roy Carr; *The Rolling Stones* written and edited by David Dalton; *Mick Jagger* by Tony Scaduto; *Janis* by Myra Friedman; *Janis* edited by David Dalton; *Hendrix* by Chris Welch; *Jimi Hendrix* by Curtis Knight; *Jim Morrison* by Hervé Muller; *Bruce Lee Lives?* by Max Caulfield; *The Legend of Bruce Lee* by Alex Ben Block; *Kung-Fu: Cinema of Vengeance* by Verina Glaessner; *Che Guevara* by Andrew Sinclair; *Evita* by W. A. Harbinson.

Reference Books
The Great Movie Stars by David Shipman; *The Filmgoer's Companion* by Leslie Halliwell; *The Encyclopedia of Rock* edited by Phil Hardy and David Laing; *The Age of Rock* edited by Jonathon Eisen; *The NME Book of Rock* edited by Nick Logan with Bob Woffinden; *The 'Rolling Stone' Illustrated History of Rock and Roll* edited by Jim Miller; *The Country Music Encyclopedia* by Melvin Shestack; *The Illustrated Encyclopedia of Jazz* edited by Brian Case and Stan Britt.